T0302117

Innovation, Investment and the Diffusion of Technology in Europe

German Direct Investment and Economic Growth in Postwar Europe

Edited by

RAY BARRELL and NIGEL PAIN

 CAMBRIDGE
UNIVERSITY PRESS

CAMBRIDGE
UNIVERSITY PRESS

University Printing House, Cambridge CB2 8BS, United Kingdom

Cambridge University Press is part of the University of Cambridge.

It furthers the University's mission by disseminating knowledge in the pursuit of education, learning and research at the highest international levels of excellence.

www.cambridge.org
Information on this title: www.cambridge.org/9780521620871

© The National Institute of Economic and Social Research 1999

First published 1999

A catalogue record for this publication is available from the British Library

Library of Congress Cataloguing in Publication data

Innovation, investment and the diffusion of technology in Europe:
German direct investment and economic growth in postwar Europe
edited by Ray Barrell and Nigel Pain.
p. cm.
ISBN 0 521 62087 2 (hb)
1. Investments, German–Europe. 2. Investments, Foreign–Europe:
3. Diffusion of innovation–Europe. 4. Europe–Economic
conditions–1945- I. Barrell, Ray. II. Pain, Nigel.
HG4538.I4728 1999
332.67'34304–dc21 98-41842 CIP

ISBN 978-0-521-62087-1 Hardback

Innovation, Investment and the
Diffusion of Technology in Europe
German Direct Investment and Economic
Growth in Postwar Europe

The globalisation of the world economy has raised many fears for
employment and growth in the advanced economies. Foreign investment
by multinational companies is one of the major factors driving
globalisation. Such investments are an effective way of transferring techniques, processes and products into new markets. Firm-specific assets
transferred in this way can raise productivity in the host country without
costing jobs in the home country. The papers in this volume examine the
role of German foreign investment in the European growth process. The
implications for the German economy are addressed, as are the determinants of outflows, and the effects of foreign investment in host countries.
The editors draw conclusions for future economic development in the
European Union.

RAY BARRELL is a Senior Research Fellow at the National Institute of
Economic and Social Research. He has written widely on European
economic integration, labour markets, and on the processes affecting the
pattern of trade and investment. Previous books include *The UK Labour
Market: Comparative Aspects and Institutional Developments* (Cambridge, 1994).

NIGEL PAIN is a Senior Research Fellow at the National Institute of
Economic and Social Research. He has written widely on international
economics, trade, investment, capital markets and the UK economy.

THE NATIONAL INSTITUTE OF
ECONOMIC AND SOCIAL RESEARCH
XXXIX

2 DEAN TRENCH STREET, SMITH SQUARE, LONDON, SW1P 3HE

The National Institute of Economic and Social Research is an independent, non-profit-making body, founded in 1938. It has as its aim the promotion of realistic research, particularly in the field of economics. It conducts research by its own research staff and in cooperation with universities and other academic bodies.

Contents

Contributors

Jamuna Prasad Agarwal *Kiel Institute of World Economics*
Ray Barrell *National Institute of Economic and Social Research, London*
Marian Beise *Centre for European Economic Research, Mannheim*
Heike Belitz *German Institute for Economic Research, Berlin*
Pontus Braunerhjelm *Research Institute of Industrial Economics, Stockholm*
Karolina Ekholm *Research Institute of Industrial Economics, Stockholm*
Holger Görg *Department of Economics, University College Cork*
Neil Hood *Strathclyde International Business Unit, Strathclyde University*
Florence Hubert *National Institute of Economic and Social Research, London*
Nigel Pain *National Institute of Economic and Social Research, London*
Frances Ruane *Department of Economics, Trinity College, Dublin*
James Taggart *Strathclyde International Business Unit, Strathclyde University*
Stephen Young *Strathclyde International Business Unit, Strathclyde University*

1 Introduction

RAY BARRELL and NIGEL PAIN

This collection of papers arises from a conference held at the National Institute in February 1997.[1] The objective of the conference was to address the related issues of globalisation, growth and integration in Europe through a discussion of the determinants and effects of foreign direct investment (FDI). In organising the conference we set out to bring together a diverse range of approaches to the study of FDI and multi-national firms, ranging from econometric studies, through survey-based analysis, to detailed discussions of published statistics. The rapid expansion in cross-border investments in recent years has led to increasing interest in the topic, both from theorists and from the policy community. Approaches to the causes and effects of the location of production have become more rigorous and now play a significant role in the debate over the sources of growth and the impact of distinctive institutions and policies at both the national and supranational level.

This volume focuses largely, but not exclusively, on the role of German FDI in Europe. Overseas investment by German companies has attracted considerable attention because of its recent growth and the associated policy debate in Germany concerning the hollowing out of the economy. World-wide, German firms have the fourth largest stock of overseas assets of all investing countries. Within Europe they are the second most important investors after the United States. At the end of 1994 just under 1.2 million workers were employed in the foreign affiliates of German firms located in the European Union. However the debate over whether or not Germany and some other European economies have become unattractive business locations because of high costs and stringent regulations is rather negative in its approach. In particular it ignores the other

1

factors behind the decision of German firms to invest overseas, such as the desire to exploit technological advantages, and the consequent importance of FDI as a potential bearer of structure in the globalisation of the world economy.

The process of globalisation of economic activities is much discussed, but not always fully understood. The existence of national borders, even within the European single market, does still matter, but they are becoming more permeable. Changes in production technology, along with the removal of barriers to the movement of goods and capital, have meant that economic activities have changed their locations, frequently whilst still under the control of the initial parent firm. This can be driven by numbers of factors, including the characteristics of home countries and host countries. This has led to a debate about the impact of relocation on growth and employment in both home and host countries and empirical investigation of the claim that multinational companies help to transmit innovations and ideas throughout the global economy (Romer, 1993; Helpman, 1997). This book contributes to this debate with a particular focus on European issues.

The location decision is a more pervasive one than the decision to become a multinational. There are important agglomeration effects and external economies of scale that have to be taken into account. The gains from network externalities in industries with large numbers of horizontally and vertically integrated firms have formed an important part of the study of location decisions for many years (Estall and Buchanan, 1966). Recent, more rigorously founded studies have stressed the importance of product differentiation, imperfect competition and economies of scale. These developments have led to the location and relocation decisions of firms being incorporated into theories of trade and of (the new) economic geography (Krugman, 1991; Krugman and Venables, 1995; Markusen and Venables, 1996). Firms may decide to move across borders for many reasons, including the comparative advantage of different nations and the need to obtain market access. Comparative advantage encompasses factors such as lower cost labour as well as country-specific characteristics such as the educational attainment of the labour force and an abundance of natural resources. Any of the comparative advantage-based reasons are contingent, in that they depend upon history rather than inherent characteristics, but can still be long lasting or even irreversible. Market-access reasons depend upon the specificity of products and on barriers to trade. Removal of barriers could lead either to more concentration, if there are unused economies of scale within the plant or industrial complex, or to more dispersed production if there are unexploited economies of scale at the level of the firm.

If products are differentiated and firms have specific knowledge-based assets, then they may have reasons for wishing to set up multiple plants. The multi-plant firm would exist in a single country world if economies of scale at the plant level were not sufficient to offset the costs of transportation to markets. Indeed such multi-plant firms may be becoming more common with the move beyond mass production of standardised products to more specialised production for niche markets. Broadberry (1997) provides a useful historical perspective on the sources and implications of these developments. The desire and ability to adapt products to particular national markets has increased over time. As a result firms increasingly make use of subsidiaries overseas to develop R&D facilities in host countries to help design and customise products. Such subsidiaries often bring new investments by supplier firms and downstream corporate services such as banking and advertising in their wake, leading to further agglomeration economies.

This change in the nature of production reflects both increased levels of income, with consumers more willing to pay for variety, and changes in the nature of technical progress. New advances are increasingly based around specific ideas and organisational innovations rather than machines and methods of increasing the efficiency of homogeneous production. If the firm is based on a specific portfolio of patents and ideas, rather than on economies of scale in mass production, multi-plant production becomes more common. These forces are strengthened by rapid advances in, and reliance on, information technology. This increases the feasible span of managerial control whilst reducing the scale of the minimal cost plant. All these forces help to multinationalise firms, taking specific products to particular markets.

There are other forces at work that also increase the multinationalisation of firms. Whilst barriers to trade, and hence the costs of entering foreign markets, have been reduced in Europe in recent years, significant differences remain in national economies owing to differences in culture, consumer preferences and regulations in areas such as health and safety and the environment. As a result of such barriers multi-plant firms are perhaps more common within a space such as Europe. Because of national borders, more of these firms will be multinationals than they would be in the United States, and conversely the average size of firm in an industry, for example in the manufacture of motor cars, will be smaller in Europe than in the US.

The determinants of FDI

All of the papers in the book discuss the determinants of FDI in one way or another. Three important themes emerge: the role of knowledge and of innovative activity in the growth of multinational firms, the importance of home and host country characteristics and the impact of European integration. Barrell and Pain (Chapter 2) provide a general overview of these factors and their importance in the recent expansion of FDI in Europe. Developments within Europe are also discussed in relation to the recent pattern of FDI in the global economy. It is clear from their analysis, along with the more detailed figures for Germany described by Agarwal (Chapter 7) and Hubert and Pain (Chapter 8) that the majority of foreign direct investment undertaken by German firms is located in other developed economies, especially in Europe. This indicates that explanations for the recent growth of FDI must involve more than just a desire to move to locations with low labour costs, although this is clearly one part of the explanation for some investments, particularly in Central and Eastern Europe.

Two papers particularly emphasise the extent of the interlinkages between research and development (R&D) activities and foreign direct investment. The study of the determinants of German FDI by Hubert and Pain suggests that investment overseas by German firms may be closely related to technological developments in the domestic economy, with innovating industries being more likely to have a significant overseas presence. Belitz and Beise (Chapter 5) look at the internationalisation of R&D by German firms abroad and foreign firms in Germany as a result of FDI. Their analysis highlights the extent to which the internationalisation of R&D by multinational companies follows the internationalisation of production, with firms wanting to adapt products to meet the needs of foreign markets and expand linkages with research expertise in other countries (Cantwell and Harding, 1998). One important implication of these papers is that foreign direct investment from Germany and elsewhere may be an important vehicle for the transmission of firm-specific innovations throughout Europe and the wider world economy. A second is that the future technological capacities of national economies are likely to become increasingly dependent on the restructuring of R&D within multinational companies.

The internationalisation of R&D cannot just be seen as a mechanism for transferring technology from the host country. Belitz and Beise argue that the establishment of research facilities outside the home country has led to new forms of specialisation in R&D. In particular, German firms have acquired R&D companies abroad to try to obtain access to technological resources. This in part reflects domestic regulations, especially in the environmental field. German chemical and pharmaceutical firms wishing to be involved in biotechnology-based research had no option but to invest abroad, at least until 1993, when restrictions on domestic research were relaxed. The location and relocation of R&D abroad can be seen as a threat to the longer-term technological capacity of the German economy and, to the extent that it is, it may require a policy response in terms of domestic regulation and research policy. This would in turn change the specific characteristics of the home economy, and hence change the location and pattern of German R&D and FDI.

Patterns of comparative advantage are clearly not the only factors affecting FDI. Cost factors do matter, but the nature of industrial and educational policies as well as the structure of industry also matter. The specific characteristics of home and host countries are stressed by Braunerhjelm and Ekholm (Chapter 6), who look at the multinationalisation of Swedish firms, and by Ruane and Görg (Chapter 3), who study Irish experience. The contrasting pattern of FDI in these two countries is particularly interesting. Sweden, for its size, has, like Germany, been a major source of successful R&D. This has been reflected in the industrial pattern of outward direct investment. Ireland is a small country, and has grown very rapidly in the last decade, in part because of the successful use made of industrial policies to attract FDI. Contrasting patterns of education may also help explain differences between the experiences of these countries. In particular, higher education enrolments have been rising rapidly in Ireland over the last twenty years, helping to expand the supply of skilled, numerate graduates in the economy, whilst enrolments have been stable or falling in Sweden.

Sweden has been a major exporter of FDI for many years, and has begun to receive significant inward investment only recently. As Braunerhjelm and Ekholm argue, the nature of production in Sweden and its recent decision to join the European Union are important factors behind this pattern. Sweden has had an unusually concentrated industrial structure, dependent upon history as much as necessity, and whilst outside the EU it had barriers to inward investment that could not be maintained once it was a member. The authors utilise a unique data set held at the IUI in Sweden based on a regular survey of Swedish multinational companies that was first conducted in 1965. The broad picture shown is one of a trend towards increasing internationalisation of production, employment and R&D, with the proportion of the employees of Swedish multinational companies in foreign affiliates rising from 33 per cent in

1965 to over 60 per cent by 1994. Despite policy reforms in Sweden and entry into the EU the share of activities accounted for by foreign production has continued to rise in the 1990s.

However there does appear to be some evidence of a change in the regional pattern of investments, with Swedish multinationals now less concerned to establish operations within other EU member states. This has coincided with the removal of the actual, or potential, barriers to trade that were present whilst Sweden remained outside the EU. Such barriers may have induced Swedish firms to increase their activity in the EU to avoid losing market share. Their removal appears to have allowed Swedish firms to re-establish the search for new markets and low cost locations, such as the Baltic States and Central Europe. There has also been a rise in investment in the NAFTA economies and in East Asia in the 1990s.

Braunerhjelm and Ekholm also examine whether there is a 'large-country' effect in the pattern of location in Europe. A number of models arising out of the new literature on economic geography suggest that the initial stages of a decline in barriers to trade could simply generate increased agglomeration of activities in large markets, rather than a broader geographical dispersion of industries in line with comparative advantage (Baldwin and Venables, 1995). Regional differentiation within such models is driven by the interaction between scale economies and transport costs. Agglomeration effects may arise under the combination of intermediate levels of trade costs and increasing returns to scale. Firms located in densely populated areas can economise on fixed costs by concentrating production in a single plant and on transport costs by being close to a large market. On these grounds small countries, particularly within a wider market such as Europe, may not provide sufficient demand to justify the establishment of new facilities. Braunerhjelm and Ekholm examine the scale of Swedish investments in France, Germany and the UK relative to those elsewhere in Europe. Little consistent evidence is in fact found in favour of the 'large-country' hypothesis, although the UK does appear to have been a particularly favoured location.

Ireland has been in the EU for more than two decades and has received significant inward investment. Over two-thirds of output in the manufacturing sector is now produced by foreign-owned firms. Even before joining the EU Ireland pursued policies designed to make it attractive to FDI, with significant investment to improve educational attainment and fiscal incentives for foreign investors. Ruane and Görg stress the specific nature of the investment promotion policies followed, and hence the difficulties in transferring them to other countries. The proactive nature of policy, as well as the emphasis placed on continuity and certainty in the implementation of policy, was particularly important in its success. Potential investors were sought to fill gaps in the industrial structure of the economy, with a conscious stress on high-technology firms. For long periods fiscal incentives were exceptionally strong, although these have now become increasingly constrained by EU regulations. It is interesting that the evidence from the survey of German manufacturing affiliates reported by Hood, Taggart and Young (Chapter 4) reveals the marked impact of government financial assistance on affiliate location in Ireland.

Hubert and Pain find that national labour market characteristics affect the level of inward investment by German companies, especially in the UK. This is also consistent with the relatively strong growth in Swedish multi-nationals in the UK noted by Braunerhjelm and Ekholm and the relative labour intensity of US multinationals in Britain highlighted by Barrell and Pain. Another important aspect of the UK is the relative openness of capital markets and the ability of foreign firms to make investments by means of mergers and acquisitions. Agarwal stresses the extent to which the particular structure of corporate equity holdings acts as an impediment to new inward investments of this type in Germany. However it is important to remember that the total stock of inward investments can still rise by other means, such as the reinvestment of profits by exisiting investors and the transfer of additional funds from parent companies to their affiliates. These appear to have been particularly important sources of inward investment in Germany in recent years (Jost, 1997).

The analysis by Hubert and Pain also sheds light on the debate about whether Germany has become an unattractive business location (see, for instance, Jungnickel, 1995). Relative labour costs in Germany and potential host countries do influence investment decisions, but the extent to which they do so does not differ significantly from the findings from earlier studies of the experience of the 1960s and 1970s. Basic wage costs are high in Germany, as Agarwal illustrates, but in part this may reflect high average levels of labour productivity (Broadberry, 1997). Hubert and Pain argue that the evidence that outward FDI has been partially motivated by the development of firm-specific products and processes implies that high levels of outward investment could be seen as an indication of competitive health rather than weakness. Processes and products are being taken to new markets, rather than jobs being exported to low cost locations.

A number of chapters stress the extent to which European integration has affected the pattern of FDI in recent years. The Single Market Programme (SMP) has pushed the process of European integration forward significantly since 1986. Barrell and Pain illustrate the rapid growth in foreign direct investment in Europe that has occurred since then. The experience of the EU economies as a whole differs significantly from the other member states of the OECD. FDI in Europe by other European firms and by firms from Japan and the United States has risen more rapidly than would otherwise have been predicted as a result of the SMP, with the primary gains arising in the service sectors. Thus the removal of barriers to the mobility of capital appears to have acted as a substitute for a lack of labour mobility in Europe. This is somewhat different from the pattern beginning to emerge in North America following first the US-Canada Free Trade Agreement and then NAFTA. Mexico, the relatively low cost location, has gained considerable extra inflows of FDI, but the growth in cross-border investments between the United States and Canada has slowed.

Outward investment from Germany conforms to the pattern for Europe as a whole, as noted both by Agarwal and by Hubert and Pain. The latter report evidence of regional and industrial heterogeneity in the factors determining foreign investments by German manufacturing industries, with significant differences in the factors behind investment decisions inside and outside the European Union. These appear to arise largely from the investments undertaken by firms in the road vehicles sector. The importance of trade arrangements at the supranational level may be particularly apparent in such sectors that are characterised by a greater degree of intra-firm trade and production switching in response to changes in national labour markets and tax regimes. In contrast the production process, although not necessarily the research base, in other more capital-intensive sectors such as chemicals is more typically concentrated in a single site within the supranational market, particularly in the absence of internal barriers to trade. Pain and Lansbury (1997) find that the Single Market Programme has acted to encourage a greater concentration of chemicals production in Germany after allowing for change in market size and relative costs.

The opening up of the economies of Central and Eastern Europe has also led to rapid growth of FDI by German and Austrian firms, with investors tending to favour geographically proximate economies with relatively advanced reform programmes and a likelihood of eventual EU membership. The pattern of inward investment in Spain and Sweden strongly suggests that membership of the European Union improves the prospects for attracting inward investment, with firms concerned to be within the external barriers arising from EU trade policies such as the use made of contingent protection (Barrell and Pain, 1998). However, distance from the major national markets of Europe and national competencies still matter as the contrasting experience of Greece reveals. Moreover it should be remembered that economic integration and even monetary union are far from irreversible, as Ruane and Görg illustrate for UK FDI in Ireland. The monetary union between the UK and Ireland came to an end in 1978. Employment in UK manufacturing affiliates in Ireland halved between 1975 and 1995.

The impact of FDI on home and host economies

In recent years renewed attention has been paid to the factors affecting technological change and economic growth. Much of the literature on endogenous growth focuses on the impact of innovation and knowledge accumulation. Grossman and Helpman (1991) introduce a number of models in which the rate of technological progress is endogenised and driven by the rate of introduction of new products discovered in the research sector. International knowledge spillovers, whether through trade, migration or capital mobility, expand the stock of ideas that may be used for research in each country.

Trade carries new ideas, either embedded in machinery or through a process of discovery by interaction. Foreign direct investment may also be a major channel for the diffusion of ideas and the transfer of technologies. Blueprints, organisational and management techniques (Ferner, 1997) and products that would not otherwise have been available can all arrive with inward investment. Romer (1993) points to the experience of the automobile industry over the past century, with international investments being the conduit for the transmission of ideas such as mass production and subsequently 'just-in-time' inventory control techniques. One important difference between these two is that the latter has a much wider applicability, being used in service industries as well as manufacturing ones.

FDI has become an increasingly important part of the process of convergence of income levels between countries as new technological developments have become more dependent on information technology and tacit knowledge. Ideas can be difficult to copy or to license to other producers. Hence FDI may be necessary to carry them. Blueprints for 'ways of doing' are more complex than blueprints for basic machinery; modern research-based production is increasingly related to the former rather than the latter. The nationality of ownership appears to be an important factor in the management of human resources in firms in the UK (Wood, 1996). In particular, German and Japanese firms have had a major impact on productivity and organisational techniques in firms and sectors where they have made significant investments in the last two decades.

It is often felt that FDI is a zero sum game, in that for every gainer there is a potential loser. In particular there have been worries expressed in Germany and in Sweden about the hollowing out of domestic manufacturing capacity. The scale of capital exports has recently prompted concern because of the potential effects on the home economy, and in particular on domestic employment. The effect of outward FDI on employment and fixed investment in Germany is discussed by Agarwal; he suggests there is little negative impact, with the possible exception of some relocation into the Czech Republic by small and medium-sized enterprises in southern Germany. The issue is also addressed more specifically for R&D employment by Belitz and Beise, and is covered in the discussion of Swedish experience by Braunerhjelm and Ekholm. They show that the proportion of R&D by Swedish multinationals that is undertaken abroad has risen from 9 per cent in 1970 to 25 per cent by 1994. This reflects both the general growth in the international operations of Swedish multinationals as well as specific problems with research capacities in Sweden.

The rapid growth in outward investment from Germany has tended to overshadow the fact that Germany remains an important host location for inward investment in Europe, both because of the size of the domestic market and because of the relatively highly skilled workforce. Although inflows of FDI as recorded in the balance of payments appear rather disappointing in recent years, the recorded stock of inward investment has continued to grow rapidly (Jost, 1997). Barrell and Pain highlight the fact that Germany is preferred to the UK as a host for manufacturing production in Europe by US multinationals, and is the primary location for R&D expenditure by their European affiliates. The estimates reported by Belitz and Beise suggest that foreign-owned firms now account for around 16 per cent of R&D expenditure in Germany, balancing the level of R&D expenditure overseas by German-owned firms.

The impact of FDI on the domestic economy is often misunderstood. The level of output and the growth rate of the economy depend to a large extent upon the resources used for investment in fixed capital. There need not be a simple accounting relationship between domestic investment and foreign direct investment. It is obviously true that a deficit in the current account of the balance of payments, and hence a net capital inflow, augments national saving and allows domestic investment to be held at a higher level than it would otherwise have been. However FDI is only one component of the overall capital account of the balance of payments. The UK, for instance, has frequently been a net exporter of FDI even in periods when it ran a current account deficit and hence had aggregate net capital inflows from abroad. Foreign direct investments do not depend on the existence of a current account imbalance. If the current account is in balance, then net outflows of FDI would be matched by net inflows of portfolio and banking sector investments.

This is not to say that the composition of capital flows does not matter, nor does it mean that there are no other factors affecting growth. The level of productivity in an economy depends upon the stocks of capital and of knowledge, and hence the composition of the skills of the workforce and the technical capacity of firms does matter. FDI is different from other forms of capital inflow, in that investors gain a controlling interest in the firms in which investment takes place. This allows them to change the way in which production is organised, which they cannot do if they are passive portfolio investors. They receive a 'rent' in the form of profit for this activity.

It is important to distinguish changes in the structure of national economies from changes in national income. There may obviously be some short-term job losses if industries such as textiles move from developed economies to developing ones. Such relocation is part of the process of restructuring that all progressive economies go through. In other more technologically advanced industries foreign investments may be undertaken in order to maximise the rate of return to an investment in knowledge. Ultimately, as Agarwal points out for the United States, the income from foreign investments can actually more than offset the value of any new outward investments. Firms have more funds available for new investment and shareholders have higher returns. This distinction is also important for an economy such as Ireland, where gross national income is 88 per cent of gross domestic output, with the difference constituting net royalty, profit and interest payments to foreign investors.

In a similar vein, the fact that foreign-owned firms account for a rising proportion of employment in many developed economies does not in itself tell us anything about their effect on economic growth and national income. If such firms were to withdraw overnight, the resulting decline in the relative price of labour should raise the the amount of labour demanded by indigenous companies. However, there is increasing evidence to suggest that growth is augmented by the spread of ideas associated with FDI. Barrell and Pain (1997) find that inward direct investment has had a positive impact on the level of technical progress in both the UK and Germany. Foreign-owned firms matter as they bring specific assets and standards which are not used by domestic firms. It is otherwise difficult to explain why domestic firms should not be able to take advantage of any profitable opportunities, unless they face significant financial constraints. Ruane and Görg argue that FDI in Ireland has played an important role in the overall development of the Irish economy for more than three decades, assisting the process of adjustment across geographic regions and within the manufacturing sector from traditional industries to more high-tech ones.

In many developed countries new inward investments primarily occur by means of mergers and acquisitions rather than by investments in 'greenfield' sites, which directly boost final demand. However it is not necessarily the case that the benefits of inward investment must thus be limited. Takeovers and the associated reorganisation of existing capacity and introduction of new ideas and standards may raise the rate of technical progress and hence the long-run rate of economic growth, even if they do not add to final demand directly. In developing countries FDI can help to close 'object gaps' (Romer, 1993) as well as 'idea gaps'. The paper by Agarwal highlights the extent to which FDI inflows have added considerably to fixed capital formation in the Central European economies.

An important policy issue is the extent to which linkages can be developed between inward investors and local firms (Blomström and Kokko, 1996). It is clear, both from the Irish experience (Barry and Bradley, 1997) and from other studies of local regional economies in the UK (Hood and Young, 1976) that the beneficial linkages between foreign and domestic firms may take some time to emerge. The survey of German manufacturing affiliates described by Hood, Taggart and Young in this volume suggests that to date the majority of German subsidiaries in the UK solely serve the UK market, rather than act as one component in an integrated global, or European, production network. Hence they have had only a limited effect on export performance. However over half the firms report significant sourcing of material inputs from UK suppliers. There appear to be significant national differences in the characteristics of foreign affiliates, with Japanese affiliates in the UK being more export orientated than German ones, but with less decision-making autonomy. The authors argue that UK regional policy has concentrated on maximising the quantity rather than the quality of inward investment and point to a need to develop local agglomeration economies to retain and expand multinational involvement in regional economies.

The development of local linkages is important both to maximise the benefits from inward investment and because such linkages may help to retain inward investment even if the initial source of comparative advantage for the host economy disappears. As Ruane and Görg comment, even in Ireland where there has been significant inward investment in high-tech industries, some concern remains about the growing dependency of the national economy on investment decisions made in the United States.

There is also increasing evidence of linkages between domestic firms and their foreign subsidiaries. This is brought out clearly by the survey evidence for Sweden reported by Braunerhjelm and Ekholm. The intensified integration of Swedish and foreign production units is reflected in the increase in intra-firm trade. Between 1990 and 1994 imports by affiliates from parent companies increased by almost 14 per cent. Similarly, exports from the foreign affiliates back to the parent company as a share of total affiliate sales almost doubled in that period. This may reflect changing patterns of specialisation that have developed as a consequence of Swedish membership of the EU.

Panel discussion

The papers were complemented by a lively panel discussion led by representatives from the UK Treasury, the Foreign Office and the Bundesbank. The discussion was undertaken on the basis of 'Chatham House' rules, and so comments are not attributed to particular speakers in the following summary.

Several speakers emphasised the extent to which firms had increasingly started to carry technologies across national borders. However it had to be remembered that foreign direct investment was still small in comparison with global economic activity. Some activities appeared to have become particularly prone to internationalisation, with patterns of foreign direct investment beginning to show the cross-hauling characteristics apparent in trade flows. Given the apparent scope for exploitation of economies of scale through concentrated production at a single location, especially in Europe, more research was needed in order to explain why firms were increasingly choosing to set up overseas affiliates. The need for a local market presence in order to expand demand and the desire to protect investments in firm-specific knowledge were widely agreed to be important elements of these decisions.

More attention also needed to be paid to the overall benefits of foreign investment rather than just to its determinants. Inward investment could affect only the types of jobs available rather than the quantity, unless it could be shown that it had wider effects on the growth process. A key question was whether higher foreign investment, both inward and outward, raised national income. There was a case for arguing that the effects on the host country were more likely to be beneficial if inward investment involved process innovations which helped enhance the skills and knowledge of the indigenous workforce. A number of speakers expressed surprise at the absence of any timely information in the UK on the activities of the foreign affiliates of British companies, particularly given the large stock of outward investments. This was in marked contrast to the detailed statistics available on US, Swedish and German multinational companies and made it impossible to investigate whether the activities undertaken overseas by UK multinationals had any bearing on the industrial structure and composition of employment in the United Kingdom.

There was general agreement that some caution was needed in drawing policy conclusions from the present high level of net outward investment in Germany. A high level of outward investment was to be expected from a capital rich economy such as Germany. The scale of outward investment relative to the size of the German economy was not at all unusual – broadly in line with France – and below that of the United Kingdom. Part of the reason for the recent growth in outward FDI was simply that German firms were beginning to seek new ways of expanding their presence in foreign markets. This could be done either through the establishment of distribution facilities to support exports or through the expansion of R&D facilities in core industries such as chemicals and electronics to adapt products to meet the specific requirements of local markets. The maturity of many German foreign affiliates was much lower than that of American and Swedish affiliates, suggesting that further internationalisation of R&D could be expected in the future.

There was some debate about the question of whether the claim that Germany had become an unattractive business location could be substantiated by the current low (absolute) level of capital inflows. Several participants stressed that this might be misleading. The German data on inflows of foreign direct investment were poor and gave different signals to the statistics of investing countries. Moreover it was not possible to judge what the 'right' level of capital inflows should be. Using alternative criteria such as employment the picture was somewhat different as many foreign-owned firms in Germany had been there for several decades. By 1994 they accounted for 10 per cent of total employment in western Germany, and 18 per cent of employment in manufacturing, broadly in line with the share of employment in foreign-owned firms in the United Kingdom. There was only a case for concern about a 'shortfall' in new investments if there was evidence that foreign firms brought new firm-specific advantages which were otherwise not available in Germany. This was more likely to be in the retail sector and other service industries than in manufacturing ones. It was suggested that the more general argument that the German economy needed less regulation and greater flexibility in parts of the labour market was best made independently, on the basis of comparative macroeconomic performance and constraints on the aggregate level of fixed capital investment, rather than on the specific level of net capital inflows.

The research agenda

It is clear from the papers in this book that there is a growing body of research into the interrelationships between trade, investment and economic growth. A body of work discussed in this volume and elsewhere has begun to discuss the factors affecting trade patterns, including relative costs, production capacity, the qualities of the indigenous workforce and the degree of international investment in a particular location. It is also important to understand the forces driving foreign investment, including relative costs, barriers to trade, the increasing differentiation and customisation of products, and the process of innovation and the diffusion of technology. Some progress has been made in this area, but more detailed studies at the sectoral and firm level are needed. The research agenda has begun to be expanded to include the factors influencing economic growth and total factor productivity, including domestic innovation and investment in education and international spillovers from other countries via trade and foreign investment.

Research has been undertaken in all these areas, but much more remains to be learned. As Eaton *et al.* (1994) emphasise, many formal analyses of the effects of FDI have neglected particular aspects of foreign investment. Traditional textbook general equilibrium approaches based on the Heckscher-Ohlin framework treat technological change as exogenous, whilst the policy interest in FDI arises from the extent to which it affects technological change. Yet all too often the popular focus is purely in terms of the number of jobs in foreign-owned firms, without any consideration of the overall costs and benefits to other sectors or the economy as a whole. A full general equilibrium analysis taking account of the endogenous linkages between trade, investment and technological change is required.

One example is provided by the experiments undertaken by Bayoumi *et al.* (1996) on a version of the IMF multi-country macroeconometric model Multimod modified to incorporate the estimates of Coe *et al.* (1997) of the impact of domestic and foreign R&D on total factor productivity growth. In this particular model international spillovers occur only via trade linkages. Models of this type extended to incorporate potential production relocation are essential if policy options such as fiscal incentives, corporate tax reforms, R&D subsidies, infrastructure investment and exchange rate regimes are to be properly evaluated. All may have very different costs and benefits if allowance is made for the extent to which they could permanently change the industrial structure of the nation.

Of course, the focus should not be only on one factor affecting technical change, albeit an important but empirically neglected one. The restructuring of the economic geography of Europe does not come about solely through FDI, although this is clearly an important part of the process. Any study of the impact of FDI on growth should also seek to allow for the role of domestic research activity and investment in education before conclusions can be drawn. Evidence from developing economies suggests that it is not simply the level of foreign investment, but the interaction between domestic institutions, social capabilities and foreign investment which affects economic growth. Borensztein *et al.* (1994), in a study of flows of FDI from industrial countries to sixty-nine developing countries, find that its impact on growth is dependent upon the existence of adequate human capital in the host economy. The discussions of the Irish experience by Ruane and Görg (this volume) and Barry and Bradley (1997) also add weight to the view that the quantity and quality of domestic human capital is important, both in terms of its direct effect on productivity and through the ability it can give to attract and adopt new technologies.

All the research methodologies utilised in this volume have an important part to play in the study of multinational companies. Microeconomic analysis is essential to discover the many diverse influences on the decision of the firm to become a multinational, and the extent to which new products and processes are thereby transferred across national borders. Many fruitful insights have been gained from the international business literature (Dunning, 1993). Macroeconomic analysis serves to complement such findings by allowing a fuller evaluation to be made of the overall impact of foreign-owned firms on national economies. Panel data analysis has helped to confirm the hypothesis that the Single Market Programme in Europe has affected direct investment patterns by allowing the impact of the different measures in the programme to be evaluated after controlling for the other factors that are known to influence investment decisions (Pain, 1997). Case studies of individual multinational firms could usefully complement studies of this kind by enabling more to be learnt about the forms of activities undertaken by newly established subsidiaries within the EU. We hope that the diverse range of studies presented in the volume will encourage further cooperation amongst researchers in this area.

Note

1   Funding for the conference was provided by the Anglo-German Foundation. The preparation of the conference volume and the research reported by the two editors was financed by the ESRC under grants R00023606 and R02220091. The editors are grateful to the providers of funds for their support.

References

Baldwin, R.E. and Venables, A.J. (1995), 'Regional economic integration', in Grossman, G.M. and Rogoff, K. (eds.), *Handbook of International Economics Volume III*, Elsevier, North-Holland.

Barrell, R. and Pain, N. (1997), 'Foreign direct investment, technological change and economic growth within Europe', *Economic Journal*, 107, pp. 1770–86.

(1998). 'Trade restraints and Japanese direct investment flows', *European Economic Review*, forthcoming.

Barry, F. and Bradley, J. (1997), 'FDI and trade: the Irish host country experience', *Economic Journal*, 107, pp. 1798–811.

Bayoumi, T., Coe, D.T. and Helpman, E. (1996), 'R&D spillovers and global growth', International Monetary Fund Working Paper WP/96/47.

Blomström, M. and Kokko, A. (1996), 'Multinational corporations and spillovers', CEPR Discussion Paper No. 1365.

Borensztein, E., De Gregorio, J. and Lee, J. (1994), 'How does foreign direct investment affect economic growth?', International Monetary Fund Working Paper WP/94/110.

Broadberry, S.N. (1997), *The Productivity Race: British Manufacturing in International Perspective 1850–1990*, Cambridge, Cambridge University Press.

Cantwell, J. and Harding, R. (1998), 'The internationalisation of German companies' R&D', *National Institute Economic Review*, 163, pp. 99–115.

Coe, D.T., Helpman, E. and Hoffmaister, A.W. (1997), 'North-South R&D spillovers', *Economic Journal*, 107, pp. 134–49.

Dunning, J. (1993), *Multinational Enterprises and the Global Economy*, Wokingham, Addison-Wesley.

Eaton, B.C., Lipsey, R.G. and Safarian, A.E. (1994), 'The theory of multinational plant location in a regional trading area', in Eden, L. (ed.), *Multinationals in North America*, Calgary, The University of Calgary Press.

Estall, R.C. and Buchanan, R.O. (1966), *Industrial Activity and Economic Geography*, London, Hutchinson.

Ferner, A. (1997), 'Country-of-origin effects and human resource management in multinational companies', *Human Resource Management Journal*, 7, pp. 19–37.

Grossman, G.M. and Helpman, E. (1991), *Innovation and Growth in the Global Economy*, Cambridge, Mass., MIT Press.

Helpman, E. (1997), 'R&D and productivity: the international connection', NBER Working Paper No. 6101.

Hood, N. and Young, S. (1976), 'US investment in Scotland: aspects of the branch factory syndrome', *Scottish Journal of Political Economy*, 23, pp. 279–94.

Jost, T. (1997), 'Direct investment and Germany as a business location', Economic Research Group of the Deutsche Bundesbank Discussion Paper 2/97.

Jungnickel, R. (1995), 'Foreign direct investment, trade and employment: the experience of Germany', in OECD, *Foreign Direct Investment, Trade and Employment*, Paris, OECD.

Krugman, P. (1991), *Geography and Trade*, Cambridge, Mass., MIT Press.

Krugman, P. and Venables, A.J. (1995), 'Globalisation and the inequality of nations', *Quarterly Journal of Economics*, 110, pp. 857–80.

Markusen, J.R. and Venables, A.J. (1996), 'The increased importance of direct investment in North Atlantic economic relationships: a convergence hypothesis', in Canzoneri, M.B., Ethier, W.J. and Grilli, V. (eds.), *The New Transatlantic Economy*, Cambridge, Cambridge University Press.

Pain, N. (1997), 'Continental drift: European integration and the location of UK foreign direct investment', *The Manchester School Supplement*, pp. 94–117.

Pain, N. and Lansbury, M. (1997), 'Regional economic integration and foreign direct investment: the case of German investment in Europe', *National Institute Economic Review*, 160, pp. 87–99.

Romer, P. (1993), 'Idea gaps and object gaps in economic development', *Journal of Monetary Economics*, 32, pp. 543–73.

Wood, S. (1996), 'How different are human resource practices in Japanese "transplants" in the United Kingdom?', *Industrial Relations*, 35, pp. 511–25.

2 The growth of foreign direct investment in Europe

RAY BARRELL and NIGEL PAIN

Introduction

Interest in the long-term comparative economic performance of nations has risen considerably in recent years, helped by the development of new theories of economic growth which stress the potential for international linkages to affect the productivity performance and economic growth of national economies. Two important channels are international trade, which makes available products that embody foreign knowledge, and foreign direct investment (FDI), which may involve the direct transfer of technology or new ideas. Increasing attention is now being paid in Europe to the question of why firms invest abroad. This reflects both the rapid growth in FDI within Europe as well as recent improvements in the quality and availability of data. At the heart of the debate is a focus on the costs and benefits of foreign investment, such as whether inward investment affects employment and economic growth and whether outward investment is simply 'job exporting', with firms moving to low-cost, labour-abundant locations.

The answers to these questions have potentially important implications for the design of national and supra-national policies in Europe. The Single Market Programme (SMP), with the removal of internal barriers to trade and capital mobility in the European Union, has changed the comparative advantages of countries and regions and highlighted the role of distinctive national institutions in location decisions. At the same time supra-national trade policies still affect the investment decisions of firms outside the European Union. In this chapter we provide an overview of recent trends in FDI in Europe and attempt to place these within the wider context of the ongoing evolution of European Union institutions and

19

policies. We investigate the factors affecting FDI flows, the extent to which government policies can affect such flows, and the wider implications for home and host economies.

Recent trends in foreign direct investment

Foreign direct investment has expanded rapidly throughout the world economy over the past two decades, helped by the removal of many national barriers to capital movements. The aggregate stock of FDI in the world economy is estimated to have risen from 4½ per cent of world output in 1975 to 9½ per cent in 1995, with the value of sales by the foreign affiliates of domestic companies estimated to exceed the value of world exports by around one-quarter.[1]

The broad pattern of foreign direct investment stocks is shown in table 2.1. It is clear that the vast majority of investments have been made by firms from the developed economies of the OECD and are located within other developed countries. The global level of FDI has risen particularly sharply since the middle of the 1980s, especially within Europe in the aftermath of the common deregulation of national capital and product markets. The proportion of the aggregate stock of world FDI located within EU member states is estimated to have risen from 31 per cent in 1985 to 39 per cent by 1995. During this time there have been rising levels of investment in the EU both by non-EU nationals and EU firms themselves.

The geographical distribution of existing investments suggests that foreign direct investment cannot simply be characterised as the movement of production to low wage economies. However in recent years there does appear to have been an increasing tendency to locate investments outside the major economies. United Nations estimates suggest that the proportion of new investments located in developing economies doubled from 18 per cent between 1985 and 1990 to 36 per cent between 1991 and 1996 (UNCTAD, 1997).[2] This primarily appears to have been at the expense of the non-EU OECD economies.

The pattern of investment flows within the OECD is summarised in table 2.2. The largest investors overseas are the United States, the UK, France, Germany and Japan. Whilst the first three of these economies also receive a high level of inward investment as well, less investment takes place in Japan. The situation of Germany is unclear; recorded FDI inflows are low, but this may in part reflect differences in their national definition of the inflow of direct investment (Jost, 1997). The change in the stock of

Table 2.1 *Global foreign direct investment stocks*

		1980	1985	1990	1995
Outward FDI					
World	$ billion	513.7	685.5	1,684.1	2,730.1
	% of GDP	4.9	5.9	8.1	9.7
OECD	$ billion	501.9	657.4	1,606.2	2,503.2
	% of GDP	6.8	6.1	10.6	13.2
	% of total	[97.7]	[95.9]	[95.4]	[91.7]
EU-15	$ billion	213.2	286.5	777.2	1,208.8
	% of GDP	7.4	7.1	13.8	17.4
	% of total	[41.5]	[41.8]	[46.1]	[44.3]
Inward FDI					
World	$ billion	481.9	734.9	1,716.9	2,657.9
	% of GDP	4.6	6.3	8.3	9.4
OECD	$ billion	356.4	526.3	1,361.4	1,922.0
	% of GDP	4.8	4.9	9.0	10.1
	% of total	[74.0]	[71.6]	[79.3]	[72.3]
EU-15	$ billion	185.0	226.5	712.2	1,028.1
	% of GDP	6.4	5.6	12.7	14.8
	% of total	[38.4]	[30.8]	[41.5]	[38.7]

Source: Authors' calculations from UNCTAD (1996), and OECD National Accounts.

inward investment in Germany between the end of 1990 and the end of 1995 is $92bn, considerably greater than the recorded capital inflow over this period.

The flow of investment from EU firms into other EU member states and North America from 1982 to 1994 is discussed in Pain and Lansbury (1997). From 1982 to 1987 investment in North America was greater than investment within the EU. However intra-EU investment exceeded investment in North America from 1988, after the start of the Single Market Programme, reaching a peak of 1¼ per cent of GDP in 1990. Over the five years to 1994, intra-EU FDI flows were equivalent to 4½ per cent of gross domestic fixed capital formation in the EU on average. Such data appear to suggest that moves towards greater European integration and the eradication of barriers to cross-border capital mobility have generated a significant change in investment patterns. Inward direct investment in countries such as Belgium, Denmark, France and Ireland during 1991–5 was more than twice the level in the previous five-year period.

Table 2.2 *FDI flows in selected OECD economies ($ billion, period totals)*

		1976–80	1981–5	1986–90	1991–5	1995 GDP ($ billion)
USA	Outflows	82.2	42.8	130.3	292.9	6,954.8
	Inflows	37.6	92.9	266.8	204.9	
Japan	Outflows	10.1	25.5	160.4	103.4	5,114.0
	Inflows	0.6	1.7	1.6	5.2	
UK	Outflows	39.1	46.1	140.5	127.1	1,101.8
	Inflows	27.8	21.6	108.7	85.8	
France	Outflows	9.6	13.5	83.4	116.0	1,537.6
	Inflows	11.2	10.8	40.4	95.0	
Germany	Outflows	18.7	21.1	71.9	110.3	2,412.5
	Inflows[a]	5.9	3.8	13.5	18.3	
	Inflows[b]	13.8	22.1	71.5	92.3	
Belgium	Outflows	2.9	1.0	21.1	33.7	269.2
	Inflows	6.3	5.6	23.4	49.1	
Denmark	Outflows	0.9	1.0	5.5	12.6	173.3
	Inflows	0.9	0.4	3.0	13.4	
Greece[c]	Inflows	2.4	2.3	3.8	5.3	114.3
Italy	Outflows	2.2	8.4	20.4	31.4	1,087.2
	Inflows	2.7	5.3	19.4	16.3	
Ireland[d]	Outflows	n.a.	n.a.	3.3	11.6	64.3
	Inflows	n.a.	n.a.	6.9	16.8	
Netherlands	Outflows	21.0	19.2	50.2	62.9	395.5
	Inflows	6.3	7.6	31.9	35.1	
Portugal	Outflows	0.0	0.1	0.3	2.2	99.8
	Inflows	0.4	0.9	6.0	7.8	
Spain	Outflows	0.9	1.5	7.4	16.7	559.6
	Inflows	5.2	8.9	37.5	49.5	
Sweden	Outflows	3.0	7.0	41.2	25.3	230.6
	Inflows	0.5	1.5	7.0	30.5	
Switzerland[e]	Outflows	n.a.	6.2	25.7	40.2	306.1
	Inflows	4.6	2.6	12.6	11.3	

Sources: Direct investment statistics from IMF *International Financial Statistics Yearbook 1996* and *International Financial Statistics*, June 1997, and *Deutsche Bundesbank Monthly Report*, August 1997. GDP from OECD *Main Economic Indicators*, June 1997.
Notes: (a) Figures from FDI flow data in balance of payments. (b) Figures based on change in stock of inward investment. (c) Outflow data not available. (d) Data based on Eurostat figures in *European Union Direct Investment Yearbook*, 1996. (e) National data only available from 1983. Data prior to then from US, German and UK statistics.

Borders and institutions at the supra-national level seem to have a significant impact on the pattern of investments. Membership of the dominant regional trading bloc appears to matter. The level of inward investment into Spain (Bajo-Rubio and Sosvilla-Rivero, 1994; Barrell and Pain, 1998) and Portugal rose significantly after their accession into the EU in 1986. Sweden appears to have had a similar experience in more recent years.[3] However the contrasting experience of Greece since entry into the EU in 1981 suggests that membership of the regional 'club' is necessary but not sufficient, implying that national institutions and social capabilities may also affect location decisions (Barry and Bradley, 1997).

While it is clear that new foreign direct investments have risen significantly in real terms over the past decade, they remain small in comparison to total fixed capital investments in Europe. The aggregate *stock* of FDI in Europe is approximately the size of the annual *flow* of gross fixed investment in the European Union. The scale of national direct investment inflows should also be judged against the size of the economies in question. Although the US was the largest recipient of inward FDI between 1985 and 1995, it is also the largest economy. The level of inward and outward investment from the United Kingdom is higher than in Germany and France if expressed as a proportion of GDP, but less than in some of the smaller European economies such as Belgium and Ireland. Foreign-owned firms account for over three-fifths of value added in the manufacturing sectors of these economies.

The pattern of the data suggests that FDI in Western Europe is not simply a reflection of capital being invested in locations with 'flexible' labour markets and few direct regulatory burdens on business, as is sometimes claimed (Eltis and Higham, 1995). Comparisons between the UK and Italy and, to a lesser extent, Germany, might appear to give some weight to this argument. Comparisons with more heavily regulated economies such as France and Belgium, which have succeeded in attracting a significant level of inward investment, suggest that many other factors are likely to be important.

Indeed despite the supposed advantages offered by the flexible labour market and the deregulated business environment in the UK, the UK remains a net outward investor, both within Europe and elsewhere, even in the manufacturing sector. UK companies have for instance been the largest single investors in France since 1990. The drift of foreign direct investments by UK companies towards continental Europe has accelerated in recent years, with over a third of all investments now located within EU member states, compared to a little over a fifth a decade ago. It could be argued that labour flexibility in countries such as the UK is presently higher than in some continental economies. However, the rising level of investment by companies within mainland Europe does not suggest that the Social Chapter and the myriad different labour market regulations in many European countries are seen by large multinational firms as obstacles that cannot be overcome.

Why do firms invest overseas?

Factor endowments and relative costs

Cross-border investments are made for many different reasons. Traditional general equilibrium models based on the Heckscher-Ohlin framework concentrate on the relation between trade, capital mobility and relative factor endowments (Mundell, 1957). If two autarkic countries have the same production function, then the capital rich country will have a lower rate of return to capital if there are no trade or capital flows. Capital flows to equilibrate returns could take place if there were limited trade, and the stronger are barriers to trade, the larger the potential flows of capital. If this was the only factor causing capital flows, then we should see a simple pattern of flows, with capital rich countries, generally those with high incomes, exporting capital to poor (in terms of both capital and income) countries. However, whilst models of this type provide an explanation for the observed net flows of capital from developed economies to developing ones, they can say little about direct investments within developed countries themselves, or indeed why capital should flow by means of direct rather than portfolio investments. As table 2.1 suggests, the leading investing countries – the UK, the US, France, Germany, and Japan – have tended to invest in other OECD countries rather than in the more capital scarce developing economies. Within the OECD there are, of course, labour-abundant low wage economies, and some such as Spain, Portugal and Mexico have specific locational advantages arising from their membership of a regional trade area. However, key destinations for inward investment in recent years such as the US, the UK, France and Belgium are relatively high cost, at least in terms of wages per hour, and relatively capital rich. Hence we can conclude that simple general equilibrium models do not provide a full explanation of firms' decisions to invest abroad.

    If capital flows cannot be explained in a simple general equilibrium framework we could posit that relocation takes place in response to relative costs of production, with the ultimate market for the product unchanged.[4] It is clear from our recent research into the foreign investments of US, German, Japanese and British companies that relative unit labour costs, which take account of wage and productivity differences, remain an important element in the investment decision.[5] However they cannot account fully for the observed pattern of foreign investment between developed economies in recent years, nor for why individual companies may elect to have multi-plant operations rather than produce in a single location and serve foreign markets by trade. Models which stress relative factor endowments and relative factor costs thus need to be augmented in order to explain the patterns of investment that we observe.

Proximity, knowledge-based assets and trade costs

Comparative advantage has to be seen as path dependent. Account needs to be taken of imperfect competition, product differentiation and the gains arising from the agglomeration of complementary activities when constructing models to explain the location of investments (Krugman, 1995; Venables, 1996). A number of recent papers have stressed that the extent to which firms elect to engage in trade rather than establish foreign affiliates depends on the benefits of proximity to final markets relative to the benefits of concentrating production in one location and exploiting scale economies (Markusen and Venables, 1996; Brainard, 1997). If trade costs are high, then firms have an incentive to locate close to final markets. If there are strong, plant-level, scale economies, then firms have an incentive to centralise production and serve foreign markets by exports. If firms possess knowledge-based, firm-specific assets, then they may become multinationals.

Knowledge-based assets consist of factors such as firm-specific process or product innovations as well as intangible assets such as managerial or marketing skills or reputation. With the changing nature of technology and production such assets appear to be coming more common (Patel and Pavitt, 1995). The linkages between multinational companies and their level of firm-specific assets have long been recognised, see Caves (1996) and the references therein, but have recently been given renewed attention following new developments in the theories of economic geography and international trade.

Such assets encourage foreign investment in two ways. First, as Markusen (1995) stresses, they act as a joint input across plants, giving economies of scale at the level of the firm rather than at the level of the individual plant. In some circumstances a single multi-plant firm may therefore have a cost advantage over two separate single plant firms. It can locate production nearer to the market, setting up cloned plants using common knowledge-based assets. Such possibilities appear to have increased with the move away from Fordist modes of production based on mass assembly of identical products to more customised production. As Prais (1995) argues, these changes have been facilitated by, and require, improved computer techniques and better education, especially numeracy, in the workforce. Foreign investment can ensure that brand images and specific products reap extra profits for their owners, with product differentiation for niche markets now much easier than it was thirty years ago. Developments in telecommunications and information technology have also helped to create global markets for some non-tradable products.

The existence of knowledge-based assets also affects the choice over the method of expansion overseas. For instance firms may prefer to undertake foreign direct investment rather than license existing foreign firms to undertake production. Licensing has the dual risks that product quality may not be maintained and that potential competitors can acquire technical secrets (Horstman and Markusen, 1987). The changing nature of innovation and ideas has also changed the type of investments made. New fixed capital investments in 'greenfield' sites were required to exploit ideas such as mass production. Process innovations and managerial expertise can often be introduced as easily by reorganising an existing firm, with investment being undertaken through mergers and acquisitions.

In a large market, such as the US, a firm with a specific product can have a multi-plant operation without investing abroad. In a large economy such as Europe, which has many countries, a similar firm would be described as a multinational, as its optimal plant structure requires dispersed production. Grossman and Helpman (1991) argue that R&D intensive small countries are the most likely to invest abroad. Such countries are common in Europe, with Sweden and Switzerland being the prime examples. At the end of 1994 the stock of outward FDI by Swedish and Swiss firms is estimated to have been equivalent to 26 per cent and 39 per cent of GDP respectively (UNCTAD, 1996, Annex table 6).

Markusen and Venables (1996) argue that continuing integration, and hence expansion in market size, may lead to a gradual substitution of 'horizontal' foreign investment for intra-industry trade between countries within integrated regions. This is because the variable cost advantage of multinational firms arising from the use of a joint input across plants comes to dominate the higher fixed costs of multi-plant operations. However, such a result would depend upon the structure of both industries and countries. The example of development in South Asia, and especially the role of Singapore, discussed in Barrell et al. (1997), indicates the limits to such patterns, as the size of the industry can exceed the capabilities of the country. The optimal pattern of location within Asia has, to date, led to multi-country involvement in a single chain of production in industries such as electronics and computer manufacture, with 'vertical' direct investment raising trade.

It has also long been recognised that changes in regional trade arrangements can have an important effect on both the level and location of overseas investments (Eaton *et al.*, 1994). For instance trade liberalisation appears to have altered the economic geography of Mexico (Hanson, 1997), with Mexico City declining in importance relative to areas on the US–Mexico border as trade barriers between Mexico and the United States have been lowered and new investments have been made by US firms in the maquiladora sector.

The initial eradication of tariff barriers within the then European Community prompted considerable empirical study into the question of whether investment was diverted into the region (Yannopoulos, 1990). More recently, integration within Europe has involved the removal of internal non-tariff barriers to market entry under the Single Market Programme, although external barriers to trade have remained. Common internal scientific and labour standards are being developed and a carefully constructed industrial policy put in place. Measures based on the single licence principle have meant that the SMP has opened new markets for firms in non-tradable sectors as well as those in tradable ones. The continued existence of external barriers may induce firms from outside the 'closed' region to set up production facilities inside the barriers in order to be able to enhance their product specific rents by gaining barrier- and tariff-free access to the regional wide market (Balasubramanyam and Greenaway, 1993).

The issue of whether European integration has affected production location is important. Integration may have had effects on the demand for factors of production, and especially labour, in different nations. A priori it might be expected that the removal of internal barriers to trade and capital flows should cause some industries to agglomerate, whilst other may disperse away from core centres. The forces at work will depend on the economies of scale at plant and firm level within the industry, and on transport costs for the products involved. The similar sized US market for automobiles, for instance, has fewer producers, and in general fewer plants than the European industry. Hence one might expect that the process of European integration, and the removal of country-specific implicit protection and national currencies, should ultimately lead to a restructuring of the industry, concentrating locations in key economies.

What determines investment patterns in Europe?

There is a growing body of empirical evidence that suggests that firm-specific assets and trade barriers are an important part of the explanation for the observed patterns of FDI in Europe. Empirical work in Pain (1997) and Hubert and Pain in this book shows that registered patents help to explain the industrial pattern and level of overseas investment by British and German companies, with 'innovating' companies being more likely to invest overseas. This suggests that foreign direct investment may act as an important channel for the diffusion of new ideas and products across national boundaries.

Evidence from the recent pattern of outward investment by Japanese and German corporations suggests that the location of such investments is affected by regional trading arrangements and trade policy instruments. Hubert and Pain report evidence of significant differences between the factors determining foreign direct investment from German firms within the EU and other Northern Hemisphere economies with separate free trade agreements. Relocation within Europe appears to be more sensitive to cost factors, such as relative labour costs and corporate tax burdens, whilst relocation outside appears to be associated with large markets and the existence of specialised products.

Barrell and Pain (1998) illustrate the extent to which the scale and pattern of Japanese direct investment in Europe and North America have been influenced by the intensity of contingent protection within the European Community and the US. As increasing use was made of anti-dumping procedures in the EU in the 1980s FDI flows from Japan rose independently of other factors, with a switch from trade to foreign production. The key objective was to locate within the EU to gain access to the wider regional market. Particular locations within the EU were then chosen on the basis of their cost competitiveness with other possible EU locations, with the UK gaining the largest share of such investments. In this instance national characteristics, such as the structure of the UK labour market, did affect the level of inward investment, but only because the supra-national tools for creating a 'closed' region forced Japanese firms to invest within Europe. Cost differentials between individual EU economies and Japan were not found to be an important factor in the investment decision.

There is also econometric evidence that the Single Market Programme has helped to raise intra-EU FDI, with the effects of the programme found to differ significantly across industries and countries (Pain, 1997; Pain and Lansbury, 1997).[6] Investment has risen more rapidly than might otherwise have been expected in those sectors that previously had the highest barriers to cross-border market entry. This is true of both the industrial and service sectors, with limited evidence, especially for the UK, that industries have chosen to concentrate production in a single location, despite the reductions in barriers to trade.[7] Taken together the models imply that the SMP had raised intra-European FDI by German and British companies by $27 billion by 1992 (at constant 1990 prices), or around 0.5 per cent of EU GDP. Over two-thirds of this gain occurred in the service sectors.

There is also some support for the hypothesis that the SMP may have served to divert investment into the EU at the expense of other locations in the econometric results of Aristotelous and Fountas (1996) and Pain (1997). The former find that the level of inward investment in Europe by US and Japanese firms has been significantly higher than might otherwise have been expected since 1987, whilst the latter finds some evidence that UK companies have raised investment in Europe since 1990 at the expense of investment in the United States.

The brief discussion above along with the results reported in the other chapters of this volume suggest that labour market institutions, social capabilities, fiscal incentives and exchange rate policies can all influence the location of investments. From a policy perspective it is of interest to ask whether we can identify factors which affect the type of activities placed in different locations within Europe. One approach, adopted in the Hubert and Pain paper, is to use econometric evidence to estimate the importance of particular factors in the growth of FDI. Their results indicate that the UK has clearly benefited from changes in the performance of the labour market in recent years, but appears to have performed relatively poorly in attracting investments from those sectors in Germany where innovations have risen most rapidly.

This pattern of results is consistent with other studies that highlight both the higher level of technical and scientific skills in the workforce in many continental countries and the lower level of labour market regulation in the UK. Prais (1995) surveys a number of comparative studies undertaken at NIESR that have highlighted the extent to which the skills of much of the broader workforce in the UK have fallen behind those in the Netherlands and Germany. Patterns of investment elsewhere have also been influenced by the availability of qualified personnel, with Japanese investment in the US being particularly attracted to regions with high levels of research capacity, especially in semiconductor based technologies.

The research findings discussed above also have a number of interesting implications for European countries, particularly for those in Central and Eastern Europe. It appears that membership of the EU and access to its market are important factors behind high levels of inward investment. Labour costs and tax competitiveness do matter, but only if a firm wishes to locate within the European market. However if these were the sole factors in investment decisions it would be difficult to account for the continued, positive, level of inward investment into Germany and the high level of net outward direct investment from the UK. Other characteristics of the host country also affect the investment decision. Labour costs are not as important an element in many investment decisions as they once were, particularly for companies making high technology products. Cultural factors such as language matter as does contiguity to the major investing economies (Thomsen and Woolcock, 1993), the skills and abilities of the host country workforce, the quality of infrastructure and existence of supportive institutional arrangements for knowledge transfer between the science base and private industry.

American multinationals in Europe

Up until this point we have confined our discussion to foreign direct investment. This is only one indicator of the type and scale of activities carried out by multinational firms. It is also possible to learn from the detailed statistics available in some source countries on the operations of the foreign affiliates of domestic companies. In particular we can draw on the long-established surveys undertaken into the operations of US multinationals, the most important source of investment in Europe from non-European countries.

Table 2.3 reports figures on the geographical distribution of employment and the gross product of majority-owned foreign affiliates of US companies.[8] Gross product is a measure of value-added output in the affiliates. The increasing concentration of production in Europe over time is readily apparent from these figures, particularly since the early 1980s. Outside Europe the proportion of output produced in Asia has also risen significantly. In contrast the proportion in Canada has fallen sharply since the start of the Free Trade Agreement between Canada and the US in 1989, with a number of US multinationals closing subsidiaries within Canada and substituting exports for FDI as a result of the improvements in market access (Niosi, 1994).

Within Europe, the UK and Germany are the two most important sites for production. Output in affiliates in France, Spain and Ireland has also risen sharply in recent years, in line with the pattern revealed by the aggregate capital flow data reported in table 2.2. By 1995 the gross prod-

Table 2.3 *The geographical distribution of the activities of US majority-owned foreign affiliates (per cent)*

	Gross product					Employment		
	1977	1982	1989	1994	1995	1989	1994	1995
Europe	43.0	50.3	56.2	58.7	59.2	45.1	45.3	45.2
UK	10.5	17.2	16.5	15.5	15.3	12.4	10.6	10.3
Germany	11.2	11.1	11.2	13.7	13.3	9.7	9.6	9.2
France	6.0	5.5	7.1	7.9	7.5	6.5	6.4	6.3
Italy	3.6	3.8	5.2	4.6	4.5	3.1	2.9	3.1
Netherlands	2.6	2.4	4.1	3.6	3.8	2.3	2.4	2.2
Belgium	2.6	2.3	2.7	2.9	3.1	2.2	1.7	1.7
Ireland	0.5	0.8	1.4	1.6	2.2	0.8	0.9	0.9
Spain	1.3	1.1	2.3	2.0	2.1	2.3	2.2	2.3
Switzerland	1.3	1.4	1.6	1.7	1.9	0.8	0.8	0.8
Sweden	0.7	0.8	0.7	0.6	1.1	0.5	0.5	0.8
Other	2.7	3.9	3.4	4.6	4.4	2.2	4.2	4.3
Canada	17.2	15.2	16.3	11.9	11.1	17.7	14.2	13.9
Latin America	10.0	12.5	9.3	10.3	9.9	18.8	19.3	18.5
Asia	10.2	12.7	14.6	16.7	17.2	15.0	18.8	19.8
Rest of the world	19.6	9.3	3.6	2.4	2.6	3.4	2.4	2.5
Memorandum								
World total[a]	161.1	223.7	320.0	403.7	463.0	5.11	5.71	5.97

Source: *Survey of Current Business*, various issues.
Note: (a) Gross product, $ billion; employment, millions.

uct of US affiliates in Ireland represented some 16 per cent of Irish GDP. The gross product of US affiliates also amounts to over 5 per cent of GDP in both the UK and Belgium (Barrell and Pain, 1997).

The UK is continually regarded as the prime destination in Europe for investment by non-European firms. This is particularly apparent in the US foreign direct investment data, which suggest that, at the end of 1995, some 39 per cent of US FDI in the EU member states was held in the United Kingdom.[9] The UK had over three times the level of investment as the next most popular host, Germany. However such figures give a misleading impression of the scale to which the UK is preferred to other countries. As can be seen from table 2.3 the output of US affiliates in the UK represented only 25 per cent of the total gross product of US affiliates in the EU. Indeed, as we show below in table 2.5, the gross product of manufacturing affiliates within Germany was higher than those located in the UK.

Table 2.4 *1995 industrial composition of the gross product of US majority-owned foreign affiliates (per cent)*

	Europe	UK	Germany	France	Neths	Belgium	Ireland	Spain
Manufacturing	51.0	40.4	65.3	54.7	48.7	54.8	74.4	68.9
Food & Drink	*5.1*	*4.0*	*4.9*	*5.2*	*8.8*	*4.2*	*7.5*	*9.2*
Chemicals	*11.3*	*7.8*	*8.6*	*15.3*	*12.3*	*23.5*	*27.6*	*14.6*
Machinery	*8.0*	*7.2*	*11.3*	*13.8*	*3.9*	*3.9*	*8.7*	*3.2*
Electronics	*4.7*	*3.8*	*4.1*	*4.6*	*3.0*	*2.1*	*16.8*	*5.0*
Transport	*7.6*	*7.4*	*14.7*	*2.7*	*0.8*	*7.1*	*0.4*	*25.8*
Other	*14.3*	*10.2*	*21.7*	*13.1*	*19.9*	*14.0*	*13.4*	*11.1*
Petroleum	21.9	32.3	17.0	17.4	15.6	15.2	8.0	2.5
Wholesale	12.5	7.3	6.2	14.0	21.8	15.4	9.6	16.4
Other services	14.6	20.0	11.5	13.9	13.9	14.6	8.0	12.2

Source: Authors' calculations from Mataloni (1997).

Again this suggests that relative labour costs are not the sole determinant of investment patterns, even in the tradable goods sector within the single European market. In part the higher level of compensation per employee in economies such as Germany and France is a reflection of a higher level of productivity per head. Also, whilst employers' social security costs do tend to be higher in mainland Europe than in, say, the UK, it needs to be remembered that their impact depends on their eventual incidence. Studies of wage formation within Europe point to the absence of long-run 'wedge' effects, so that the eventual incidence of higher employers' taxes is on the employee not the employer (Layard *et al.*, 1991). Greater mobility of capital might in any case ultimately be expected to help equalise overall labour costs across countries within Europe, even if social security systems differ across countries.

Differences between the industrial composition of US investments in the UK and other European nations are brought out in table 2.4. Value added in petroleum industries accounts for one-third of the total gross product of US affiliates in the UK, well above the EU average. A similar picture is true of service industries. Manufacturing activities are relatively less important in the UK than elsewhere. Transport and electronics investments are relatively important in Spain and Ireland respectively; Ireland, along with Belgium, also has a relatively high proportion of investment in the chemicals industries.

Table 2.5 provides more details on the operations of US foreign affiliates within Europe. The figures suggest that the activities located within

Table 2.5 *Selected data for US nonbank foreign affiliates In Europe (1995 unless otherwise stated)*

	All sectors				Manufacturing	
	Gross product ($bn)	Employ-ment (000s)	R&D expenditures (1989– 95 average)		Gross product ($bn)	Value added per head[a] (1993 prices)
			Total ($bn)	as % of gross product		
EU15	273.9	2701	7.66	3.46	139.8	100.0
UK	70.6	813	1.85	3.12	28.5	83.3
Germany	61.5	549	2.53	5.02	40.1	111.6
France	34.7	378	1.02	3.41	19.0	89.0
Italy	20.9	184	0.36	1.89	9.5	104.4
Netherlands	17.5	129	0.44	3.12	8.5	129.2
Belgium	14.1	101	0.35	3.75	7.7	129.8
Ireland	10.0	56	0.45	7.83	7.4	176.1
Spain	9.6	136	0.21	2.60	6.6	83.2
Sweden	5.1	49	0.16	4.78	2.7	71.5

Sources: calculated from annual articles on 'Operations of US Foreign Affiliates', *Survey of Current Business*, selected issues.
Note: (a) Average based on four years from 1992–5.

the UK have been relatively employment intensive, with the UK accounting for a larger share of employment than output. Labour productivity in manufacturing measured in terms of gross product per employee over the four year period 1992–5 is over 16 per cent lower in UK affiliates than the European average. Even so, the productivity of US affiliates in the UK appears to be somewhat higher than the productivity of UK firms overall. For example, in manufacturing the US affiliates only account for some 10½ per cent of total employees in employment, but produce around 13½ per cent of value added.[10] The research intensity of affiliates in the UK, measured as R&D expenditures relative to sales, is also below the European average, with the most research intensive affiliates being located within Germany, Sweden, Belgium and Ireland. However it is noteworthy that on average the United States affiliates have a greater propensity to undertake R&D expenditures in all countries than domestic firms (as measured by the share of business enterprise R&D in GDP).

The implications of these detailed statistics on the operations of US

affiliates mirror those from econometric studies of foreign direct investment. Both suggest that whilst the UK has clearly been able to attract relatively labour intensive investments, it has fared relatively poorly in attracting more capital intensive investments. The UK has performed comparatively well in attracting investments in the non-manufacturing industries.
However it is in these sectors where the evidence for the existence of beneficial supply-side effects from foreign investment is weakest.

The impact of FDI in Europe

In recent years renewed attention has been paid to the factors affecting
technological change and economic growth. Much of the literature
on endogenous growth focuses on the impact of innovation and knowledge accumulation (Grossman and Helpman, 1991). International
knowledge spillovers expand the stock of ideas that may be used for research in each country. At present much more is known about the role of
trade than about the role of FDI (Helpman, 1997). The majority of
empirical studies have followed Coe and Helpman (1995) in analysing the
extent to which the growth of total factor productivity is affected by the
diffusion of technological activities between industrialised countries as a
result of trade flows.

One approach to the evaluation of FDI might be to estimate the extent
to which it affects productive capacity within national economies or to
add up the number of new jobs created by inward investment. This might
suggest that its benefits are limited in many developed economies given
the relatively high proportion of investments that are mergers and acquisitions rather than investments in 'greenfield' sites. However the impact
of FDI is not simply a matter of the extent to which it creates new capacity, but also the extent to which it acts as a channel through which new
ideas, technologies and working practices can be established in the host
economy (Romer, 1993). Takeovers and the associated reorganisation of
existing capacity may raise the rate of technical progress and hence the
long-run rate of economic growth, even if they do not add to final demand
directly. Survey evidence suggests that, in general, the mode of entry of
foreign firms makes relatively little difference to the impact of such firms
on domestic suppliers in the UK (PACEC, 1995). A more appropriate
means of assessment would therefore be to ask whether inward and outward FDI raise the incomes of factors of production owned by residents
of the particular economy above the levels they would otherwise be at in
the absence of any such investments.

Products and processes that would not have otherwise have been produced within the host economy can arrive with inward FDI, whilst outward investment can enable domestic firms to open up markets that would not otherwise have been available and maximise the rents accruing to their firm-specific assets. In this sense the foreign investment process need not be a zero sum game, with winners in host countries being matched by losers in the investing countries. Foreign investment is important because the characteristics of foreign-owned firms are different from those of purely domestic ones. If they were not, then, in the absence of any capital market constraints, there is no reason why domestic companies should not take advantage of any profitable investment opportunities, and the economy would be at the same point on its production possibility frontier.

Inward investment and technical progress

Microeconomic evidence on licensing and direct investment suggests that inflows of new technology and working practices from the affiliates of multinational firms create a significant potential for spillovers to local firms in the host country (Blomström and Kokko, 1996). Such effects can be direct, if foreign-owned firms are more productive or expand final demand through new investment on 'greenfield' sites, or indirect, through growing contact with local suppliers, learning by doing and observation, and the movement of knowledge with workers leaving foreign firms for domestic ones. Such indirect spillovers are likely to take some time to emerge, particularly in developing economies. In either case new investment has shifted the production possibility frontier of the economy and raised the marginal product of capital in the economy for each level of the capital stock.

Most of the existing empirical evidence on the spillovers from foreign investment relates to developing countries. There is widespread evidence that inward investment has raised the growth rate of many developing countries, particularly those with open economies (Balasubramanyam *et al.*, 1996). Much less is known about the impact of foreign investments on economic performance in developed economies, especially in Europe, or indeed the extent to which government policies can affect the pattern of investment.

At a general level, there is agreement about the key role played by the transfer and adaptation of American technologies to European conditions during the so called 'golden age' of economic growth in the postwar period (Crafts and Toniolo, 1996). The high level of inward investment in manufacturing activities has clearly been particularly important in the economic development of many smaller European economies such as Ireland and Belgium (Cassiers *et al.*, 1996). Studies of manufacturing inward investment in countries such Australia (Caves, 1974), Canada (Globerman, 1979), Mexico (Blomström, 1986) and Portugal (Farinha and Mata, 1996) also suggest that the presence of inward investors can exert a positive influence on the productivity of local firms. Within the UK, the Competitiveness White Papers in 1995 and 1996 have stressed the importance of FDI in the supply-side transformation of the UK economy (Eltis and Higham, 1996). Innovative production and managerial techniques appear to have been spread to many UK owned companies (PACEC, 1995) and foreign-owned firms have improved export performance (Blake and Pain, 1994).

However the increased attention recently paid to foreign investment by many policy-makers within Europe has not yet been matched by empirical developments within the large-scale general equilibrium models often used for policy evaluation. Most models of this type have little to say about the impact of multinational enterprises, and implicitly assume that foreign-owned assets held within particular economies are as productive on average as those owned by indigenous residents (Pain, 1996). This would seem to question why foreign-owned firms exist, particularly within developed economies.

In recent work at the National Institute we have begun to provide empirical evidence of the wider consequences of foreign direct investment on home and host economies. This work has used time series analyses of sectoral labour demand in Germany and the UK, with labour productivity allowed to vary with the level of inward investment in the respective sector (Pain, 1996; Barrell and Pain, 1997). One advantage of an aggregate approach of this kind is that it captures inter-industry spillovers as well as intra-industry effects in the industries in which the inward investment takes place. The results suggest that inward FDI has been a major source of technological progress in both economies.

The beneficial effects of inward investment in the UK appear to have been concentrated in the manufacturing sector, with a 1 per cent rise in the stock of inward manufacturing investment estimated to raise the aggregate level of labour-augmenting technical progress in the sector by 0.26 per cent. Barrell and Pain (1997) calculate that around 30 per cent of the growth in UK aggregate manufacturing productivity since 1985 can be attributed to the impact of inward investment.

The lack of any discernible effect from FDI in non-manufacturing industries on labour productivity in the non-manufacturing private sector suggests that some caution be applied to the extent to which the benefits of inward investment are extolled. Some two-thirds of all inward investment in the UK is in sectors outside manufacturing. One possible explanation is that the benefits offered by inward investment are more apparent and more quickly felt in those sectors where domestic producers are at a comparative disadvantage and relatively less productive. Inward investment in the manufacturing sector often reflects the technological advantages of investing firms, whereas investment in sectors such as financial services in the UK may in part be motivated by the ability to benefit from agglomeration economies. It is possible that service sector investments may transfer new managerial or financial practices, but the diffusion of such skills is likely to prove difficult to track.

Direct investment and trade performance

In order to examine the effects of FDI on patterns of output as well as of technical progress it is necessary to address the issue of the size of nations and assess the impact of FDI on trade patterns. Foreign investments can serve to change the range and technological characteristics of indigenous products, factors that are widely thought to be important determinants of trade performance (Grossman and Helpman, 1991). In accounting terms foreign investments may change the proportion of the (given) world market accounted for by exports from that country. Consider the case of a car manufacturer who moves from one location in Europe to another. Such a move will do little to affect the relative costs of production in different locations or the total size of the market for cars in Europe, assuming that price discrimination is not pursued in national markets. However the market share of cars produced in the original location will decline, whilst the export performance of the new location will improve. These changes may be partially offset by a higher level of exports of intermediate products from the source country to the new host location.

Whilst it is possible to conceive of situations in which both inward and outward investment may either create or displace exports, on balance the available evidence points to a complementary relationship in Europe between inward investment and exports, particularly in open economies such as Ireland (O'Sullivan, 1993), Portugal (Cabral, 1995) and the UK (Blake and Pain, 1994). Any evaluation of the impact of FDI on trade also needs to address the effects of outward FDI, and ask if it is a substitute for exports, or raises them by providing better marketing facilities or expanding market size and demand for intermediate products. We should also ask if outward FDI raises imports, although there appears to be little available research in this area at present (WTO, 1996).

The evidence on the relationship between outward investment and export performance is mixed. Many early cross-sectional studies found a complementary relationship between the two, either in particular sectors, or at the level of the firm. A useful overview of this literature is given by WTO (1996), although their conclusion that there is little empirical evidence of any substitution between outward investment and exports is somewhat misplaced. Exports and FDI have both risen over time owing to general economic growth. The relevant question is whether national export performance, that is exports relative to foreign market size, has been affected by FDI.

Most recent time series evidence provides a different picture, as shown in the detailed surveys in Pain and Wakelin (1998a,b). They also report new panel data studies of the impact of outward and inward investment on export demand for a wide range of OECD economies. Their results provide evidence of a statistically significant negative relationship between net outward investment and export performance for many European countries and the US, after controlling for relative price and non-price competitiveness.[11] Thus while inward investment does help to improve export prospects, market entry by outward investment can be at the expense of export sales, even if there is some boost to sales of intermediate goods to foreign affiliates. In contrast there was evidence of a positive long-term relationship between outward investment and exports for Japan.

One possible explanation for the differences between these findings and those from earlier cross-sectional studies on data in the 1960s and 1970s is that the effects of foreign direct investment depend on the maturity of the investments and the accumulation of investments over time, with long-established foreign affiliates now having a relatively high local content in their output, after having initially been established with capital goods imported from the investing country. Pain and Wakelin (1998b) also find that the negative relationship between outward FDI and exports for most European economies appears to have strengthened significantly since the start of the Single Market Programme.

Even if the direct effects of FDI on trade performance appear deleterious, it is important to take account of the beneficial effects of the income from those investments on the national product. For instance the earnings from UK direct investments overseas were equivalent to 2¾ per cent of GDP per annum on average between 1990 and 1995, whilst the earnings from direct investment in the UK averaged 1¼ per cent of GDP per annum. Indeed in some cases it should be recognised that the only option available is to undertake FDI or withdraw from the area of production, and hence the effects may be unambiguously positive, with

the income stream from specific activities protected by foreign investment.[12]

It would not be appropriate to conclude that outward investment 'exports' jobs simply because we find a negative relationship between outward investment and net trade performance. Account also needs to be
taken of the factors responsible for the higher level of outward investment.
If this has arisen as a result of the creation of a higher level of firm-specific assets, and hence a faster rate of domestic innovation, then domestic
economic growth and non-price competitiveness may have been enhanced.
What is required is a full general equilibrium analysis taking account of
the endogenous linkages between trade, investment and technological
change.

Conclusions

Changing patterns of demand for products inevitably change the pattern
of locational advantage. The process of the growth and decline of countries and regions is not, however, autonomous. Industrial, trade and other
policies, such as the Single Market Programme, change patterns of advantage because they change the environment within which firms work. The
restructuring of the economic geography of Europe does not only come
about through FDI, although this is clearly an important part of the process. As we have shown in this chapter, recent moves to deepen European
integration have helped to raise the level of FDI in Europe both from outside Europe and from within.

There are also developments and policies that are more idiosyncratic,
at least at the intra-European level, which change locational advantages.
Labour market institutions appear to have an impact on the fortunes of
nations, as do tax structures and the stock of human capital available to
producers. Such factors inevitably influence the processes affecting output and growth, the policies that are available to increase growth and the
direction and impact of future European integration.

Notes

1   It is difficult to get a fully reliable measure of this ratio. The estimates in UNCTAD
    (1996, Table I.6) are based on the sales of the foreign affiliates of French, German,
    Japanese and US firms.
2   In part this reflects the high level of investment in China. However even if this is
    excluded some 25 per cent of new investments were located in other developing

economies during 1991–6.

3 A similar picture is apparent in North America. The cumulated inflow of foreign direct investment in Mexico rose from $10.6 billion over 1986–90 to $31.5 billion over 1991–5, reflecting in part a higher level of investment as a result of the North American Free Trade Agreement.

4 Firms maximise total profits, and hence can choose to relocate to undertake the same level of activity at a lower cost, or they could expand the level of their activities. As their capital base is not fixed they can expand by borrowing capital at home and investing it abroad. We would expect that the marginal return would be the same in all locations.

5 Representative results for the US, Japan, the UK and Germany can be found in Barrell and Pain (1996, 1998), Pain (1997) and the chapter by Hubert and Pain in this book.

6 The results in these papers update the earlier results of the authors in the review of the Single Market Programme by the European Commission, subsequently made available in *The Single Market Review, Subseries IV Volume 1, Foreign Direct Investment*, published by Kogan Page, London in 1998.

7 This evidence is consistent with other developments since the advent of the SMP as reported by the European Commission (1996, Chapter 6). Concentration ratios, measured as the market share of the four largest firms, rose at the EU level between 1987 and 1993, but not at the national level, and intra-industry trade has increased. Thus adjustments appear to have taken place within firms rather than within industries.

8 A majority-owned foreign affiliate is one in which US investors hold more than 50 per cent of the equity stake and hence have a clear controlling interest.

9 Calculated from Table 17 in 'US Direct Investment Abroad: Detail for Historical-Cost Position and Related Capital and Income Flows', *Survey of Current Business*, September 1997.

10 The gross product of US manufacturing affiliates in the UK in 1994 was $25.74 billion. At the average sterling/dollar exchange rate for 1994 this translates to £16.79 billion. Total value added in UK manufacturing was £124.34 billion (*UK National Accounts 1996*, Table 2.2). Total employees in employment in the US affiliates and the UK manufacturing sector overall were 402,400 and 3.827 million respectively (*Economic Trends*, April 1997, Table 4.2). This implies that output per employee in UK-owned firms was around three-quarters of that in the US-owned affiliates.

11 Similar findings are reported by Barrell and Pain (1997) from separate time series studies of manufacturing exports from the UK, France, Germany and Sweden, four of the major outward investors in Europe.

12 This provides a further reason why the negative impact of outward investment on exports we report may have strengthened over time. Investments in the 1960s were often to bypass trade barriers and thus expand the total market size. Investments in more recent years are more likely to reflect cost differentials.

References

Aristotelous, K. and Fountas, S. (1996), 'An empirical analysis of inward foreign direct investment flows in the EU with emphasis on the market enlargement hypothesis', *Journal of Common Market Studies*, 34, pp. 571–83.

Bajo-Rubio, O. and Sosvilla-Rivero, S. (1994), 'An econometric analysis of foreign direct investment in Spain, 1964–89', *Southern Economic Journal*, 61, pp. 104–20.

Balasubramanyam V.N. and Greenaway, D. (1993), 'Regional integration agreements and foreign direct investment', in Anderson, K. and Blackhurst, R. (Eds), *Regional Integration and the Global Trading System*, Brighton, Harvester Wheatseaf.

Balasubramanyam, V.N., Salisu, M. and Sapsford, D. (1996), 'Foreign direct investment and growth in EP and IS Countries', *Economic Journal*, 106, pp. 92–105.

Barrell, R., Anderton, R., Lansbury, M. and Sefton, J. (1997), 'FEERs for the NIEs', in Collignon, S., Park, Y.C. and Pisani-Ferry, J. (eds), *Exchange Rate Policies in Emerging Asian Countries*, London, Routledge.

Barrell, R. and Pain, N. (1996), 'An econometric analysis of US foreign direct investment', *Review of Economics and Statistics*, pp. 200–207.

(1997), 'Foreign direct investment, technological change and economic growth within Europe', *Economic Journal*, 107, pp. 1770–86.

(1998), 'Trade restraints and Japanese direct investment flows', *European Economic Review*, forthcoming.

Barry, F. and Bradley, J. (1997), 'FDI and trade: the Irish host country experience', *Economic Journal*, 107, pp. 1798–811.

Blake, A.P. and Pain, N. (1994), 'Investigating structural change in UK export performance: the role of innovation and direct investment', NIESR Discussion Paper No.71.

Blomström, M. (1986), 'Foreign investment and productive efficiency: the case of Mexico', *Journal of Industrial Economics*, 35, pp. 97–110.

Blomström, M. and Kokko, A. (1996), 'Multinational corporations and spillovers', CEPR Discussion Paper No. 1365.

Brainard, S.L. (1997), 'An empirical assessment of the proximity-concentration trade-off between multinational sales and trade', *American Economic Review*, 87, pp. 520–44.

Cabral, S. (1995), 'Comparative export behaviour of foreign and domestic firms in Portugal', *Banco de Portugal Economic Bulletin*, March, pp. 69–78.

Cassiers, I., De Villé, P. and Solar, P.M. (1996), 'Economic growth in postwar Belgium', in Crafts, N. and Toniolo, G. (eds), *Economic Growth in Europe Since 1945*, Cambridge, Cambridge University Press.

Caves, R.E. (1974), 'Multinational firms, competition and productivity in host-country markets', *Economica*, 41, pp. 176–93.

(1996), *Multinational Enterprise and Economic Analysis* (2nd edition), Cambridge, Cambridge University Press.

42   Innovation, investment and technology in Europe

Coe, D.T. and Helpman, E. (1995), 'International R&D spillovers', *European Economic Review*, 39, pp. 859–87.

Crafts, N. and Toniolo, G. (eds) (1996), *Economic Growth in Europe since 1945*, Cambridge University Press

Eaton, B.C., Lipsey, R.G. and Safarian, A.E. (1994), 'The theory of multinational plant location in a regional trading area', in Eden, L. (ed.), *Multinationals in North America*, Calgary, The University of Calgary Press.

Eltis, W. and Higham, D. (1995), 'Closing the UK competitiveness gap', *National Institute Economic Review*, 154, pp. 71–84.

European Commission (1996), *The Single Market and Tomorrow's Europe*, London, Kogan Page.

Farinha, L. and Mata, J. (1996), 'The impact of foreign direct investment in the Portugese economy', Banco de Portugal Working Paper No. 16–96.

Globerman, S. (1979), 'Foreign direct investment and "spillover" efficiency benefits in Canadian manufacturing industries', *Canadian Journal of Economics*, XII, pp. 42–56.

Grossman, G.M. and Helpman, E. (1991), *Innovation and Growth in the Global Economy*, Cambridge, Mass., MIT Press.

Hanson, G.H. (1997), 'Increasing returns, trade and the regional structure of wages', *Economic Journal*, 107, pp. 113–33.

Helpman, E. (1997), 'R&D and productivity: the international connection', NBER Working Paper No. 6101.

Horstmann, I. and Markusen, J.R. (1987), 'Licensing versus direct investment: a model of internalization by the multinational enterprise', *Canadian Journal of Economics*, 20, pp. 464–81.

Jost, T. (1997), 'Direct investment and Germany as a business location', Economic Research Group of the Deutsche Bundesbank Discussion Paper 2/97.

Krugman, P.R. (1995), 'International trade theory and policy', in Grossman, G. and Rogoff, K. (eds), *Handbook of International Economics Volume III*, Amsterdam, Elsevier.

Layard, R., Nickell, S. and Jackman, R. (1991), *Unemployment: Macroeconomic Performance and the Labour Market*, Oxford, Oxford University Press.

Markusen, J.R. (1995), 'The boundaries of multinational enterprises and the theory of international trade', *Journal of Economic Perspectives*, 9, pp. 169–89.

Markusen, J.R. and Venables, A.J. (1996), 'The increased importance of direct investment in North Atlantic economic relationships: a convergence hypothesis', in Canzoneri, M.B., Ethier, W.J. and Grilli, V. (eds), *The New Transatlantic Economy*, Cambridge, Cambridge University Press.

Mataloni, R. (1997), 'Real gross product of U.S. companies' majority-owned foreign affiliates in manufacturing', *Survey of Current Business*, 77 (April), pp. 8–17.

Mundell, R.A. (1957), 'International trade and factor mobility', *American Economic Review*, 47, pp. 321–35.

Niosi, J. (1994), 'Foreign direct investment in Canada', in Eden, L. (ed.), *Multinationals in North America*, Calgary, The University of Calgary Press.

OECD (1995), *Foreign Direct Investment, Trade and Employment*, Paris, OECD.

O'Sullivan, P.J. (1993), 'An assessment of Ireland's export-led growth strategy via foreign direct investment: 1960–80', *Weltwirtschaftliches Archiv* 129, pp. 139–58.

PACEC (1995), *Assessment of the Wider Effects of Foreign Direct Investment in Manufacturing in the UK*, Report by PA Cambridge Economic Consultants for Department of Trade and Industry.

Pain, N. (1996), 'Foreign direct investment, trade and economic growth within Europe', paper presented at ESRC Macroeconomic Modelling Bureau Annual Conference, University of Warwick, July.

(1997), 'Continental drift: European integration and the location of UK foreign direct investment', *The Manchester School Supplement*, pp. 94–117.

Pain, N. and Lansbury, M. (1997), 'Regional economic integration and foreign direct investment: the case of German investment in Europe', *National Institute Economic Review*, 160, pp. 87–99.

Pain, N. and Wakelin, K. (1998a), 'Export performance and the role of foreign direct investment', *The Manchester School*, forthcoming.

(1998b), 'Foreign direct investment and export performance in Europe,' in Read, R., Thompson, S. and Milner, C. (eds), *New Horizons in International Trade and Industry*, London, Macmillan.

Patel, P. and Pavitt, K. (1995), 'Patterns of technological activity: their measurement and interpretation', in Stoneman, P. (ed.), *Handbook of the Economics of Innovation and Technological Change*, Oxford, Basil Blackwell.

Prais, S.J. (1995), *Productivity, Education and Training*, Cambridge, Cambridge University Press.

Romer, P. (1993), 'Idea gaps and object gaps in economic development', *Journal of Monetary Economics*, 32, pp. 543–73.

Thomsen, S. and Woolcock, S. (1993), *Direct Investment and European Integration: Competition among Firms and Governments*, London, Pinter.

UNCTAD (1996), *World Investment Report 1996*, Geneva, United Nations.

(1997), *World Investment Report 1997, Transnational Corporations, Market Structure and Competition Policy*, Geneva, United Nations.

Venables, A.J. (1996), 'Localisation of industry and trade performance', *Oxford Review of Economic Policy*, 12/3, pp. 52–60.

WTO (1996), *World Trade Organisation Annual Report*, Geneva, WTO.

Yannopoulos, G.N. (1990), 'Foreign direct investment and European integration: the evidence from the formative years of the European Community', *Journal of Common Market Studies*, 28, pp. 235–59.

3 Irish FDI policy and investment from the EU

FRANCES RUANE and HOLGER GÖRG[1]

1 Introduction

Over the past forty years the Republic of Ireland, hereafter referred to as Ireland, has pursued an industrial strategy characterised by promoting export-led growth in Irish manufacturing through various financial supports and fiscal incentives, and by encouraging foreign companies to establish manufacturing plants in Ireland, producing specifically for export markets. As a consequence of this strategy, any comparison of the Irish economy with other economies in the European Union (EU) immediately notes the enormous significance of foreign direct investment (FDI) in the Irish manufacturing sector and the manufacturing sector's very high export ratio, especially among foreign-owned companies.[2] The significance of FDI for the Irish economy is reflected in, *inter alia*, the significant gap between GNP and GDP; in 1994, GNP was roughly 88 per cent of GDP in Ireland. As regards the manufacturing sector, the high shares of output and employment in foreign-owned companies in Ireland also indicate the importance of foreign firms. As we discuss in some detail in Section 3, foreign companies produced roughly 69 per cent of total net output and accounted for 45 per cent of employment in Irish manufacturing industries in 1993.

FDI has played a crucial role in the overall development of the Irish economy over three decades. From the 1930s until the mid-1960s the Irish manufacturing sector had some of the highest rates of effective protection of any manufacturing sector in the world (McAleese, 1971). In particular, these tariffs protected Irish manufacturing industry against imports from the UK. Reductions in tariffs began in 1966 as a consequence of the Anglo-Irish Free Trade Area Agreement, and the process of tariff reduction was eventually completed in 1978, following a five-year adjustment after Ireland joined the European Economic Community (EEC). The scale of structural adjustment necessary for free trade was on a par with that undertaken by many developing economies over the past decade under the auspices of the structural adjustment programmes of the IMF and the World Bank. In the absence of FDI, the reduction of high tariffs in Ireland would have required a massive devaluation against sterling, when policy at the time was fully committed to maintaining that link at parity. The scale of FDI coupled with some restructuring support for import-substituting Irish firms allowed the exchange rate to be maintained, and an inevitable shakeout in the indigenous manufacturing sector to take place without any massive decline in total jobs in manufacturing.

Furthermore, FDI has assisted in the process of adjustment within the manufacturing sector and across geographic regions. The sectoral composition of FDI overall is less concentrated on traditional and food-sector activities than that of indigenous manufacturing, and thus the growth of the FDI component in manufacturing has meant that the share of these activities in total manufacturing output has declined over the past thirty years.[3] The extent of restructuring is more apparent the lower the level of sectoral disaggregation. In terms of regional employment, FDI became a vehicle for spreading manufacturing employment across the country and away from the traditional manufacturing bases in Dublin and Cork. Since the Irish economy was still heavily dependent on agricultural employment in the 1960s, the regional dispersal of foreign-owned firms created new jobs in regions where existing employment opportunities were declining.[4]

The focus of this chapter is on FDI from countries within the European Union. It describes the policies used and analyses their effects on sectoral adjustment within the Irish manufacturing sector. The chapter is essentially micro in its approach to examining the impact of FDI on Ireland.[5] Some reference is made to indigenous industry in order to establish a benchmark against which we can assess the impact of foreign-owned firms.[6] We concentrate on FDI in the manufacturing sector, as this is the sector where FDI has hitherto had its greatest impact, and we do not analyse foreign investment in service activities.[7] In the context of the manufacturing sector we assess the major impact of foreign-owned industries in Ireland by focusing primarily on the associated employment because employment has always been the major target of the policy-makers and we have an employment time series which allows us to distinguish some elements of sectoral dynamics.

The outline of the chapter is as follows. In Section 2 we look at three characteristics of the policy which has been used to promote FDI, namely, its employment focus, its combination of automatic and discretionary policies and its emphasis on certainty. In Section 3 we look at how policy is currently implemented – an issue which is typically ignored by economists and which we consider merits more attention. In Section 4 we examine the overall impact of FDI in Ireland in terms of employment, concentrating on European-sourced FDI, distinguishing the UK, Germany and a residual category 'Other European'. In Section 5 we consider some of the current concerns about industrial policy in Ireland and make some concluding comments.

2   Key characteristics of Irish policy towards FDI[8]

The decision to promote FDI actively in the 1950s represented a dramatic change in policy for the Irish economy. In the period dating from the 1930s, when the Irish economy introduced high rates of tariff protection on manufactured goods, FDI had been legislatively prohibited directly through the Control of Manufactures Acts. The purpose of these Acts was to ensure that indigenous 'infant' industry would benefit from the protectionist strategy and in particular that UK firms would not benefit by establishing manufacturing plants in the protected Irish market into which they had previously been exporting. UK-owned firms already established in Ireland prior to 1932, however, were not forced to leave, so that there was a considerable amount of UK FDI in the 1950s. The change in the 1950s can be seen as Ireland's finally managing to decouple the link between FDI and its colonial past, as hitherto the presence of FDI companies was seen by many as evidence that Ireland had not established its economic independence from the UK.[9] From this time onwards, attitudes in Ireland to FDI, irrespective of source, have typically been extraordinarily positive right across the socio-political spectrum.

Employment focus

The change from an anti- to pro-FDI strategy was driven primarily by the real failure of the prewar protectionist strategy to generate a viable manufacturing sector, which was capable of providing enough jobs to counteract the falling number of agricultural jobs in rural areas. Indeed the highly protected 'infant' industries established in the 1930s had become 'geriatric' industries by the 1950s, exhibiting many of the features of X-inefficiency which might be expected from such a prolonged period of protection. Despite the high levels of protection, indigenous firms were continually losing market share to imports and almost none of them were exporting. In the mid-1950s the economy was in decline with high unemployment and emigration rates, especially in and from rural areas. Consequently employment in FDI firms and their regional distribution, rather than firm numbers, capital expenditures, exports, and so on have been the major focus of policy and the key indicator of its success or failure. In the past decade, policy has also focused on other attributes of FDI, in particular on profits (because of the growing significance of the corporate tax yield), on technology (because of possible spillover effects), and on linkages (because of the potential positive effects for indigenous companies). None the less employment remains the key variable for measuring policy success or failure and the availability of a young educated labour force is promoted heavily by the national agency for industrial development.

Automatic and discretionary policies

Proactive policy has taken two major forms: fiscal and financial. Initially the main element in the fiscal policy for foreign manufacturing companies was an *automatic tax holiday* on the profits from all new export sales.[10] When introduced in the mid-1950s, the tax holiday was given for ten years but this was subsequently extended to fifteen years with a further five years of partial relief; the holiday was set to terminate in 1990. Prior to 1990, however, Ireland was forced by the European Commission to alter the policy for new firms, as the tax holiday created a bias towards exports which was incompatible with the Treaty of Rome. Since 1982, all new firms have been entitled to an automatic preferential corporate tax rate of 10 per cent which has applied to all profits and not merely those arising from export sales.[11] Given the small size of the Irish market and Ireland's membership of the EEC from 1973, Ireland's attractiveness for foreign companies lies in its being an investment base for exporting, especially for extra-EU companies.[12] Consequently the switch to a trade-neutral incentive away from a pro-exporting incentive had little effect on firms' sales behaviour, with exporting remaining the driving force behind the investment of foreign-owned firms in Irish manufacturing. The automatic fiscal incentives are backed by double tax agreements to maximise the benefit of the tax incentives to FDI companies. In the case of the continental European countries, these agreements incorporate tax-sparing, that is, the home country tax authorities deem tax to have been paid at the standard rate for computing home country additional tax liabilities. In the case of the US and the UK, the agreements do not incorporate tax-sparing, so that the benefits of the reduced tax rates lie essentially in tax deferral.[13]

Financial supports for foreign firms locating in Ireland in the 1950s were primarily in the form of cash grants towards the cost of the plant and machinery which would be used to produce goods for export markets.[14] As with the tax holiday, the basis for grant eligibility had to be changed in 1982, so that the grants now apply to all manufacturing firms and not merely those which are exporting.[15] By contrast with the fiscal incentives which are available to all firms automatically, these are *discretionary grants*, available up to certain maxima (determined by legislation) and implemented at the discretion of the Industrial Development Authority (IDA). While the discretionary option was rarely if ever exercised in the 1950s and 1960s, in the sense that the maximum grant was virtually always paid out, it has had a lasting effect on industrial policy in Ireland, in that for over forty years industrial policy has always operated at project level.[16] This issue is discussed further in the next section.

It is worth noting that, compared with other countries, Ireland has had a rather different approach to FDI, in actively promoting manufacturing investments by foreign companies which were greenfield and export-orientated. Furthermore, this was done is such a way that indigenous firms were in a sense 'protected' from direct competition with FDI firms on the local market.[17] By contrast, those semi-developed and developing countries which began to promote FDI positively in the 1960s based their strategies on attracting FDI specifically to produce for the local market which was typically protected by high tariffs and other trade barriers. In effect, these countries were adopting the very strategy which Ireland had ruled out in the 1930s, namely of allowing FDI companies to partake in the growth induced in domestic production by the tariff walls. More recently, the economies of Eastern Europe seem to be preoccupied with attracting FDI to take over existing 'brownfield' plants rather than to establish new greenfield plants.[18] Furthermore, while Ireland is not unusual in Europe today in promoting FDI, in the 1950s when it introduced this policy, most countries in Western Europe were at best indifferent towards FDI.

Policy certainty

Thus the primary characteristics of Irish FDI strategy are its employment focus, and its promotional approach combining automatic fiscal incentives with discretionary grants. A further additional characteristic worthy of note is the emphasis placed on certainty. Recognising the negative effects of uncertainty on investment, the Irish system has always attempted to give as much certainty as possible to the incoming and established investor through policy continuity.[19] With regard to fiscal incentives, certainty is achieved by providing the investing firms with a long and certain time horizon.[20] Promotional FDI fiscal policies are essentially independent of the annual budgetary process and of changes in government.[21] With regards to financial policies, which are also independent of the budgetary process, uncertainty on the part of firms has been minimised by the payment of the cash grant up-front, with repayment required if the firm fails to meet its agreed employment objectives. The government's money is secured by linking the payment to fixed assets lest the project fail. This gives certainty and security to both investor and government.[22] In effect, there is a strong commitment to make the FDI policy work and generate as much policy certainty in the system as possible – a strategy of particular importance to Ireland since it is a small country still attempting to establish its name as an attractive location for FDI.

3 Characteristics of implementation

We have drawn a distinction between the characteristics of policy and the characteristics of implementation because we feel that this distinction can be important to understanding the success and outturn of policy. Indeed policy can have quite different effects depending on how precisely it is implemented. While different governments offer various investment incentives, as listed by Yuill *et al.* (1995), the decision to invest in one country rather than another is influenced by a complex set of factors, many of which materialise during the actual implementation of policy.

Financial incentives and factor choice

One example of how the operation of policy impacts can be seen by looking at how developments in the capital grant system influence factor choice. As noted above, when the grant policy was introduced, it operated as a straight capital grant – that is, an exporting firm entitled to a grant of 50 per cent towards the cost of machinery would receive that grant on receipt by the agency of proof that the machine had been purchased and was in operation. In response to criticism that such an incentive was capital-biased and hence inappropriate, the grant system became more discretionary, with the amount of grant money given being influenced by the number of jobs expected to be created. The grant money was then expressed in terms of a capital grant rate to the cost of machinery (say 45 per cent) and paid out, as before, when the machine was purchased and put into operation. Following further criticisms that capital bias was still possible, because firms had an incentive to exaggerate the number of jobs which they expected to generate, limits were set in terms of both grant per unit capital *and* grant per unit labour. Also, while grants were still paid out in relation to capital purchases, firms were legally contracted to re-pay grants if they did not reach their stated employment target. Thus while Ireland might appear to have had the same capital grant policy since the early 1950s, changes in how it is implemented have considerably altered its effects on factor choice, so that where once it generated a capital bias, today it operates in a more or less factor neutral way.

Project selection

As noted in Section 2, Irish policy has always operated at project level and has become increasingly proactive and selective since the 1970s. While good projects in virtually all sectors of internationally-tradable economic activity are in principle eligible for support,[23] not only has the level of grant support varied, but resources have been increasingly deployed in the IDA to select potential projects on a market-driven basis – that is, where market growth potential is greatest. The first stage of this selection involves identifying high-growth market niches, in which projects are internationally mobile (footloose) and in which Ireland could provide a reasonably competitive base; the second stage seeks to discover the strong companies which are operating in those niches and which might be considering diversifying their production internationally.[24] The third stage requires having project executives initiate contacts with the companies identified in the second stage. Finally, the fourth stage involves getting the company to visit Ireland in the context of a specific project proposal. The precise pattern of FDI projects which come to Ireland is strongly influenced by this process, which might more accurately be described as 'market-led intervention'.

Bargaining

The fact that grant supports have been discretionary up to a maximum means that all FDI projects involve bargaining between project executives and potential investors. While foreign project investors argue for more grants on the basis of the attractiveness of alternative international investment locations, Irish project executives limit the grants they offer on the basis of a form of cost–benefit analysis, which considers factors such as employment potential (in terms of both job numbers and skill mix) and location of the projects within Ireland.[25] The grant maxima ensure that the amount of assistance given is bounded and when the absolute amount of the capital grant support exceeds a defined number, presently £2.5 million, the grant support requires Cabinet approval.[26] All grant payments are in the public domain so that transparency is assured about the final payment but not the process of arriving at it.

Sectoral selectivity

With regard to sectoral selectivity, in the 1970s the IDA identified the electronics and pharmaceutical sectors as providing the most promising opportunities for foreign investment projects for Ireland. Furthermore, the US was identified as the most likely market source for such projects. The creation of industrial clusters has been central to policy and particular sub-sectors of electronics and pharmaceuticals have been heavily targeted for over twenty years; since the late 1980s and early 1990s this targeting has begun to yield very significant benefits especially with US companies (see Section 4).[27] The present sectoral strategy for the manufacturing sector is to consolidate on building clusters in the electronics and pharmaceutical sectors and to promote outsourcing linkages with domestic firms in these sectors. In addition, within existing sectors executives are mandated to seek to promote the location of headquarter and R&D functions in Ireland, as there is a desire to have the Irish operation as the sole or key production/distribution centre for the EU. This is seen as important from the point of view of achieving high-income jobs and of encouraging a deepening of the firms' commitment to Ireland. Finally, increasing resources have been devoted in recent years to promoting FDI in internationally traded services, which accounted for some 19,000 jobs in 1995. A detailed discussion of services, however, lies beyond the scope of this chapter (see Ruane and Görg, 1997).

4   Impact of FDI in Ireland

Overview

We now turn to look at some empirical measures of the significance and impact of foreign direct investment on the Irish economy. Table 3.1 shows shares of net output, employment and exports by sector for 1993. Over two-thirds of total net output in manufacturing in 1993 was accounted for by foreign-owned companies, with the share of total net output generated by foreign-owned companies varying quite considerably by sector. This variability is to be expected, both because of differences in the

Table 3.1 *Significance of foreign firms for the Irish economy, 1993*

	Net output		Employment		Exports	
	Sectors	Foreign	Sectors	Foreign	Irish-owned firms	Foreign-owned firms
	As % of total				As % of output	
Food, drink & tobacco	27.6	52.5	23.2	29.0	38.5	72.4
Textiles	1.7	63.5	5.0	61.8	46.2	93.0
Clothing & footwear	1.5	37.2	5.6	26.0	46.4	89.9
Timber & furniture	0.8	24.0	4.4	4.3	16.1[a]	93.2[a]
Paper & printing	11.7	60.8	6.8	12.6		
Chemicals	22.7	94.3	8.3	78.9	26.2	96.3
Non-metallic minerals	3.0	15.7	5.0	24.0	20.0	66.9
Metals & engineering	25.7	78.3	36.1	62.5	48.6	86.6
of which:						
Electric & Electronic	12.8	92.2			49.8	88.2
Instruments	4.8	90.0			80.0	94.4
Transport equipment	1.8	30.6			36.3	95.2
Other	6.4	54.8			36.1	91.1
Miscellaneous	5.2	56.8	5.8	37.1	34.2	74.6
Total manufacturing	100.0	68.4	100.0	44.7	35.2	87.7

Source: Authors' estimates based on preliminary data on output and exports from the Central Statistics Office and on employment data from the *Forfás Employment Survey*.
Note: (a) export ratio is for sectors 'timber & furniture' and 'paper & printing' combined.

degree of international mobility of investments across sectors and because of the selective way in which policy is implemented. Looking at sectors, we find that this share ranges from less than 20 per cent in non-metallic minerals to over 90 per cent in chemicals and in the high tech sub-sectors of metals & engineering (M&E), namely, electrical & electronic and instruments. As discussed above, these are exactly the sectors targeted by Ireland's industrial policy.

One might argue that the output data overstate the significance of the value-added of foreign-owned companies, to the extent that companies understate the value of inputs used and overstate the value of the sales generated. Firms may try to artificially raise their net output figures in Ireland by engaging in transfer pricing in order to transfer profits to Ireland (Foley, 1991). The employment figures reported in the table can be seen as giving a more conservative measure of the significance of foreign firms.

The overall share of foreign firms in total manufacturing employment is 44 per cent, less than two-thirds the share of net output. The foreign share of net output by sector exceeds the foreign share of employment in all but one sector showing a similar but not identical pattern (the correlation coefficient between sectoral shares of net output and employment is 0.796). These differences could be due to (i) differences in sectoral activities, (ii) differences in factor intensities in the same sectoral activity, resulting in foreign firms being less labour intensive than indigenous firms, or (iii) transfer pricing. Nevertheless, the employment figures confirm the importance of the *high-tech* sectors.

Table 3.1 also shows the export ratios for foreign-owned and indigenous manufacturing companies by broad industrial sector. Foreign-owned firms have considerably higher export ratios than indigenous firms, with over 85 per cent of the gross output of foreign firms being exported – two and a half times the comparable figure for indigenous firms. Note that the export ratios in foreign-owned companies are close to 90 per cent in most of the manufacturing sectors; only foreign companies in the food, drink and tobacco, non-metallic minerals and miscellaneous sectors appear to serve the local market to any great extent.

Sources of foreign companies

As discussed above, employment creation has been the overriding focus of Ireland's industrial strategy and the figures in table 3.2 suggest that this aspect of the strategy has been successful. While manufacturing employment in Irish-owned firms decreased by approximately 19 per cent between 1975 and 1995, employment in foreign-owned firms increased by some 27 per cent during the same period. Both effects sum up to a net decrease in manufacturing employment of roughly 3 per cent, in a period when manufacturing employment in the EU declined by more than 20 per cent (European Commission, 1996).

Looking at the source of foreign investment, table 3.2 shows that the US was by far the biggest investor in Ireland in 1995, with more than half of the employment in foreign-owned firms being in US-owned firms. Employment in US firms has almost trebled between 1975 and 1995, lending some support to the conclusion that the policy of attracting FDI projects from the US has been successful over the last twenty years. This success is evident in Ireland's increasing its 'market share' of US investment in manufacturing industries (measured in terms of capital

Table 3.2 *Total employment by company nationality, 1975–95*

Nationality	1975		1995		Percentage
	Employ-ment	In % of total	Employ-ment	In % of total	change in employment 1975–95
Ireland	143,387	65.7	116,273	55.0	−18.9
UK	29,669	13.6	12,260	5.8	−58.7
Germany	6,074	2.8	9,700	4.6	59.7
Other European	17,776	8.1	13,929	6.6	−21.6
US	18,418	8.4	51,615	24.4	180.2
Other non–European	2,997	1.4	7,611	3.6	154.0
Total foreign	74,934	34.3	95,115	45.0	26.9
Total	218,321	100.0	211,388	100.0	−3.2

Source: Authors' estimates based on data from the *Forfás Employment Survey*.

expenditures by US affiliates) in the EU from 2.6 per cent in 1983 to 5.8 per cent in 1994.[28] Employment in companies originating in other non-European countries has also increased considerably since 1975, though it still only accounts for a relatively small share of total employment in Irish manufacturing industries. In the remainder of this section, we focus on the employment performance of European companies in Ireland, and our analysis indicates different trends in the pattern of investment by different European nationalities. We distinguish three nationality groups, namely the UK, Germany, and a group 'other European';[29] as noted above, in general the benefit of the low tax rate is much greater to companies from continental European countries than to those from the UK. Figure 3.1 complements the analysis in table 3.2 by showing annual employment figures by nationality.

Employment in German firms increased relatively modestly between 1975 and 1985 (by around 1,500), but grew by 2,100 between 1986 and 1995. This represents a total increase in employment of more than 50 per cent between 1975 and 1995 and suggests that German firms have responded positively to both Ireland's accession to the EEC in 1973 and to the impact of the European Single Market Programme in the late 1980s. The availability of a relatively cheap and skilled labour force and of relatively generous fiscal and financial incentives has always made Ireland attractive to German investors, and this attractiveness was enhanced by Ireland's membership of the European market. An additional attraction is the increased level of education and training in the Irish workforce, as evidenced in the annual OECD *Education at a Glance* publications.

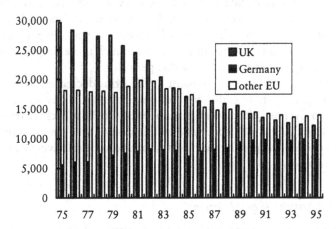

Figure 3.1 *Employment by company nationality, 1975–95*
Source: Authors' estimates based on data from the *Forfás Employment Survey.*

On the other hand, employment in companies from other European countries shows a more volatile development. It increased between 1975 and 1982 by approximately 500, but decreased by roughly 3,000 between 1983 and 1986. Since then it has stabilised at around 14,000. This trend may indicate that in a more integrated European market, Ireland has lost part of its attraction for investors from other continental European countries beside Germany. This may partly be due to the fact that some of the European investment came from countries which have since joined the EU and, thus, they have no need for a base in an EU country to serve the EU market.

In contrast to the firms from continental Europe, UK-owned firms show a much more dramatic development – employment has declined by over 50 per cent since 1975. The fall in employment of approximately 13,000 between 1975 and 1985 is not surprising for several reasons. Firstly, the Anglo-Irish Free Trade Area Agreement in 1965 reduced Ireland's high tariffs on manufacturing, which had not only protected indigenous firms, but also protected a large number of UK firms which had established in Ireland prior to 1932. The introduction of the Free Trade Area not only reduced the profitability of the Irish plants, it also removed the need to maintain plants in Ireland in order to serve the Irish market competitively – this could now be achieved through exports from the UK. Secondly, UK firms were heavily concentrated in those sectors which have declined over the period or which have grown more slowly (see below). Thirdly, the break in the link between sterling and the Irish punt in 1979 and the subsequent punt–sterling exchange rate volatility would have had a further negative effect, particularly on the UK firms which had located more recently in order to export. Fourthly, UK regions, especially Scotland, Wales and Northern Ireland, began to compete much more directly with the IDA for foreign investment during this period.

Between 1986 and 1995, employment in UK firms decreased by a further 4,000, indicating that the downward trend has slowed down, primarily owing to a decline in the average number of jobs lost each year; the average number of new jobs generated in this decade was lower than in the previous decade, suggesting that Ireland has become relatively less attractive to UK investors.

Sectoral composition of employment

We now turn to look at the sectoral composition of employment in European companies in Ireland. Following the policy orientation towards high-tech industries, most closely measured here by the mechanical and electrical engineering (M&E) and chemicals sectors, we would expect employment in these sectors to have grown particularly strongly.

Table 3.3 shows the sectoral breakdown of employment in European firms in Ireland. Particularly noteworthy is that almost 80 per cent of employment in German firms in 1995 was concentrated in the M&E sector and that employment in this sector more than doubled between 1975 and 1995. The remaining employment is spread across the other sectors. By contrast, employment in firms from other European countries is less concentrated and spread across the chemicals (20 per cent) and the M&E (33 per cent) sectors. Employment in the latter sector actually fell over the period while employment in chemicals increased by approximately 50 per cent. Thus, as measured in terms of employment, the response of German firms in the M&E sector and other European firms in the chemicals sector is in line with Irish industrial strategy.

Employment in UK-owned firms shows a sectoral breakdown which is very different from the continental European countries. The sectoral spread is much less concentrated in both 1975 and 1995, and such concentration as occurs is in the food and drink & tobacco sectors, which accounted for almost 50 per cent of jobs in UK-owned firms in 1995. This reflects the significance of long-standing UK firms and of Irish raw material resources for UK firms in those sectors. Indeed, as we concluded elsewhere (Ruane and Görg, 1996, 1997), the experience for the UK companies over this period resembles much more that of Irish-owned firms than of other foreign-owned firms in Ireland.

Table 3.3 *Sectoral breakdown of employment by company nationality, 1975-95*

	1975			1995		
	UK	Germany	Other European	UK	Germany	Other European
Food	4,932	34	4,108	3,262	386	1,868
	(16.6)	(0.6)	(23.1)	(26.6)	(4.0)	(13.4)
Drink & tobacco	5,862	0	1,208	2,759	56	803
	(19.8)	(0.0)	(6.8)	(22.5)	(0.6)	(5.8)
Textiles	2,986	201	1,206	831	219	957
	(10.1)	(3.3)	(6.8)	(6.8)	(2.3)	(6.9)
Clothing & footwear	3,971	533	806	731	79	956
	(13.4)	(8.8)	(4.5)	(6.0)	(0.8)	(6.9)
Timber & furniture	135	308	0	0	0	201
	(0.5)	(5.1)	(0.0)	(0.0)	(0.0)	(1.4)
Paper & printing	820	108	319	386	63	83
	(2.8)	(1.8)	(1.8)	(3.1)	(0.6)	(0.6)
Chemicals	2,201	647	1,941	1,651	824	2,839
	(7.4)	(10.7)	(10.9)	(13.5)	(8.5)	(20.4)
Non-metallic minerals	2,032	422	506	762	75	290
	(6.8)	(6.9)	(2.8)	(6.2)	(0.8)	(2.1)
Metals & engineering	4,525	3,620	6,801	1,330	7,670	4,522
	(15.3)	(59.6)	(38.3)	(10.8)	(79.1)	(32.5)
Miscellaneous	2,205	201	881	548	328	1,410
	(7.4)	(3.3)	(5.0)	(4.5)	(3.4)	(10.1)
Total	29,669	6,074	17,776	12,260	9,700	13,929
	(100.0)	(100.0)	(100.0)	(100.0)	(100.0)	(100.0)

Source: Authors' estimates based on data from the *Forfás Employment Survey*.
Note: Employment figures in 000s; percentages shown in brackets.

Composition of employment change

Thus far, we have compared employment figures in 1975 and 1995, which provided us with a snapshot at two particular points of time. However, such an analysis cannot reflect the full extent of changes taking place within particular sectors over the period between the two benchmark years. Industrial policies can be expected to have some effects on job gains but only a weaker influence on the employment stock, since the latter reflects

Table 3.4 *Job gains and losses by company nationality and sector, 1975–95*

	UK			Germany			Other European		
	Gains	Losses	Net	Gains	Losses	Net	Gains	Losses	Net
Food	3226	4896	–1670	609	257	352	2774	5014	–2240
Drink & tobacco	1489	4592	–3103	64	8	56	873	1278	–405
Textiles	1712	3867	–2155	444	426	18	2294	2543	–249
Clothing & footwear	3212	6452	–3240	873	1327	–454	2718	2568	150
Timber & furniture	117	252	–135	198	506	–308	287	86	201
Paper & printing	515	949	–434	152	197	–45	166	402	–236
Chemicals	1921	2471	–550	901	724	177	3662	2764	898
Non–metallic minerals	1022	2292	–1270	237	584	–347	235	451	–216
Metals & engineering	4366	7561	–3195	12096	8046	4050	8772	11051	–2279
Miscellaneous	1159	2816	–1657	623	496	127	2245	1716	529
Total	18739	36148	–17409	16197	12571	3626	24026	27873	–3847

Source: Authors' estimates based on data from the *Forfás Employment Survey.*

the impact of past history and policies. (This is particularly so in the case of UK firms which accounted for a very large part of the stock in 1973.) To take some account of these dynamics, we now turn to look at job gains and losses across manufacturing sectors. A sector can show job gains and job losses in the same year due to (i) firms that expand (through firm entry or firm expansion) and (ii) firms that contract employment (through exit or contractions) over the same period. Thus, our measure of job gains includes all new jobs generated in firms in sector j over a given period (whether or not they still existed at the end of the period) while the measure of job losses includes all jobs lost in firms in the same sector over the same period. Net job change is the summation of job gains and job losses in a given sector. The data on job gains and losses per firm are compiled annually at firm level by the data collecting agency, and we aggregate these for the period 1975 to 1995.

The data in table 3.4 indicate that, relative to 1975 or 1995 stocks, there have been huge job gains and losses over the period analysed. In order to compare the employment performance for different nationalities we generate two indicators,

$$A_j = \frac{g_j}{n_j}$$

where g_j and n_j denote total job gains between 1975 and 1995 and total employment in sector j at the end of 1975 respectively, and

$$B_j = \frac{(g_j - l_j)}{g_j} \,,$$

where l_j represents the total number of jobs losses in the period 1975 to 1995.[30]

The A-ratio expresses job gains relative to the employment base in 1975, which allows us to benchmark the extent of job creation across source countries that started from very different employment bases in 1975. The B-ratio expresses the net job change relative to job gains which can yield some insights into the relationship between gross and net job creation – that is, whether or not gross gains translated into persistent net job creations. These are presented in table 3.5.

The large numbers of total job gains and losses in table 3.4 indicate considerable activity of job generation and destruction taking place which is not reflected in the net figures of employment change in table 3.3. In the nationality comparison it is apparent that, of the three nationality groups, German firms have both the highest A- and B-ratios, while the UK has the lowest A- and B-ratios. The B-ratio of –0.93 for UK firms in fact indicates that the job losses were almost twice as high as job gains (–1 would indicate that job losses were double the job gains).

It is also evident from the table that job gains and losses were not uniform across manufacturing sectors. UK firms show net job reductions in all manufacturing sectors; despite the quite considerable job gains in the M&E and chemicals sectors, the job losses by far exceeded even in these sectors. The A-ratio indicates that the job gains compared with the base employment in 1975 were among the highest in the M&E and chemicals sectors, while they also show some of the highest values for the B-ratio (though they are still very low compared with the other countries). This suggests, to some extent, that the policy measures did result in job gains in the M&E and chemicals sectors, though, in the case of UK firms, these were more than outweighed by job losses.

The UK figures are quite different from those for continental European countries. German firms have the highest job gains in the M&E sector (around 75 per cent) and also a relatively high number of job gains in the chemicals sector. This is confirmed by the A-ratio which shows that the

Table 3.5 *Employment indicators by company nationality and sector, 1975–95*

	A-ratio			B-ratio		
	UK	Germany	Other European	UK	Germany	Other European
Food	0.65	17.91	0.68	−0.52	0.58	−0.81
Drink & tobacco	0.25	0.00	0.72	−2.08	0.88	−0.46
Textiles	0.57	2.21	1.90	−1.26	0.04	−0.11
Clothing & footwear	0.81	1.64	3.37	−1.01	−0.52	0.06
Timber & furniture	0.87	0.64	0.00	−1.15	−1.56	0.70
Paper & printing	0.63	1.41	0.52	−0.84	−0.30	−1.42
Chemicals	0.87	1.39	1.89	−0.29	0.20	0.25
Non-metallic minerals	0.50	0.56	0.46	−1.24	−1.46	−0.92
Metals & engineering	0.96	3.34	1.29	−0.73	0.33	−0.26
Miscellaneous	0.53	3.10	2.55	−1.43	0.20	0.24
Total	0.63	2.67	1.35	−0.93	0.22	−0.16

Source: Authors' estimates based on data from the *Forfás Employment Survey*.
Note: The very high value of *A* in the sector food is due to the fact that in 1975 German firms in the food sector accounted for only thirty-four jobs.

gains relative to base employment in 1975 is relatively high especially in the M&E sectors. While the figures suggest that German-owned firms have invested relatively strongly in the sectors which proxy high tech, they also show that these sectors accounted for some of the highest job losses in German firms in Ireland. None the less, the *B*-ratio ratio is still positive— that is, the gross gains have translated into net gains. These results remind us that these sectors are not only innovative growth sectors, but also sectors with high job turnover. It also points to the danger of having policies which are aimed only at generating new jobs without reference to the sustainability of those jobs.

In the case of firms whose parent companies come from other continental European countries, we can also see that the bulk of job gains accrued in the M&E and chemicals sectors, although considerable job losses are recorded in these sectors as well. Note that the chemicals sector has the highest *B*-ratio for other European firms – that is, the gross job gains translated into the highest net job gains in this sector.

Overall, the empirical analysis suggests that the investment incentives offered in Ireland appear to have led to significant gross job gains in the targeted high tech sectors, as proxied here by the M&E and chemicals sectors. However, these gross gains have not necessarily translated into net gains of anything like the same magnitude. To interpret this result fully a further sectoral disaggregation is required to ascertain whether the job gains occurred in the same or different sub-sectors to the job losses. For example, it may be the case that job gains occurred in the electronics and pharmaceuticals subsectors of M&E and chemicals respectively, while the job losses may have occurred in the more traditional sub-sectors, such as mechanical engineering or basic industrial chemicals. Unfortunately, the data here do not allow us to analyse this issue.

5 Current concerns

Ireland's recent success in winning large-scale FDI projects from the US has led to renewed concern in some quarters that the country is becoming too dependent on FDI.[31] The fact that indigenous companies appear to be prospering at present with increasing employment and profits rates has reduced concerns about 'crowding out', so that the attitude to FDI is not hostile but rather marks a concern with dependency *per se* – the 'what would happen if FDI globally declined' scenario. Of perhaps more significant concern is the dependency on the US market, as the portfolio of investment sources has concentrated dramatically over the past five years, at the same time as it has concentrated sectorally. Furthermore, it has also become more concentrated geographically within Ireland, with the four largest centres (Dublin, Cork, Limerick and Galway) receiving more than 80 per cent of the new jobs in the last couple of years. These concerns are somewhat counteracted by the phenomenal growth in the high tech sectors world-wide, the scale and dynamism of the US economy at present, and the fact that the absolute number of new jobs is so significant.

As noted above, Ireland was well ahead of the field in introducing incentives to encourage FDI in the 1950s and 1960s. Now governments throughout the world, and of particular relevance to Ireland, EU governments, are promoting FDI projects by means of a range of incentives, typically offered by agencies at sub-national levels. Thus the relative impact of Ireland's incentives has been eroded over the past decade. Although hitherto there is not much evidence of direct competition from Eastern Europe, where foreign direct investment appears to be going more into existing commercial activities rather than into new projects, one can expect that this situation is unlikely to continue as existing opportunities get taken up and as EU membership becomes a reality for these countries. The implications of these developments have been recognised in Ireland (Forfás, 1996), reinforcing the search for projects which build on comparative national advantage as well as lower basic wage costs and fiscal and financial incentives. In tandem, domestic policy has focused increasingly on programmes of skill enhancement (through training and increased numbers of skilled workers) and improvements in basic infrastructure.

It also seems inevitable that the increasing use of incentives to attract FDI projects across EU countries will soon receive more attention from the European Commission – at present only minimal attention is paid to it in connection with Article 92 of the Treaty of Rome. Furthermore, clarification of the future of the 10 per cent corporate tax rate, due to terminate in 2010, is now essential – in industrial policy terms Ireland has benefited enormously from having a stable investment environment in the past.

Irish policy towards FDI has evolved since the 1950s as a strategy driven primarily by the use of fiscal incentives to enhance the profitability of locating in Ireland, with grants as required to achieve a particular bargaining advantage in competing against alternative international locations. While employment in Irish-owned manufacturing firms decreased by around 19 per cent between 1975 and 1995, employment in foreign-owned firms rose by approximately 27 per cent during the same period, mostly due to the very strong performance of US firms. In effect the major benefit to Ireland from foreign investment comes from its attractiveness as a base for extra-EU investment rather than as a base for intra-EU investment.

Thus the strategy of moving to free trade while retaining employment in the manufacturing sector could be said to have succeeded, with foreign companies generating more or less the same number of jobs as was lost in indigenous manufacturing firms. In terms of sectoral composition, FDI from continental Europe made some contribution to the sectoral restructuring of the Irish manufacturing sector, through its increasing concentration in the chemical and M&E sectors but, as is apparent in Ruane and Görg (1997), the major structural change which occurred in foreign investment in Ireland over the 1975–95 period was the shift out of traditional sectors which were historically dominated by UK companies, towards high tech sectors, currently dominated by US-owned companies.

Notes

1 Department of Economics, Trinity College, Dublin 2. Telephone x353 1 608 1325, Fax x353 1 677 2503, email fruane@tcd.ie and georgh@tcd.ie. We are grateful to Jim Bourke, Forfás and Kieran McGowan, IDA Ireland, for valuable comments on an earlier version of the paper and to Ray Barrell, Nigel Pain and their colleagues at NIESR, and participants at the conference on Investment, Innovation and the Diffusion of Technology in Europe German Foreign Direct Investment and its role in European Growth for comments on the draft presented to the conference. We also benefited from helpful discussions with John FitzGerald and Patrick Honohan, ESRI, and Donal de Buitléir, AIB Bank, on various aspects of FDI in Ireland. Frances Ruane gratefully acknowledges support from the Royal Irish Academy Social Science Research Council.

2 These two features have been well documented in the literature. See, for example, the relevant chapters in Foley and McAleese (1991) and O'Hagan (1995).

3 The major exception here is investment from the UK, whose pattern of sectoral distribution is much more akin to that of indigenous industry.

4 As Killen and Ruane (1993) discuss, Irish industrial policy in effect avoided the problems generated by industrial development in many LDCs where the growth of industrial employment concentrated in urban areas led to massive rural–urban migration, a phenomenon modelled formally by Harris and Todaro (1970).

5 Clearly the scale of FDI is such that it has significant macro implications, which are evident in the high ratio of FDI stocks to GDP and differences in the levels and rates of growth of GNP and GDP.

6 Developments in the indigenous sector, however, cannot be seen as indicating what would have happened overall in the absence of the FDI which occurred. In practice, the outcome could not have been such because the structural adjustments to free trade without FDI would have required macro interventions, which would have altered the environment faced by the indigenous sector. Furthermore, the presence of FDI companies may have had some negative impact on indigenous firms, say through crowding out especially in the factor markets, or some positive impact, say through generating additional markets for the products of indigenous firms, enhancing the level of technology in use and in improving the levels of management and so on in the manufacturing sector.

7 We recognise both that foreign direct investment in services in the EU has been increasing rapidly over the last decade and that this rapid growth is likely to continue in the light of the technology- and market-driven globalisation of services and the reduction of barriers to service trade. See Ruane and Görg (1996, 1997) for further discussion.

8 There are various extant reviews of policy with regards to FDI, the most recent substantial one being found in Foley and McAleese (1991). Other recent commentaries include O'Sullivan (1995) and Ruane (1991).

9 For an overview of the change, see, for example, Lee (1989), Chapter 5 and O'Malley (1989), Chapters 4 and 5.

10 Since the 1970s, other fiscal policies have facilitated foreign companies in

obtaining cost-effective tax-based financing on the Irish market. In some cases these policies have had a very significant impact on attracting foreign companies to locate in Ireland.

11 This compares with the standard rate of corporate tax which has been reduced gradually from 50 per cent in the 1970s to 36 per cent in 1997.

12 Double tax agreements are very important in this context, since the value of a tax incentive against corporate tax in the host country depends crucially on how it is viewed by the tax authorities in the home country. Comparing tax incentives with other incentives, various surveys have concluded that the tax incentives are the most important incentive encouraging manufacturing investors to locate in Ireland. For example, a recent Deloitte Touche Tohmatsu survey indicated that almost 60 per cent of foreign companies interviewed found the 10 per cent rate to have been very influential in their location choice. Furthermore, IDA Ireland personnel would suggest that tax incentives are particularly popular with US firms.

13 For US firms such tax deferrals can be very important because of the scale of operations; they would be much less so for UK firms which, because of the way ACT operates, currently find themselves with little incentive to locate in Ireland.

14 While companies were not totally prohibited from selling on the domestic market, they could not do so using grant-aided equipment and the return to domestic sales was significantly lower because of the high rate of corporation tax such profits attracted (*circa* 50 per cent).

15 Additional assistance in the form of training grants, subsidised rents, technology-transfer supports and so on, have also formed part of the policy package and in the case of some projects the training grants can be an important component of the total financial support given.

16 While in many countries intervention is increasingly made at a proejct level, in the 1950s and 1960s this was extremely rare, except in, say, the nationalised industries in the UK. Such intervention as occurred was only likely in the case of extremely large projects, whereas in Ireland the smallest of projects was analysed and evaluated for grant purposes.

17 While this protection effectively disappeared when the tax holiday came to an end, it is still the case that grants are not given to firms which are clearly going to add to competition for Irish based producers on the domestic market.

18 However, this is mainly due to their different industrial structures. They attract investors to take over existing formerly state-owned companies which are being privatised.

19 The continuity in policy has been possible primarily because there is widespread consensus in Ireland on the strategy of promoting FDI and on the use of the financial and fiscal incentives in that process. That is not to say that there are not occasional disagreements about the support given or not given to particular projects, but by and large there is no major political debate on the fundamental issues and consequently policy has remained broadly unchanged over long periods.

20 Thus, for example, firms locating in Ireland in the 1960s were given a fifteen-year

tax holiday and those locating in the 1980s were assured that the corporate tax system which they would face would be unchanged until 2000; in 1990 this was extended to 2010. Furthermore, the ending of the tax holiday was 'grandparented' so that individual firms who had been given tax-holiday status were able to hold on to it, despite the changes for new firms after 1982.

21 Where changes have been made, such as the reduction in the rates of asset depreciation for tax purposes as rates of inflation declined in the late 1980s, these have been preannounced and done in a very steady and gradual way, minimising uncertainty for firms.

22 Since the policies are operated in a discretionary manner, firms do not know precisely what grant they can expect to get until the negotiations with the IDA are complete, but they have the advantage of dealing with one agency in a centralised system so that at the earliest possible date they are in a position to know what support they can expect.

23 An exception to this is the tourism sector which has always been treated separately from manufacturing and other internationally traded services, presumably on the grounds that it is different since the consumers rather than the outputs move.

24 In a sense IDA personnel were collecting and responding to market information about particular firms which were likely to expand. Implicit in their approach to looking at potential foreign investment was the kind of framework developed by Dunning (1988), who suggests that foreign investment depends on (i) special firm characteristics which enable companies to produce profitably abroad, (ii) an incentive to internalise this advantage, and (iii) location characteristics in the host countries. IDA Ireland's approach involves (i) identifying industries (and firms) which had the ability to profitably locate in foreign locations, (ii) considering the means of how this foreign involvement could be achieved (in general through FDI), and (iii) analysing whether Ireland could offer locational advantages for these particular industries (and firms).

25 The grant maxima were higher in the designated compared with the nondesignated areas and within those areas executives were in a position to respond in offering grants to particular pressures which might exist, for example, the recent closure of a large plant at a particular location.

26 For firms with large employment training grants, there is a maximum also subject to Cabinet review.

27 For example, recent high profile investors in Ireland, such as Intel, Hewlett Packard, Gateway, Dell, Compaq and IBM have been targeted by IDA for many years, with regular presentations and so on. This points to the long lead time required to realise the benefits of such a strategy and the fact that the success in this area has been heavily influenced by the method of implementation.

28 We have documented the growth and significance of US investment in Ireland in more detail elsewhere (Ruane and Görg, 1996, 1997).

29 As regards this nationality group, note that investment from non-EU European countries is virtually non-existent in Ireland. Therefore, one can think of the 'other European' group as investment from continental EU countries other than Germany.

30 To put it formally, we calculate

gains: $g_j = \Sigma_i g_{ji}$

losses: $l_j = \Sigma_i l_{ji}$

net: $(g_j - l_j) = \Sigma_i(g_{ji} - l_{ji})$ $i \in \{76, 77, ..., 95\}$

Note that the first gains and losses are reported in 1976, since 1975 is our base year. Note also that the calculation of job gains and losses is not readily comparable to the calculation of gross flows of jobs as introduced by Davis and Haltiwanger (1990) and used recently by, for example, Konings et al. (1996). In particular, the two indicators described are different from the measures used in those papers.

31 Obviously the scale of FDI also generates some concerns in macro terms, but these are not the focus of this chapter.

References

Davis, S.J. and Haltiwanger, J. (1990), 'Gross job creation and destruction: microeconomic evidence and macroeconomic implications', *NBER Macroeconomics Annual*, 5, pp. 123–68.

Dunning, J.H. (1988), *Explaining International Production*, London, Unwin Hyman.

European Commission (1996), 'Annual economic report for 1996', *European Economy*, 61, Brussels, European Commission.

Foley, A. (1991), 'Interpreting output data on overseas industry', in Foley and McAleese, pp. 29–53.

Foley, A. and McAleese, D. (eds) (1991), *Overseas Industry in Ireland*, Dublin, Gill and Macmillan,

Forfás (1996), *Shaping our Future: A Strategy for Enterprise in Ireland in the 21st Century*, Dublin, Forfás.

Harris, J.R. and Todaro, M.P. (1970), 'Migration, unemployment and development: a two sector analysis', *American Economic Review*, 60, pp. 126–42.

Killen, L. and Ruane, F. (1993), 'The regional dimension to industrial policy and performance in the Republic of Ireland', paper presented to the conference: Economic Change and Development: Prospects for Peripheral Regions, Queen's University Belfast, 2–4 September 1993.

Konings, J., Lehmann, H. and Schaffer, M.E. (1996), 'Job creation and job destruction in a transition economy: ownership, firm size, and gross job flows in Polish manufacturing, 1988–91', *Labour Economics*, 3, pp. 299–317.

Lee, J.J. (1989), *Ireland 1912–85: Politics and Society*, Cambridge, Cambridge University Press.

McAleese, D. (1971), *Effective Tariffs and the Structure of Industrial Production in Ireland*, Dublin, Economic and Social Research Institute.

O'Hagan, J.W. (ed.) (1995), *The Economy of Ireland: Policy and Performance of a*

Small European Economy, Dublin, Gill and Macmillan.

O'Malley, E. (1989), *Industry and Economic Development: The Challenge for the Latecomer*, Dublin, Gill and Macmillan.

O'Sullivan, M. (1995), 'Manufacturing and global competition', in O'Hagan, pp. 363–96.

Ruane, F. (1991)'The traded sector: industry', in O'Hagan, pp. 345–77.

Ruane, F. and Görg, H. (1996), 'Aspects of foreign direct investment in Irish manufacturing since 1973: policy and performance', *Journal of the Statistical and Social Inquiry Society of Ireland*.

(1997), 'The impact of foreign direct investment on sectoral adjustment in the Irish economy', *National Institute Economic Review*, 160, pp. 76–86.

Yuill, D., Allen, K., Bachtler, J., Clement, K. and Wishlade, F. (eds) (1995), *European Regional Incentives 1993–94*, 13th edition, Glasgow, Bowker Saur.

4 German manufacturing investment in the UK: survey results and economic impact

NEIL HOOD, JAMES TAGGART and STEPHEN YOUNG

Introduction

The research reported in this chapter investigates the relatively unexplored topic of the impact of German foreign direct investment (FDI) in manufacturing industry in the United Kingdom. The main body of the text presents the results of a sample survey of German multinational (MNE) affiliates, with the principal issue examined being that of the roles of subsidiaries in the early growth phase of German FDI. This theme is important in that it provides indicators of the developmental impacts and potential of German affiliate operations, and is one which has attracted much attention, albeit chiefly from a business strategy perspective, in recent literature.

The economic impact of inward investment in the UK

Multinational firms have been an important part of the UK economy for many years. Britain was the location for the first FDI from the United States in the 1850s, and for German direct investment, in the form of Siemens, in 1858 (Schröter, 1993). After the Second World War inward investment from the US, and more recently Japan, has expanded rapidly. During the 1980s UK inflows (and indeed outflows) of FDI were a greater proportion of GDP than in any other G7 country. In stock terms, the UK in 1992 was second to the US as a recipient of inward investment on a worldwide basis.

There have been a variety of studies of inward FDI since the pioneering research on US manufacturing investment in the UK by Dunning (1958).

68

The most comprehensive research on economic and political issues was undertaken by Steuer *et al.*(1973). They concluded that 'on economic grounds and grounds of national autonomy we express few arguments against inward investment' (p. 15) and that 'concerns over the multinational firm and inward investment on the grounds of monopoly power, technology and the balance of payments are not well founded. At the same time, some drawbacks have been indicated' (p. 12). Young *et al.* (1988) confirmed the conclusion that the net impact of inbound FDI was probably beneficial but were more qualified in their conclusions. Among the positive contributions identified were the role of international investment as a complement to cross-border trade, the competitive stimuli induced by MNE activity and the transfer of managerial skills and knowledge. The qualifications included the cyclical variability and relative decline in the competitiveness of inward foreign affiliates (particularly those of US origin), the lack of strong linkages to domestically owned firms in many sectors (which has at least as much to do with UK competitiveness as with multinationals) and the limited decision-making capacity of most MNE affiliates. Indeed there remain concerns in the peripheral areas of the UK about the 'branch plant syndrome' (Hood and Young, 1976).

Although much of the inward investment into the UK has taken the form of takeovers and mergers there has been little research on the topic. Ashcroft and Love (1993) analysed the effect of inward acquisitions on the Scottish economy for the period 1965–89. Their conclusion was that there were net benefits for the acquired companies, with improved availability of investment funds, improved financial and managerial techniques and a greater supply of technical help. By contrast, the external effects seemed to be unfavourable to the Scottish economy, with some reduction in local linkages and organisational functions as the firms' demands shifted away from Scotland.

As is evident from the above, the microeconomic concerns about the impact of FDI on the UK economy have changed little over the years. The basic conclusion is still that the static effects of inward investment are positive, whereas the long-term, dynamic benefits are limited, at best. However globalisation has changed the nature of many of these debates.

The internal and external environments for foreign direct investment have begun to change rapidly in recent years, with moves towards global manufacturing and service activities, global sourcing and global customers, the emergence of integrated international production systems, new forms of corporate governance; and the addition of inter firm alliances and cooperation to formerly self contained business and corporate networks (UNCTAD, 1994). Globalisation might be expected to affect the economic impact of MNEs in the UK. Exploitation of a global division of labour creates possibilities for wider export roles for subsidiaries as well as greater global sourcing. Hierarchical relationships between head-quarters and subsidiaries may be partially replaced by heterarchical and network relations. In such systems, decision making units (in areas such as R&D, finance, marketing, procurement and so on) may be decentral-ised to subsidiary level in the UK or elsewhere. By contrast, shorter product life cycles and greater global competition for mobile international investment may reduce the ability to anchor FDI projects within the local economy. In this regard, MNE strategy may be increasingly affected by agglomeration economies and the 'anchors' provided by immobile local clusters (Stopford, 1995).

Cantwell and Dunning (1991) distinguish between the roles of MNEs as promoters of virtuous cycles of increasing technological capabilities or vicious cycles of declining technological capability. Interesting compari-sons may be made between the pharmaceutical and motor industries in the UK. In the latter the declining locational attractiveness of the UK con-tributed to a vicious cycle, with reduced inward investment and MNE activity directed away from high value-added activities. In turn this reduced the industry's ability to compete. It is only the recent wave of Japanese FDI which has helped convert the vicious cycle into a potentially virtuous one. In contrast, from the early 1950s foreign producers in the pharmaceutical industry acted as a competitive challenge to an already strong indigenous industry. Between them they generated a critical mass of innovatory capacity, both human and physical, producing substantial agglomerative economies and further reinforcing the attractiveness of the industry in the UK. More recently the financial services industry and the City of London reveal similar positive economies of agglomeration, although these are perhaps under threat in the light of recent events (Hood and Young, 1997).

The international management literature has discussed the emergence of 'developmental' MNE affiliates, essentially world product mandate (WPM) operations, and the regional conditions for their establishment or evolution. Birkinshaw's (1996) work on Canada highlighted the impor-tance of the subsidiary's capabilities or resources as the driver of its man-dates; whereas the case study work in Scotland by Young et al.(1993a, b) revealed a variety of influences, as well as focusing attention upon the very limited number of such WPM subsidiaries.

Young et al. (1994) argue that an integrated policy approach is required in order to derive the full benefits from inward investment. This should begin with a stable macroeconomic environment and extend through effective macroeconomic organisational policies to active and efficient microeconomic organisational policies. UK policy, however, has focused upon maximising investment flows rather than investment quality, and has not been supported by the infrastructure investment required in order to build complementary assets and develop agglomeration economies. Hence the contribution of inward FDI has been chiefly linked to the existing competitiveness of the sectors in which it has taken place (Hood and Young, 1997).

There has been little research on regionalisation processes at the European level and the particular impact of European integration and economic and monetary union. Successive enlargements of the EC and deeper integration appear to have led to the reorganisation and rationalisation of plant networks. This has taken the form of both horizontal and vertical integration. Papanastassiou and Pearce (1997) discuss the evolution of the innovatory roles of MNE subsidiaries in Europe, with those in the UK found to occupy a more strategic position than their counterparts in Belgium, Greece or Portugal. The authors suggest that UK subsidiaries are not simply low cost based operations specialising in the production of inputs as part of an EC-wide network. Instead they often play a leading creative position in the European activities of MNEs. However many UK subsidiaries did not seem to have a deep relationship with local subcontractors, research institutions or universities.

In a comparative study of enterprises in both the core and peripheral regions of the EU Amin et al. (1994) found differences in the quality of investments both between the two regional groups and amongst the peripheral regions themselves. Inward investment in Portugal was much closer to the classic 'branch plant' typology than that in the Republic of Ireland or Scotland, where, in addition, some quality improvement had taken place over time. Given that 70–90 per cent of FDI now takes the form of sequential investments undertaken by established MNEs (as opposed to initial investment by new multinational enterprises), there is growing interest in 'after care' programmes by development agencies in Europe (Young and Hood, 1994). This underlines the need to build local clusters, as well as the view that policies should be conducted at the lowest possible level, with regionally based and regionally controlled initiatives being vital (Geroski, 1989; Tomaney, 1995).

The survey evidence reported here is designed to shed light on many of the issues discussed above. In particular we focus on the role of German subsidiaries in the UK and on the dynamic linkages between these subsidiaries and the local economy.

Table 4.1 *Geographical shares of stock of German FDI (1961–90, per cent)*

Country/region	1961	1972	1980	1990
EC	14.0	35.5	33.9	40.9
France	5.3	9.9	10.3	8.5
UK	1.2	2.6	3.9	6.2
USA	8.7	8.1	21.6	27.1
Japan	n.a.	0.5	1.2	1.9
All others	73.3	55.9	43.3	30.1
Total	100.0	100.0	100.0	100.0
Total (US$bn)	1	8,312	43,105	129,100
UK share of EC total	8.5	7.3	11.5	15.2

Source: Schröter, 1993, table 2.3

The background of German foreign direct investment in the UK

German firms began to invest overseas in the latter half of the nineteenth century. The UK was host to Germany's second overseas manufacturing investment in 1858. By 1914, Germany is estimated to account for around 10 per cent of world-wide FDI. However Germany lost virtually all of its foreign direct investments in the aftermath of the two world wars (Schröter, 1993). Postwar restrictions on outward FDI were abolished in 1956, but German companies did not begin to invest heavily overseas until the mid-1970s, when the country's traditionally competitive industries of chemicals, electrical engineering and telecommunications were in the vanguard. During this phase, Europe was the main focus of FDI, with the UK accounting for a growing share as shown in table 4.1. More recent data for 1993 (Deutsche Bundesbank, 1995) conclude that the UK accounted for 6.5 per cent of the worldwide stock of FDI, and a slightly reduced share (13.5 per cent) of German direct investment in the EC.[1]

The characteristics of German manufacturing firms in the UK are summarised in tables 4.2 and 4.3. Through the 1980s there was clearly little activity, with the number of enterprises remaining nearly static. However the number of enterprises and employees grew rapidly from the end of the 1980s. This has undoubtedly continued beyond 1992. Indeed it could be argued that the BMW acquisition of Rover in 1994 and recent investments by Siemens and Bosch could have the same 'lift-off' effect in terms of enticing hesitant German investors as the Nissan project in north-east England had for Japan. Major German companies, like their Japanese counterparts, have strong domestic networks of smaller companies that underpin their competitiveness.

Table 4.2 *Selected data on foreign-owned and all private-sector manufacturing enterprises in the UK*

Year and performance measure	Germany	EC	Japan	USA	All foreign enterprises	All enterprises in the UK
1981						
Enterprises (No.)	126	340	17	827	1,522	90,068
Employment (000)	22.1	127.4	3.0	568.1	858.1	5,777.9
Employment per enterprise (No.)	175	375	176	687	564	64
Net output per head (£)	13,784	13,505	12,519	16,046	15,265	12,222
Net capital expenditure per head (£)	873	1,654	3,800	1,615	1,634	931
1985						
Enterprises (No.)	134	364	31	777	1,515	127,430
Employment (000)	18.7	95.1	6.3	416.3	677.1	4,842.8
Employment per enterprise (No.)	140	261	203	536	447	38
Net output per head (£)	26,378	23,619	17,741	27,078	25,519	18,937
Net capital expenditure per head (£)	2,214	1,882	5,524	3,074	2,723	1,740
1989						
Enterprises (No.)	122	347	86	633	1,356	139,879
Employment (000)	24.6	133.5	27.2	395.0	724.1	4,873.6
Employment per enterprise (No.)	202	385	316	624	534	35
Net output per head (£)	35,922	34,453	29,326	43,153	39,264	27,157
Net capital expenditure per head (£)	5,211	4,795	13,213	5,124	5,353	2,886
1992						
Enterprises (No.)	161	458	117	624	1,507	130,936
Employment (000)	39.0	190.3	58.0	374.8	784.2	4,341.3
Employment per enterprise (No.)	242	416	496	601	520	33
Net output per head (£)	36,646	37,214	43,904	46,097	43,035	32,175
Net capital expenditure per head (£)	4,805	3,411	14,028	4,388	4,872	2,775

Source: HMSO, *Business Monitor*, 1981, 1985, 1989 and 1992.

Table 4.3 *The performance of German manufacturing enterprises in relation to EC and all foreign manufacturing enterprises in the UK*

Year and performance measure	EC enterprises	All foreign enterprises	All enterprises in UK
1981			
Share of employment (%)[a]	17.30	2.60	0.40
Net output per employee[b]	1.02	0.90	1.13
1985			
Share of employment (%)	18.90	2.80	0.40
Net output per employee	1.12	1.03	1.39
1989			
Share of employment (%)	18.40	3.40	0.50
Net output per employee	1.04	0.91	1.32
1992			
Share of employment (%)	20.50	5.00	0.90
Net output per employee	0.98	0.85	1.14

Source: Calculated from table 4.2.
Notes: (a) Share of total employment in German enterprises. (b) Ratio of productivity in German enterprises to productivity in all enterprises.

German FDI conforms to the conventional pattern of foreign manufacturing activity, with German affiliates having higher investment and productivity levels than domestic manufacturing enterprises. The contrast with other foreign manufacturing operations in the UK reveals a different picture. On average German enterprises have fewer employees and their productivity levels, while close to the EC norm, were below the levels of all overseas enterprises in the UK. The average employment per enterprise has, however, been growing and capital expenditure per head has been above the figures for American and EC enterprises as a whole (although nowhere near the levels for Japan). The picture is thus of a limited but growing German manufacturing presence in the UK, consisting of smaller and medium sized enterprises (SMEs). This is confirmed by the results of a German Chamber of Commerce and Industry (1992) survey which, in addition, highlighted the dominance of the machinery and electrical equipment sectors in German FDI.[2]

Apart from this, rather little is known about the detailed composition of German FDI in the UK, its underlying strategic intent or the direction of its development. Our survey was undertaken to fill some of these knowledge gaps, and to enable some preliminary observations to be made on the economic impact of German inward investments in this early development phase.

Survey results on German manufacturing FDI in the UK

Our results are derived from a postal questionnaire of German manufacturing companies in the UK, supported by personal interviews with a sub-sample of firms. Appendix 4.1 provides further details. The questionnaire focused upon subsidiary development at three points over a ten year period (1989, 1994 and 1999) in areas such as markets and products, research and development and production, and a range of strategic issues. Operational characteristics of the subsidiaries were also established including size, industry sector, locational determinants and mode of entry. The UK survey was complemented by a survey of German affiliates in the Republic of Ireland. Some of the main differences between the two groups are summarised in the second part of this section. We also compare the operations and strategies of German subsidiaries in the UK with those from Japan. Finally, we discuss the status and evolution of strategy of the German subsidiaries in the UK.

German manufacturing subsidiary operations in the United Kingdom

The survey results on German subsidiaries are summarised in table 4.4, based on a sample of 77 responses to a postal survey undertaken in 1994.

Market entry. The data on market entry show that almost equal proportions of German MNEs were set up in the UK through greenfield plants (44%) and acquisitions (43%).[3] Personal interviews with a sub-sample of companies indicated that entry by means other than greenfield investment stemmed from the prior existence of a range of 'trading relationships' with UK firms. Such relationships included agent/distributorship arrangements, joint ventures with UK companies, prior marketing agreements and so on. This implies an evolutionary, iterative approach to internationalisation within Europe. We also found a gradual increase in the importance of acquisitions as a means of entry for more recently established German subsidiaries, while takeovers tended to be associated with smaller subsidiaries and lower levels of employment.

Subsidiary roles. A strong UK market sales orientation was apparent in almost two-thirds of the sample. Over the 1989–94 period, however, there was some evidence of a gradual move by German subsidiaries

Table 4.4 *Characteristics of sample German manufacturing subsidiaries in UK*

	No. of firms	% of total
Entry method		
Build a new plant	33	44.0
Acquisition of domestic firm	27	36.0
Acquisition of non-domestic firm	5	6.7
Joint venture	6	8.0
Other	4	5.3
Market area served		
Domestic	33	42.5
UK plus selected European countries	17	22.1
Europe	2	2.6
Europe and selected other parts of the world	11	14.3
Global with specific exclusions	4	5.2
Global	10	13.0
Domestic sales		
Low (0–20% of total sales)	6	8.0
Medium (21–80%)	30	40.0
High (81–100%)	39	52.0
Per cent of material inputs to subsidiary from domestic market		
0–5%	8	10.5
6–25%	25	32.9
26% and over	43	56.6
Per cent of subsidiary output to other group operations		
0–5%	61	80.2
6–25%	10	13.2
26% and over	5	6.6
R&D[a]		
Limited R&D	38	49.4
Substantive R&D	39	50.6
Decision-making on market area served		
Parent-oriented	21	27.7
Subsidiary-oriented	56	72.7

Source: German FDI Survey 1994.
Note: (a) 'Limited R&D' = no R&D, customer technical services, adaptation of manufacturing technology. 'Substantive R&D' = development of new and improved products for UK/European markets, new products and processes for world markets, generation of new technology for the corporate parent.

towards a greater continental European market focus. This would again support the notion of an evolutionary approach to affiliate development. Looking forward to 1999, around 40 per cent of the operations were expecting to have market franchises covering Europe and beyond (up from 32.5 per cent in 1994).

The German companies entering the UK market with greenfield operations showed a greater tendency to evolve towards world market franchises. This is broadly consistent with other evidence on the characteristics of acquisitions and greenfield ventures, with the former continuing for some time to display the characteristics of indigenous enterprises, including the significant dependence on the home market. Post-acquisition reorganisation is, of course, a critical issue from an economic impact perspective.

Domestic sales. The above observations are confirmed by the sample data on shares of sales into the domestic UK market. More than half the sample were heavily UK market oriented (81–100 per cent of sales domestically), as shown in the third section of table 4.4. At the other end of the scale, only 8 per cent of German subsidiaries used the UK as an export base.

Material input sourcing. Domestic sourcing of material inputs is one measure of the linkage and spillover effects of FDI. The importance of this is illustrated by the efforts made by UK inward investment organisations (IIOs) to demonstrate the relative depth and qualities of local subcontractors. The IIOs also undertake development programmes to maximise local content and spin-off potential from manufacturing subsidiaries. In certain sectors, for instance electronics, such considerations can materially influence both initial and sequential investment decisions (Bathelt, 1991, Young et al., 1994).

Our survey also showed that significant UK purchases are made by over half of the sample firms, although there was no evident correlation between local sourcing levels and either product or market decision making autonomy.[4] Within the sample, the more developed manufacturing units had higher proportions of local sourcing, as did plants with substantive R&D roles, suggesting that local embeddedness is chiefly linked to production and innovation rather than to market variables.

Integration-subsidiary output to group operations. A further indication of low levels of manufacturing integration in the sample firms is evident from the data on outputs to other group facilities. Four fifths of the sample consigned only minimal levels of output (0–5 per cent) to other group operations. The proportions were not strongly influenced by plant size, age, mode of entry or market area served. Plants with greater autonomy over decisions about the product range generally sold less of the output to group plants.

Research and development. In studies of the impact of inward investment attention is often focused upon the presence or absence of R&D facilities within manufacturing units. Their presence is deemed to provide an indication of the innovative and entrepreneurial potential of the affiliate. Subsidiaries with world or regional product mandates would certainly be expected to have R&D capabilities. Definitional issues prove very problematic in this area but, taken at their face value, the sample data indicate that one half of German affiliates undertake little or no R&D, whereas the other half claim to undertake a more substantive level of R&D. This includes work on the development of new or improved products for UK and other European markets. Subsidiaries which had a market franchise extending beyond Europe have had a history of more substantive R&D. Plans for the years to 1999 also envisaged greater commitment to research and development.

Decision-making responsibility. Existing work on subsidiary development indicates that the allocation of product and market responsibilities and the associated decision-making procedures play an important part in determining the development path and prospects of a subsidiary (Young *et al.*, 1988; Birkinshaw and Hood, 1997). The data in the fourth section of table 4.4 suggest that decisions over the market areas served are largely made at subsidiary level.[5] Decision making did not seem to be affected by the age of the operations or employment levels. Subsidiaries established by acquisitions tended to have a greater degree of autonomy than subsidiaries established by greenfield operations, although a level of convergence was evident as acquisitions were progressively internalised into group procedures and control. It is also worth observing that affiliates in the UK with annual revenues of under £5 million indicated a stronger likelihood of autonomy in product decisions in the years up to 1999.

Inter-regional differences within the UK. Our research has also sought to explore differences between the characteristics of German subsidiaries within three different regions of the UK: south-east England, the East Midlands and the rest of the UK (with Assisted Area status). The Assisted Area subsidiaries were found to have a significantly higher proportion of exports than subsidiaries in other areas. This suggests that the more mobile FDI projects were attracted to areas offering government financial assistance, and that part of their mobility lay in the fact that they produce goods with low per unit transport costs, designed to serve the wider European market. By contrast, subsidiaries based in south-east England demonstrated more independence from corporate headquarters than those in the Assisted Areas, in both market areas and product ranges. By 1994 (and projected for 1999), East Midlands operations also had greater autonomy than the Assisted Area subsidiaries. There are indications in these findings of 'branch plant' activity in Assisted Areas.

The sample results provide strong evidence of country-centred strategies in the subsidiaries, with few signs of them being deployed as part of the parents' international response to competitive conditions on a regional scale. The tentative conclusion is that, as yet, few German manufacturing subsidiaries have had a substantial net positive impact on the UK economy when judged by measures such as international or global subsidiary roles, R&D for international markets and export performance.

A comparison of German manufacturing subsidiary operations in the UK and Republic of Ireland

Comparisons of subsidiaries in the UK and Ireland are of interest as both countries have aggressive policies to attract inward investment and compete vigorously with each other, especially at the regional level (Hood and Taggart, 1997). A regional economy such as Scotland provides a broadly similar investment environment to that of Ireland, although the latter has significantly higher investment incentives. On the basis of the UK evidence the expectation might be that Irish operations would also be primarily supply points for the UK market. One difference, however, derives from the fact that the stock of German manufacturing subsidiaries is proportionately much greater than that in the UK. The reasons are partly historical, deriving from the uninterrupted trading between the two countries because of Irish neutrality in the Second World War.

Our survey data on motivations for investment revealed that the UK is preferred as a location to supply an existing customer base, and to access the UK market. By contrast the major motivating factor in the Irish results concerned the availability of government financial assistance. Labour skills and supplying continental European customers were not discriminatory factors between the UK and Ireland, nor surprisingly were labour costs.

Entry by means of new greenfield plants (64 per cent of the sample was in this category) and the acquisition of non-domestic firms (16 per cent) is more frequent in Ireland than in the UK. This probably reflects the much larger manufacturing base, and therefore takeover possibilities, in the UK. The high incidence of greenfield facilities in turn may provide an explanation for the strong 'Europe and beyond' market franchises in the majority of affiliates in Ireland.[6]

The wider international focus of German subsidiaries in Ireland is not reflected in more advanced R&D functions as a higher proportion of Irish facilities were found to be in the 'limited R&D' categories. And, as expected given the size and diversity of the UK industrial base compared with that of Ireland, German subsidiaries in the UK sourced a significantly higher proportion of inputs locally than those in Ireland.

Overall, the evidence points to Irish affiliates fulfilling a controlled and limited European production role, with restricted development potential except in regard to exports. This role was significantly different from the country-centred strategies largely played by German affiliates in the UK, although some of the Assisted Area operations were not dissimilar from their Irish counterparts.

German subsidiary operations in the UK and economic development

It would be relatively easy to play down the contribution of German multinational activity to economic development in the UK. The survey data point to 'early-stage' market entry strategies on the part of many of the German MNEs, even where the subsidiaries are well established. There is strong evidence of country-centred strategies in the affiliates and relatively little sign of them being deployed as part of a response to global competitive conditions. However, when the comparison is made with German affiliates in Ireland, it is by no means certain that the latter group of more export-oriented operations have greater developmental potential on a long-term basis.

Related research into the decision-making autonomy of German and Japanese manufacturing affiliates in the British Isles is undertaken in Taggart and Hood (1997). Despite the fact that Japanese subsidiaries were, on average, much younger than their German counterparts, they appear to have grown much more rapidly. They employed more than twice as many people, had substantially higher sales and had a higher export propensity than German affiliates. Hence from an economic development perspective, they appeared more attractive. However, German subsidiaries had on the whole become rather more autonomous in terms of both product and market decisions over the last five years and this trend was forecast to continue over the next five. Conversely, Japanese affiliates were becoming less autonomous, with signs that parent-orientated decision making was planned to increase further. Product decisions had also become more centralised in the recent past. The authors thus argued that the two categories of subsidiary presented different types of opportunity for a host country; the Japanese operations were export – and growth – oriented but tightly controlled, the German ones country-centred but more decentralised.[7]

Subsidiary status

The business strategy literature suggests that integration, coordination and local responsiveness are important determinants of strategy in global industries. It also underlines the need to match corporate and subsidiary strategies. Taggart and Hood (1996) focus on three key strategy dimensions at subsidiary level, the responsibility allocated to the subsidiary to supply the different markets available to it (market scope), the freedom to make certain key decisions (autonomy); and the integration of activities with other subsidiaries within the parent's network (integration). These three dimensions were selected because of the findings of previous empirical work (see, for example, Jarillo and Martinez, 1990; Roth and Morrison, 1990; Johnson, 1995).

Market scope was defined to cover the current market area for the subsidiary's products, export levels and the nature of production operations. Autonomy was judged using decision-making responsibility for the market areas served and the product range produced, plus local sourcing of material inputs. Integration reflected the linkages with other group plants abroad and the nature of R&D activities.[8] A typology of subsidiaries was derived by considering two states (high, low) of each strategic dimension. The subsequent statistical evaluation of the data involved factor analysis and cluster analysis.[9] Table 4.5 summarises the findings for seventy-three German manufacturing affiliates in the UK for which data were available.

There is strong evidence of host-country centred strategies throughout the sample, but especially in Groups 1, 2 and 5, which contain twenty-eight firms in all. Group 5 is termed 'Starter plants' as evidence of its being the earliest stage of manufacturing, perhaps having emerged from being a distribution and servicing unit. However, it operates with low levels of integration and this differentiates it from Group 1, the 'Slave subsidiary'. The main role of the latter firms appears to be the final assembly for the host market of components and sub-assemblies manufactured elsewhere in the international network. The 'Host market penetrator' (Group 2 and 27 per cent of the sample) is the next stage from the 'Starter plant'. While these subsidiaries have a high degree of autonomy, this is along clearly defined product, market and technology lines which allows them to focus strongly on the host market. The fact that the UK has large numbers of major MNE subsidiaries manufacturing for EU markets means that

Table 4.5 *Subsidiary groups*

Group	No. of firms	Title	Main characteristics
1	2	Slave subsidiary	Low autonomy, very low market scope, and a very high degree of integration. Likely to be a transition phase between Groups 5 and 6.
2	20	Host market penetrator	High autonomy, low market scope and low levels of integration. Mission largely to penetrate host markets with existing products/technologies. Very low dependence on exports.
3	13	Regional exporter	Fairly low autonomy, fairly high market scope, and low integration. Mission largely to service existing customers of the parent in European countries.
4	11	Emergent regional supplier	High market scope, low integration, above average autonomy, but higher export dependency to EU markets.
5	6	Starter plant	Almost direct opposite of Group 8. Relatively low level, small, initial manufacturing operations for host market.
6	5	Integrated branch plant	Very high integration. Low on decision making. Above average in market-technology scope.
7	6	Constrained subsidiary	High autonomy, very low market scope and high levels of integration. This may be a transitional phase towards Group 8, or it may merely indicate increasing centralisation by HQ.
8	10	Strategic independent	Highly autonomous, tightly integrated into parent networks. Serving many markets with high levels of product and process technology.

this group of subsidiaries serves a large and demanding market. Group 6 ('Integrated branch plants') is distinguished from Groups 2 and 5 by having a higher level of integration with other group plants and rather higher market-technology scope. These plants are less host-country oriented and may allow German group networks to effectively achieve some intra-EU integration gains across different manufacturing locations.

Groups 3 and 4 in table 4.5 are in rather different categories and are of particular interest in the context of this chapter. Group 3 subsidiaries ('Regional exporters') have high market scope, but a low level of autonomy and integration. Group 4 plants ('Emergent regional suppliers') have substantially more autonomy. Both these groups have a higher than expected incidence of export-dependent subsidiaries. It is probable that many subsidiaries are in these categories either because they have a small but distinctive product or technology advantage, or because they are parts of small German parent companies who no longer manufacture the particular product range in Germany and use the UK as an export base. The fact that some 33 per cent of the sample subsidiaries are in these two groups suggests that the UK may be becoming an EU export base for German MNEs. This may signal considerable economic development potential for the future.

Group 8 ('Strategic independent') is a distinct category, with Group 7 ('Constrained subsidiary') plants at an earlier developmental stage where substantial market scope has yet to be achieved. A large representation in Group 8 is perhaps not to be expected at this stage of German FDI in the UK, given its relatively recent growth. In that light, it is worth noting in table 4.5 that some 50 per cent of the sample are in the relatively less developed Groups 1, 2, 3, 5 and 6.

The evolution of subsidiary strategy

The grouping of subsidiaries does not provide any information about the evolution of subsidiaries over time. The two polar positions of 'Starter plant' and 'Strategic independent' can readily be established, with the latter normally resulting from a maturing process. The sequence in between them is more difficult to map out, yet it can readily be seen that there are different types of economic impact associated with them. There could therefore be merit in founding an investment after-care strategy upon this type of analysis, deploying various tools to foster the progression of subsidiaries along the value added chain wherever possible. This raises the question of the evolution of strategy within these German subsidiaries. In completing the survey, respondents were asked to make assessments for the strategy variables (autonomy, integration and market scope) for 1989 and 1999, as well as 1994.

The overall impression was one of a considerable stability of strategy over time. Among the noteworthy changes were the findings with regard to the 'Emergent regional suppliers', who gained autonomy over 1989–94 and anticipated becoming less integrated with their parent networks during 1994–9. This is perhaps to be expected, in that as a wide market base is established, together with the production technology to support it, there is likely to be a need to increase the scope of decision-making to sustain efforts to increase market penetration. The 'Host Market Penetrators' became more focused on the UK between 1989 and 1994, with little change planned for the future. 'Regional exporters' and 'Starter plants' show no significant change in either market scope or integration over the ten year period. Thus it would seem that, having reached a strategic posture that is satisfactory to both parent and subsidiary, no change is envisaged.

Overall, our results suggest that autonomy is the most volatile dimension, while integration is the most stable parameter. All of this indicates a gradual process of change in the role of these subsidiaries to date. The evolution of subsidiary strategy reported here is less marked than that reported in recent similar work such as Prahalad and Doz (1987) and Jarillo and Martinez (1990).

Concluding remarks

Affiliates operating within country-centred strategies may have a different economic impact on the host country from those operating within global strategies. Country-oriented strategies typically reflect national conditions such as unique tastes or requirements or 'buy national' attitudes. The most likely explanations for such strategies in German affiliates relate to either the early and hesitant internationalisation of the parent and/or acquisition based entry, although the single market in Europe has not entirely eliminated the bias towards domestic purchasing. Given the present growth in foreign investments by German companies, country-centred strategies seem likely to evolve so as to exploit growth possibilities (which means product and market development focusing on international markets primarily). It is possible that the medium-tech, niche market sectors in which many German MNEs concentrate, do not provide opportunities for vertical specialisation (that is geographical specialisation by process) to the same extent as, say, electronics. Therefore the outcome could be specialised UK affiliates which are increasingly integrated into parent control and decision-making as integration is pursued within the multinational groups. However, this scenario is critically dependent on both UK affiliate performance, and hence upon the capabilities and resources of the affiliate, and a favourable supply side environment including the existence of, support for, and access to local clusters.

There is also likely to be some evolution in the extent to which subsidiaries contribute to the global or regional strategies of MNEs. UK subsidiaries may play a strengthened role within the multinational groups as, for example, decision centres for regional/global markets or as regional/global product mandate operations. Again local competencies are vital. There are other significant barriers including global project competition and the fact that there are few local high tech clusters to provide support and facilitate anchoring.

As German FDI into the UK increases rapidly over the next few years, much more research will undoubtedly be undertaken. One key policy issue seems likely to be that of how to accelerate the export orientation of country-centred German subsidiaries. A second is perhaps that of anchoring local sourcing to these affiliates and encouraging suppliers to take advantage of potential opportunities elsewhere within the German MNE groups. If developments take place along these lines the German multinational enterprise will be a different animal from that of its US and Japanese counterparts.

Appendix 4.1   Sample selection

The results on German manufacturing FDI in the UK reported here were part of a wider study which included the Republic of Ireland. The data for the survey were drawn from two sources. The German Chamber of Industry and Commerce Directory (1993) for the UK yielded a list of 268 German-owned companies manufacturing in the UK, and the Industrial Development Agency (IDA) published a similar list of 141 companies in Ireland. This gave a total population of 409 for the British Isles.

A postal questionnaire addressed to the subsidiary managing director was considered the most appropriate means of obtaining the relevant data on the basic characteristics of subsidiary strategies. The sequence of initial mailing, reminder and telephone call took place over the period February to June 1994 and resulted in 102 completed questionnaires, a 24.9 per cent response. For the UK alone, 77 completed questionnaires were received, representing a 28.7 per cent response rate. The limitations of a

postal questionnaire in evaluating subsidiary development are acknowledged in that it is preferable to discuss many of the same topics at both
subsidiary and headquarters level. Our survey was however followed up
by twenty-five interviews at subsidiary level. Studies on decision-making
in multinational companies have shown that there can be significant differences in perception between the two. Care is therefore taken in present-
ing the results to attempt to offset some aspects of this problem, while the
overall focus is factual where possible. The aggregate details of the questionnaire responses are set out below.

Questionnaire Responses

| | UK sample | | Irish sample | |
	Companies	%	Companies	%
Completed	77	28.7	25	17.7
Not eligible	23	8.6	4	2.8
a) Not German	9		4	
b) Not manufacturing	14		0	
Not willing to complete	13	4.9	0	
Non-respondents	155	57.8	112	79.3
Total mailed	268		141	

Notes

1   Comparisons with the data in table 4.1 are difficult because the Deutsche
    Bundesbank figures are quoted in DM, so that exchange-rate movements may
    distort the geographical shares.
2   An indicator of the scale of German FDI is provided by recent Invest in Britain
    Bureau data which give some measure of flows:

    German FDI in UK (£m)

1986/87	1988/89	1990/91	1992/93	1994/95
58.3	174.9	544.4	402.3	1,535.4

    Source: *Financial Times*, 31 January 1997.

3   It would be incorrect to conclude that German FDI into the UK is more acquisition
    oriented than that from other countries. Many of the statistics quoted on inward
    investment emphasise greenfield projects in Assisted Areas, omitting projects in
    the non-Assisted Areas and acquisitions throughout the UK.
4   One of the dilemmas associated with multinational ventures is that integrated

global or regional operations generate high levels of exports, but also high levels of imports as MNEs recognise and exploit the opportunities for global sourcing.

5   Subsidiaries had marginally less autonomy over decisions about products.

6   Almost 90 per cent of the Irish operations indicated that by 1999 they expected to have market franchises covering Europe and beyond (the equivalent figure for the UK was 40 per cent).

7   These characteristics of German FDI abroad are confirmed for German subsidiaries in France, see Liouville and Nanopoulos (1996).

8   It is recognised that some of these variables might be linked to more than one of the strategy dimensions.

9   The statistical procedures are set out in detail in Taggart and Hood (1996).

References

Amin, A., Bradley, D., Howells, J., Tomaney, J. and Gentle, C. (1994), 'Regional incentives and the quality of mobile investment in the less favoured regions of the EC', *Progr. Plann.* 41/1.

Ashcroft, B. and Love, J.H. (1993), *Takeovers, Mergers and the Regional Economy*, Edinburgh, Edinburgh University Press.

Bathelt, H. (1991), 'Employment changes and input–output linkages in key technology industries : a comparative analysis', *Regional Studies*, 25/1, pp. 31–43.

Birkinshaw, J. (1996), 'How multinational subsidiary mandates are gained and lost', *Journal of International Business Studies*, 27/3, pp. 467–95.

Birkinshaw, J. and Hood, N. (1997), 'An empirical study of development process in foreign-owned subsidiary in Canada and Scotland', *Management International Review*.

Cantwell, J.A. and Dunning, J.H. (1991), 'MNEs, technology and the competitiveness of European industries', *Aussenwirtschaft*, 46, pp. 45–65.

Deutsche Bundesbank (1995), *Monthly Report*, 47/5, May.

Dunning, J.H. (1958), *American Investment in British Manufacturing Industry*, London, Allen & Unwin.

German Chamber of Commerce and Industry (1992), *Trends and Views on Direct Investment by German Owned companies in the UK*, London, January.

Geroski, P. (1989), 'European industrial policy and industrial policy in Europe', *Oxford Review of Economic Policy*, 5/2, pp. 20–36.

Hood, N. and Taggart, J. (1997), 'German foreign direct investment in the UK and Ireland: survey evidence', *Regional Studies*, 31/2, pp. 137–48.

Hood, N. and Young, S. (1976), 'US investment in Scotland : aspects of the branch factory syndrome', *Scottish Journal of Political Economy*, 23/3, pp. 279–94.

(1997), 'The United Kingdom', in Dunning, J.H. (ed.), *Governments, Globalization and International Business*, Oxford, Oxford University Press, pp. 244–82.

Jarillo, J.C. and Martinez, J.I. (1990), 'Different roles for subsidiaries: the case of multinational corporations in Spain', *Strategic Management Journal*, 11, pp. 501–12.

Johnson, J.H. (1995), 'An empirical analysis of the integration-responsiveness

88   Innovation, investment and technology in Europe

framework: US construction equipment industry firms in global competition',
Journal of International Business Studies, 26/3, pp. 621–35.
Liouville, J. and Nanopoulos, C. (1996), 'Performance factors of subsidiaries abroad:
lessons in an analysis of German subsidiaries in France', *Management International Review*, 36/2, pp. 101–21.
Papanastassiou, M. and Pearce, R. (1997), 'The creation and application of technology by MNEs' subsidiaries in Europe', in Burton, F., Yamin, M. and Young, S.
(eds), *International Business and Europe in Transition*, London, Macmillan, pp.
207–30.
Prahalad C.K. and Doz, Y.L. (1987), *The Multinational Mission: Balancing Local
Elements and Global Vision*, New York, The Free Press.
Roth, K. and Morrison, A.J. (1990), 'An empirical analysis of the integration-
responsiveness framework in global industries', *Journal of International Business
Studies*, 21/4, pp. 541–64.
Schröter, H.G. (1993), 'Continuity and change : German multinationals since 1850',
in Jones, G. and Schröter, H.G. (eds), *The Rise of Multinationals in Continental
Europe*, Aldershot, Edward Elgar, 28–48.
Steuer, M.D., Abell, P., Gennard, J., Perlman, M., Rees, R., Scott, B. and Wallis, K.
(1973), *The Impact of Foreign Direct Investment on the United Kingdom*,
London, HMSO.
Stopford, J.M. (1995),'Competing globally for resources', *Transnational Corpora-
tions*, 4/2, pp. 34–57.
Taggart, J. and Hood, N. (1996), 'Strategy development in German manufacturing
subsidiaries in the British Isles', Strathclyde International Business Unit, Univer-
sity of Strathclyde, mimeo.
(1997), 'Decision making autonomy in German and Japanese manufacturing
affiliates in the British Isles', paper presented at the Academy of International
Business UK Chapter Conference, University of Leeds, April.
Tomaney, J. (1995), 'Full employment and quality jobs: the regional dimension',
Business Review North, 7/3, pp. 13–16.
UNCTAD (1994), *World Investment Report 1994*, New York and Geneva, UN.
Young, S. and Hood, N. (1994), 'Designing developmental after-care programmes
for foreign direct investors in the European Union', *Transnational Corporations*,
3/2, pp. 45–72.
Young, S., Hood, N. and Hamill, J. (1988), *Foreign Multinationals and the British
Economy: Impact and Policy*, London, Croom Helm.
Young, S., Hood, N. and Peters, E. (1993a), 'Performance and employment change
in overseas-owned manufacturing industry in Scotland', *Scottish Economic
Bulletin*, 47, pp. 29–38.
(1993b), 'The contribution of foreign direct investment to the Scottish economy: a
review and re-appraisal', Department of Marketing, University of Strathclyde,
mimeo.
(1994), 'Multinationals and regional economic development, *Regional Studies*, 28/
7, pp. 657–77.

5 Internationalisation of R&D in multinational enterprises: the German perspective

HEIKE BELITZ and MARIAN BEISE

Introduction

In most industrial countries, multinational enterprises are stepping up research and development in their affiliates abroad. In many companies, the establishment and expansion of research facilities outside the home country leads to new forms of international specialisation in research and development (R&D). By acquiring companies abroad that engage in industrial research and development, they aim at new markets and know-how in new technology fields. In these new technologies, multinational enterprises try to obtain access to the technological resources of smaller technology firms abroad through cooperation, joint ventures or acquisitions.

In recent years, the tendency for multinational enterprises to internationalise research and development is seen in Germany partly as a relocation of R&D resources abroad and as a threat to the longer-term technological capacity of the German economy. The growth of foreign affiliates' research and development activities is sometimes adduced as evidence for weaknesses in the native research environment. It has therefore been suggested that the stagnation of R&D expenditures in Germany and other industrial countries since the end of the 1980s is due to many multinationals increasing R&D spending not in their home countries, but in regions with higher economic growth or lower labour costs.

The relationship between corporate technological competitiveness and national technological capacity is doubtless affected by the internationalisation of research and development by multinational companies. Recent work by Coe and Helpman (1995) and other scholars points to significant effects of international R&D spillovers on productivity growth in industrialised countries through trade. Coe and Helpman go on to suggest that direct investment could play a similar role. They suggest that the technological capacity of a national economy is not only determined by R&D conducted within the country but increasingly by R&D generated by companies abroad, associated by capital ties, such as foreign parent companies, affiliates or joint ventures.

Indeed, the expectation of many multinationals is to get access to new technology through R&D intensive foreign direct investment. Lichtenberg and van Pottelsberghe de la Potterie (1996) find evidence for the hypothesis that outward foreign direct investment is indeed used for this so-called technology sourcing. In an earlier study Mansfield and Romeo (1984) found a positive effect of R&D performed in foreign affiliates of US multinationals on productivity at home. In addition, strategies of international R&D organisations of multinational enterprises could also have an impact on the R&D pattern of national economies. By acquiring R&D-committed companies abroad, multinational companies add in-house research and production capacities and form a world-wide web of R&D and production facilities. A growing freedom to separate R&D and production geographically, due to better communication technologies, gives companies new opportunities to divide labour internationally and distribute R&D tasks among different R&D locations. More and more multinationals are reorganising their world-wide research resources in building so-called competence centres, where the R&D for special products, techniques or even technological fields are concentrated, to avoid duplicating research and to exploit the specialisation advantages offered by particular locations. This restructuring of companies' R&D organisations, mostly triggered by acquisitions, affects research resources in individual national locations. To assess the future technological capacity of a national economy is to ask how this restructuring of R&D in multinational enterprises affects a country's R&D potential and productive potential. Is the internationalisation of R&D within multinational enterprises therefore influenced by the specialisation pattern of R&D of countries and is there even a backward impact on the countries' specialisation? By measuring the specialisation of countries by their patent applications, Barré (1995) rejects the former hypothesis for Germany but confirms it for Britain, which also has a larger share of domestic R&D by foreign companies.

In this chapter we present some results of our investigation of the extent and the sectoral structure of the R&D activities conducted by German firms abroad and by foreign firms in Germany. Our aim is to assess the impact of the internationalisation of R&D in multinational enterprises on the technological resources and future competitiveness of Germany. For it is indeed important to understand technological policy: whether R&D

activities are being shifted abroad by domestic companies and whether foreign companies invest in domestic R&D and in which fields.

Approaches to internationalising corporate R&D

Earlier studies have shown that the internationalisation of R&D in multinational companies follows the internationalisation of production and is closely related to foreign direct investment.[1] To answer the question why multinational companies expand their R&D resources abroad one must start to explain foreign direct investment. There are a number of theoretical approaches to explaining foreign direct investment, but as yet no valid closed theory has been advanced.

Dunning (1979) has consolidated various attempts to explain the foreign activities of industrial enterprises into the 'eclectic paradigm'. The propensity of a company to engage in direct investment abroad is seen to depend on the following three factors:

- the ownership specific advantage of the company in serving the external market (ownership advantage)

- the higher attractiveness of foreign locations against the home country (locational advantage)

- the interest of the company in exploiting resources itself, that is to say to internalise them rather than controlling them by other organisational means through markets or cooperation with companies abroad (internalisation advantage).

Regarding the internationalisation of R&D in multinational enterprises we have to analyse the influence of both ownership advantages and locational advantages.[2]

Any explanation of production and R&D internationalisation in multinational enterprises must furthermore take account of Vernon's product cycle hypothesis, which has the innovation process as its point of departure. Vernon (1966) asserts that innovation is triggered by special home-market conditions and comes to fruition in close cooperation with customers. As soon as market volume is adequate, foreign demand is also served, initially through exports, then by means of local production in affiliates. Earlier studies of the process of internationalisation could add R&D activities to this cycle. To improve a company's capacity to react to specific market conditions, R&D has to be conducted in the production entities located in the country concerned. As affiliates assume greater responsibility, the R&D capacities accumulating in other countries advance from technical adaptation to autonomous product and process development, and finally to the generation of technical knowledge that contributes to the knowledge stock of the overall enterprise. Research in multinational enterprises nevertheless initially remains concentrated in the parent company, where all crucial innovation originates.

However, with multinational companies developing international R&D networks, this concept needs to be broadened (Cantwell 1995). The more a multinational enterprise operating in different countries responds to regional impulses for innovation emanating from the local market and R&D landscape, the less the home country will be the sole source of corporate innovation. The internationalisation of R&D that followed the production cycle has now modified the conditions for internationalisation. Foreign affiliates resemble the domestic companies more and more. After periods of expansion, many multinational companies coordinate and restructure R&D units in various locations. After a phase of decentralisation, the groups often begin to consolidate, to eliminate duplicate research and intensify intra-group technology transfers. In this phase, competence centres are formed within the group, which assume responsibility for certain areas of business and the related regional markets. The corresponding R&D resources are often concentrated in these competence centres. Companies acquire product competence by reacting to stimuli from the market and from technological development. The formation of competence centres in foreign affiliates confirms the strong market relatedness of innovation and direct investment posited by product life-cycle theory.

As Bartlett and Ghoshal (1990) point out, the 'classical' forms of internationalised research in multinational companies – central R&D for global markets and local development for local markets – are increasingly complemented by two new forms of international product and process development concomitant with technology transfer between associated companies:

- The development of products that meet special market needs can, after adaptation, be successfully introduced in other markets as well (locally leveraged innovations). Innovations in a multinational enterprise no longer come only from the home country with its specific demand but also from markets in which affiliates develop products themselves.

- Globally coordinated research programmes to which decentralised R&D units contribute their specific knowledge resources and for which simultaneous research is conducted in decentralised laboratories (globally linked innovations). In this case technology transfer is most intensive between research units distributed in different countries.

The research units of multinational companies thus have different tasks in intra-group research and development specialisation. To some extent

R&D activities are tied closely to specific regional markets and the corresponding production, and to some extent they are independent of these factors. While market-related R&D units primarily strengthen the competitiveness of the company in a (sub-)market, R&D units largely independent of specific markets and production develop knowledge that is in principle at the disposal of the entire, world-wide group of companies. Especially in the second case it is not clear where the application of research results will enhance productivity and improve technological efficiency. To evaluate the impact of internationalising R&D in multinational enterprises, it is therefore necessary to consider both the scope of R&D activities undertaken by these companies at home and abroad, and the market and production relatedness of R&D resources.

R&D by German companies abroad

Since the Second World War, major German companies have again joined the trend towards internalisation, stepping up R&D abroad from the end of the 1960s. Because the internationalisation of corporate R&D follows production, the regional and sectoral focus of German direct investment abroad is to be analysed first.

For the postwar period, a close link between high R&D intensity and high direct investment by industries abroad has been demonstrated for Germany.[3] German direct investment abroad is primarily in the research-intensive chemical, electrical engineering, and motor vehicle industries. Over two-thirds of German direct investment in manufacturing abroad is in these three sectors. The most important target regions are the developed industrial countries in Europe and North America. The foreign share of employment and sales in German-owned companies in the manufacturing sector has risen slightly over recent years. In German-owned chemical companies, 47 per cent of employees in 1994 were located in other countries. In the motor vehicle industry the figure was 37 per cent, and in electrical engineering 30 per cent (table 5.1). In 1993, over 60 per cent of all employees of German affiliates abroad were in these three large, research-intensive industries, while the figure for all companies in Germany was only 35 per cent (table 5.2).

Direct investment by acquisition

German enterprises expand abroad predominantly by taking over existing companies. In industrialised countries these companies often have their own R&D facilities. In the period from 1985 to 1994, the average ratio of

Table 5.1 *Share of sales and employment of German affiliates abroad in German companies world-wide*

	Sales (share in %)			Employment (share in %)		
	1980[a]	1990[a]	1994	1980[a]	1990[a]	1994
Manufacturing industry	16.4	21.2	25.0	17.1	21.0	23.9
R&D-intensive sectors	26.8[b]	29.2	35.1	24.1[b]	27.4	31.1
Non-R&D-intensive sectors	9.0[b]	10.6	11.7	9.6[b]	12.3	14.5
Chemical industry	38.3	48.1	50.7	42.1	45.8	46.6
Mechanical engineering	12.5	15.4	19.2	13.1	15.3	17.7
Office, computing, accounting machinery	29.2	12.4	41.8	24.4	8.6	23.1
Motor vehicles	22.1	27.4	36.5	25.2	30.9	37.1
Aerospace	n.a.	35.9	57.9	n.a.	4.4	22.4
Electrical engineering	23.0	26.8	29.2	22.7	27.1	30.3
Professional goods	18.9	18.7	24.4	15.7	18.1	22.2

Source: *Statistisches Bundesamt*; Deutsche Bundesbank; DIW/ZEW calculations.
Notes: (a) West Germany. (b) 1982.

acquisitions to newly established companies was 2 to 1 (Dörrenbächer *et al.*, 1995). In the motor vehicle industry German companies acquired just as many firms as they founded. The greater part of German corporate direct investment in Europe is by acquisition, which is also the preferred strategy in the United States. Setting up new firms is the more frequent procedure in Japan, Portugal and the developing countries. About 70 per cent of increases in the workforce through acquisitions occurs in the three major sectors – chemicals, electrical engineering, and motor vehicles. Most major acquisitions by German chemical companies were in North America, whilst companies in the other two sectors tended to buy Western European firms.

Earlier studies on the internationalisation of R&D in multinational enterprises were based on surveys and case studies in selected multinational companies.[4] In fifteen multinational companies in Germany in 1975/76, 21 per cent of production and 10 per cent of R&D was located abroad. Although individual firms had specialised in certain R&D fields within the framework of the overall group, the authors of the study came to the conclusion that, 'the establishment of globally integrated research programmes including specialised foreign affiliates is not in sight' (Jungnickel *et al.*, 1977, p. 120). Other studies record percentages of be-

Table 5.2 *Share of employment in research-intensive sectors in total employment in groups of companies 1993 (per cent)*

	Companies in Germany			Affiliates abroad
	Total	German companies	Foreign companies	
Aerospace	0.9	1.0	0.6	0.2
Office, computing, accounting machinery	1.3	0.8	3.4	0.2
Chemical industry	8.4	7.0	15.9	21.1
Electrical engineering	14.8	14.5	16.2	20.0
Motor vehicles	11.5	11.3	12.5	19.4
Professional goods	2.0	1.9	2.5	1.6
Mechanical engineering	14.5	15.0	12.1	10.2
Total (sum of above)	53.4	51.5	63.2	72.7

Sources: *Statistisches Bundesamt*; Deutsche Bundesbank; DIW/ZEW calculations.

tween 11 and 20 for the foreign share of R&D expenditure and R&D personnel in various groups of multinational companies in the 1980s.[5] These analyses show that:

• German companies were already engaged in R&D abroad in the late 1960s. The proportion of R&D conducted in other countries grew continually in the 1970s and 1980s, with almost constant rates and little faster than the proportion of the workforce employed abroad.

• The volume of foreign research was concentrated in a few major companies.

• The most important target regions for R&D commitment were the developed industrial countries in Europe (for example Britain and France) and North America, followed at some interval by Japan.

• The chemical and electrical engineering industries were particularly forward in conducting R&D abroad. The automobile industry was concentrated on less developed countries (for example Spain, South America) and had just started doing R&D in the US and Britain.

• The greater part of R&D resources abroad were acquired by taking over companies with R&D capacities.

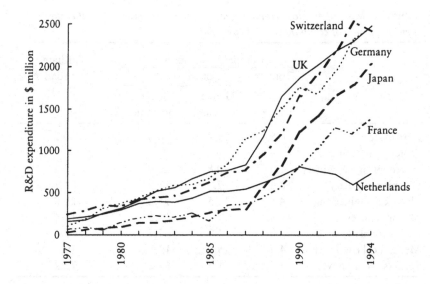

Figure 5.1 *R&D expenditure by foreign affiliates in the United States 1977–94*
Source: US Department of Commerce.

R&D of German companies in the United States

German companies engage in more research in the United States than in
any other foreign country. The direct investment statistics of the United
States Department of Commerce record R&D expenditure and personnel
in foreign affiliates operating in the United States (figure 5.1). In 1993, German affiliates in the United States spent over $2.3 billion on R&D, roughly
two-thirds of all R&D expenditures by German companies abroad and
about 9 per cent of total R&D spending by industry in Germany. With
British and Swiss firms, they thus dispose of the greatest foreign R&D resources in the United States. German-owned companies are amongst the
biggest spenders of R&D in the chemical industry.

In the 1980s, growth rates for R&D spending in the United States by
companies from the industrial countries were similar. German R&D expenditure in the US grew by an average 9.7 per cent per year between 1980
and 1994. British and French multinational R&D expenditures in the
United States display similar growth rates, while the Japanese figure is much
higher (table 5.3). Japanese companies began to conduct an appreciable
measure of R&D abroad only in the mid-1980s, but soon caught up, with
annual growth rates of over 20 per cent in the United States.

Table 5.3 *R&D expenditure by foreign companies in the United States (per cent)*

Home country of parent	Share of R&D expenditure of affiliates of foreign companies in the US		Real growth p.a. of		
			R&D		Gross product
	1980	1994	1980–94	1987–94	1987–94
All countries	100.0	100.0	11.4	9.9	6.8
of which:					
Canada	6.9	15.1	17.8	0.8	2.3
France	7.5	8.9	12.8	18.2	11.5
Germany	19.5	15.7	9.7	7.8	9.5
Netherlands	15.4	4.6	2.3	0.7	0.8
Sweden	1.8	1.7	11.0	4.0	
Switzerland	17.4	15.4	10.5	17.0	6.9
Britain	16.0	15.9	11.4	13.6	6.8
Japan	4.5	12.9	20.1	29.7	13.3
Other countries	10.9	9.7	10.5	4.7	4.1

Sources: US Department of Commerce; ZEW/DIW calculations.

The R&D activities of German companies in the United States have ahitherto been carried out primarily by companies in advanced technology sectors like industrial chemicals and electrical engineering. These are also industries with a higher share of domestic R&D expenditure in Germany that have conquered outstanding positions in international markets. Companies from other countries operating in the United States concentrate more strongly on cutting-edge technology sectors like pharmaceuticals (Switzerland, Britain), computers (France, Japan), and telecommunications and electronics (Netherlands). The technological specialisation of a company at home is apparently reflected in the structure of the company's research and development commitments abroad. The research a company conducts in other countries is thus essentially determined by owner-specific advantage.

In 1993 R&D intensity of US affiliates of German companies, where R&D personnel represented 6.3 per cent of all employees, was markedly higher than the average R&D intensity of industrial enterprises in Germany, where the figure was 3.8 per cent. In 1992, German firms had the highest R&D personnel intensity (5.7 per cent) among foreign manufacturing affiliates in the United States, followed by Swiss and Dutch companies. Highly research-intensive German companies in the United States were

Table 5.4 *R&D intensity by personnel of foreign companies in the US, 1992*

| | Percentage share of R&D personnel in all personnel of affiliates in the US | | | | | | |
| | of which parent is from | | | | | | |
	All countries	Germany	France	Nether- lands	Switzer- land	Britain	Japan
Chemical products	7.3	9.0	5.9	6.0	12.6	5.7	4.1
Drugs	14.4	15.0	12.3	–	13.6	14.5	3.9
Rubber and plastic products	2.0	2.9	3.3	0.0	0.0	1.5	0.5
Non-metallic mineral products	1.0	1.0	3.6	0.0	0.0	0.4	0.8
Iron and steel	0.9	2.2	0.0	0.0	0.0	5.1	0.6
Non-ferrous metals	1.9	4.3	–	–	1.6	1.9	0.0
Fabricated metal products	1.0	0.5	1.0	0.0	0.0	1.0	0.9
Non-electrical machinery	2.2	2.7	0.0	0.0	4.0	1.3	2.0
Office and com- puting machinery	11.8	4.2	19.0	2.3	14.3	10.0	11.6
Electrical machinery	6.0	9.3	6.1	11.6	1.7	3.7	2.3
Motor vehicles	2.2	5.5	4.8	6.7	–	2.6	1.1
Other transport equipment	3.5	4.3	0.0	0.0	0.0	4.2	0.0
Professional goods	4.5	6.6	6.1	0.0	11.3	3.6	3.7
Other manufacturing	1.1	0.7	1.0	2.6	0.7	1.4	1.1
Manufacturing industries	3.7	5.7	4.4	5.5	5.6	2.9	2.2

Source: US Department of Commerce. DIW/ZEW calculations.

manufacturers of chemicals, drugs and medicines, electrical engineering products, motor vehicles, and professional goods, industries that are also particularly research intensive in Germany (table 5.4). A comparison of the fields of technology in which German companies conduct R&D in the United States and in Germany, weighted by the proportion of company employees, reveals a relatively high degree of similarity of focus (figure 5.2).[6]

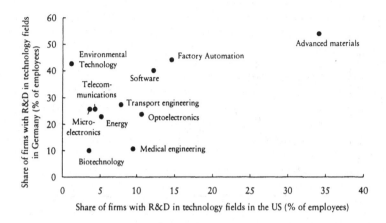

Figure 5.2 *R&D focus of German companies by technology fields in Germany and in the United States*
Source: ZEW.

Advanced materials, production engineering, and software predominate in both Germany and the United States. Environmental technology is outstandingly important only in Germany. This is due to the large, exigent market for environmental protection technology in Germany. Medical engineering, by contrast, is comparatively important in German affiliates in the United States. Overall it appears that German companies abroad are engaged primarily in fields of research that are strong in Germany as well. Ownership advantages and markets are thus also the most important motive for direct investment abroad in research-intensive sectors.

In 1993, foreign affiliates in the United States employed over 100,000 people in R&D and over 2 million in production. There is a close correlation between the employment figures in production and in R&D (figure 5.3). R&D expenditure by foreign companies in the United States grew in step with production. Indeed, between 1987 and 1993, production by German companies in the United States increased a little faster than R&D expenditure (see table 5.3). For the most part, R&D expenditure by a multinational company in the United States thus follows production. This points to a high proportion of production-supportive and market-related R&D.

German companies also operate independent research institutions in the United States that do not relate closely to production. Of the total of 96 research institutions recorded in a 1994 study by Dalton and Serapio (1995), 28 were in the field of chemicals, rubber, materials, 18 in drugs, biotechnology, 11 in automotive technology, and 4 in telecommunications.

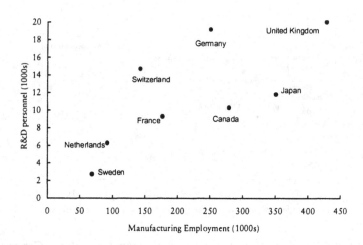

Figure 5.3 *Employment in R&D and production of foreign companies in the United States by companies' home countries, 1993*

German companies ranked third in the number of independent research facilities in the United States after Japan, which operated 230 research centres, and Great Britain, which operated 112 centres. These facilities are concentrated in a few research and technology regions within the United States in the vicinity of leading universities. The establishment of such research centres presumably serves primarily to exploit local external effects arising from the agglomeration of research resources in important new fields of technology.

R&D of German companies in France

German as well as Dutch firms are also among the most research-intensive foreign enterprises in France. American and British companies in France are considerably less active in the field of R&D in proportion to their local turnover (table 5.5). In 1993, 12.2 per cent of total industrial R&D expenditure in France was accounted for by foreign affiliates. Almost 90 per cent of foreign affiliate expenditure was in drugs and medicines, chemicals, and motor vehicles.

Financial flows for R&D in foreign affiliates

Only a small proportion of R&D in foreign affiliates is financed by the

Table 5.5 *Characteristics of large foreign companies in France engaged in R&D in 1989 (number and percentage share)*

Home country of companies	No. of companies	Share of turnover	Share of internal R&D	Share of basic research	R&D intensity
USA	140	47.3	39.6	12.8	2.06
Germany	64	9.8	17.3	24.0	4.31
Britain	49	11.4	4.0	11.0	1.09
Switzerland	46	7.0	8.7	11.5	3.06
Belgium	19	3.9	1.2	0.5	0.76
Netherlands	46	10.7	21.1	14.1	4.84
Sweden	7	0.8	0.6	4.3	2.05
Italy	14	6.7	4.6	21.0	1.69
Others	32	2.5	3.0	0.9	1.89
Total	417	100.0	100.0	100.0	2.46

Source: Ministère de L'Enseignement Supérieur et de la Recherche (1993).

parent company. This is indicated by the low share of total R&D expenditure in Germany that is financed by foreign sources, and by the low share of external R&D expenditure abroad that is financed by German companies. In each case the figure is only about 2 per cent.

Many affiliates abroad finance R&D themselves and sell the results to their parent company and related companies. R&D spending by German companies in their affiliates abroad determines the scale of R&D expenditure in the balance of payments; payments between unrelated companies play a minor role. Moreover, receipts and expenditures are concentrated in a few major multinational companies in each sector. In 1994 the three largest chemical firms accounted for 55 per cent of receipts and 43 per cent of payments, and the three largest electrical engineering companies accounted for 65 per cent of receipts and 85 per cent of payments. In motor vehicle construction, almost all payments were to the account of the three largest companies. Payments go to the companies in the group that carry out the R&D. As a rule they flow to the affiliate or fellow affiliate that carries out the research, but in some cases to the parent company, for example in the motor vehicle industry. High payments in the chemical and electrical engineering industries point to the sizeable R&D undertaken by German firms in the United States and in European countries (table 5.6).

Spending on R&D in the United States shown in the German balance of payments is attributable largely to R&D in American affiliates of German

Table 5.6 *Payments for R&D in the balance of payments of Germany by industrial sector, 1995*

	Receipts 1995 DM mn	Share 1995 %	Growth p.a. 1989–95 %	Payments 1995 DM mn	Share 1995 %	Growth p.a. 1989–95 %
Manufacturing	3,239	100.0	0.8	3,614	100.0	8.1
Chemical industry	144	4.4	3.3	765	21.2	8.1
Petroleum refining, products	12	0.4	–13.4	158	4.4	32.7
Mechanical engineering	31	1.0	5.2	37	1.0	–5.5
Office and computing machinery	673	20.8	6.9	320	8.9	13.2
Motor vehicles	1,164	35.9	4.6	794	22.0	9.6
Electrical engineering	412	12.7	–2.3	937	25.9	3.3
Professional goods	30	0.9	18.2	26	0.7	17.3
All industries	5,088		13.7	4,296		8.2

Source: Deutsche Bundesbank, ZEW/DIW calculations.

firms. This does not apply so clearly with regard to other important host countries like Britain, France, and Austria. Payments to firms in these countries are also made because companies in Germany use R&D results from associated companies. R&D income and expenditure in the German balance of payments rose steadily from the beginning of the 1980s until 1992. This is indicative of the growing integration of companies in global group research. The stagnation in R&D spending and income that occurred in 1993 was due mainly to cyclical factors, and related contemporaneous stagnation in corporate R&D spending in Germany.

Estimation of R&D expenditure by German companies abroad

There is no complete record of R&D activities by German affiliates abroad comparable to the statistics on direct investment. However, information on R&D expenditure by foreign-owned companies is available in some countries (United States, Britain, France, Japan). This data permits R&D spending by German companies abroad in 1993 to be estimated at about

Table 5.7 *Share of patent-taking by multinational companies by inventor location*

Home country of parent	European Patent Office 1990	US Patent Office 1985–90				
			of which			
	Abroad	Abroad	USA	Europe	Japan	Others
Japan	–	1.0	0.8	0.2	–	0.0
USA	–	7.8	–	6.0	0.5	1.3
Italy	11.0	11.8	5.3	6.2	0.0	0.3
France	18.0	14.3	4.8	8.7	0.3	0.6
Germany	11.0	14.9	10.4	3.9	0.2	0.4
Canada	–	33.0	24.9	7.3	0.3	0.5
Sweden	–	39.2	12.6	25.6	0.2	0.8
Switzerland	39.0	46.7	19.6	26.0	0.6	0.5
Netherlands	43.0	57.8	26.1	30.6	0.5	0.6
Belgium	–	62.8	22.2	39.9	0.0	0.6
All countries	–	10.9	4.1	5.6	0.3	0.8

Sources: Patel (1995); Barré (1994).

15 per cent of R&D expenditure by companies in Germany (in PPP terms). In the chemical pharmaceutical industry, by far the most internationalised sector, the figure is just under 30 per cent. Preliminary results of the first survey of R&D activities of German affiliates abroad in 1995 by the company SV Wissenschaftsstatistik[7] confirm this estimation. In the United States, R&D spending by American subsidiaries abroad has for some time now amounted to about 10 per cent of total domestic R&D expenditure, taking the fluctuations of the exchange rates into account.

The proportion of foreign patents taken by multinational companies by inventor location provides a further indication for the degree of home-country R&D internationalisation. According to the studies of Patel (1995) and Barré (1994), the share of patent applications by German companies with inventor location outside Germany in the late 1980s was between 11 per cent (European Patent Office) and 15 per cent (United States Patent Office). Similar shares in inventions and in R&D spending in the United States are recorded for France, Germany, Sweden, Japan and the Netherlands. However, this is not true of Britain or Canada (table 5.7). Patent data thus further confirm the 15 per cent share of foreign research in German companies. The equilibrium in the R&D balance of payments up to the early 1990s points to approximate equilibrium between R&D

spending by German companies abroad and by foreign companies in Germany.

In German manufacturing industry, the workforce employed in affiliates abroad represents 23 per cent of total sectoral employment in Germany. Average R&D intensity in all German companies abroad is thus likely to be about two-thirds of the R&D intensity in all industrial enterprises in Germany.

R&D conducted by foreign companies in Germany

For foreign investors, too, Germany has traditionally been an important industrial location. In assessing the technological capacity of the national economy, one must ask how foreign-owned firms that engage in research influence R&D resources and specialisation patterns in Germany. Most inward direct investment in Germany in manufacturing goes to the chemical and electrical engineering industries followed by petroleum refining, mechanical engineering, food and beverages, and motor vehicles.[8] The ranking of sectors in which foreign companies invest in Germany changes if the direct investment total, calculated in terms of book value, is replaced by total employees in foreign companies in 1993. Electrical engineering companies rank first in terms of employment, followed by chemicals, motor vehicles and mechanical engineering (see table 5.2). In Germany, foreign companies are hardly more strongly concentrated in research-intensive sectors than German firms. German companies in other countries, however, are predominantly concentrated in such industries (see table 5.2).

Firms from industrial countries are the most important investors in Germany. Over 45 per cent of total direct investment in manufacturing in 1993 was by companies from the European Community, a further 31 per cent by American enterprises, and only 2 per cent by companies from Japan.[9] The weight of manufacturing firms in Germany under foreign control, measured by their share in the employment and turnover of domestic companies, has remained unchanged for some considerable time. Since the beginning of the 1980s, foreign affiliates have had a quarter share in turnover and a 16 per cent share in employment (table 5.8). Among the major industrial sectors in Germany, only the chemical industry recorded an increase in the weight of foreign affiliates in the late 1980s.

Estimation of R&D expenditure by foreign companies in Germany

For the purpose of estimating R&D expenditure by foreign companies in

Table 5.8 *Share of sales and employment of foreign companies' affiliates in Germany (per cent)*

	Sales			Employment		
	1980[a]	1990[a]	1994	1980[a]	1990[a]	1994
Manufacturing industry	25.8	25.6	25.3	16.4	16.7	16.1
Technology-intensive sectors	23.3	26.2	26.7	18.5	19.4	19.3
Non-technology-intensive sectors	27.9	25.0	23.9	14.2	13.4	12.6
Chemical industry	29.6	39.0	35.1	23.7	32.9	29.9
Mechanical engineering	16.7	16.4	18.3	14.2	13.9	15.2
Office, computing, accounting machinery	72.2	73.7	85.7	49.2	53.6	52.4
Motor vehicles	19.8	22.0	24.3	19.0	17.2	18.1
Aerospace	14.4	15.9	22.2	11.1	5.8	9.2
Electrical engineering	22.8	23.2	22.5	18.3	16.8	16.6
Professional goods	20.4	28.4	28.8	15.7	24.4	20.0

Source: Statistisches Bundesamt; Deutsche Bundesbank; DIW/ZEW calculations.
Note: (a) West Germany.

Germany, the SV-Wissenschaftsstatistik GmbH carried out a special analysis of its regular annual survey for 1993 of the 500 most research-intensive companies in terms of majority ownership by Germans or foreigners. This covered about 80 per cent of domestic R&D personnel in companies and 85 per cent of total R&D spending. This analysis shows that subsidiaries of foreign companies in Germany spent at least DM 7.8 billion, offering full-time equivalent employment in R&D to at least 34,600 people. At least two-thirds of R&D personnel in foreign manufacturing affiliates are in the electrical engineering and motor vehicle sectors (tables 5.9, 5.10).

In 1993 about 15.5 per cent of R&D manufacturing personnel in Germany were employed in foreign firms. About 6 per cent of R&D personnel in domestic industry worked for companies from the United States, and the same proportion for enterprises from EU countries. While R&D personnel in American companies in Germany is concentrated in the motor vehicle industry, European companies focus more strongly on electrical engineering. If one compares the specialisation pattern in the R&D resources of German and foreign companies in Germany, it appears that foreign firms specialise more in the electrical engineering and motor

Table 5.9 *Total R&D spending by selected major companies in Germany by predominant ownership 1993*

Sector	Domestic companies	Selected companies					note: R&D by all firms in Germany
		of which					
		German companies	Foreign companies	of which			
				US	EC		
		DM million					
Manufacturing	46,339	38,582	7,756	3,685	n.a.		54,252
Chemical industry	10,151	9,469	682	272	261		10,767
Mechanical engineering	3,248	2,805	443	n.a.	n.a.		5,485
Motor vehicles	11,946	9,321	2,625	n.a.	n.a.		12,145
Electrical engineering	111,733	8,965	2,768	251	2,798		13,668
All sectors	49,079	41,274	7,805	3,685	2,673		57,787
		% share of total R&D expenditure					Coverage
Manufacturing	100.0	83.3	16.7	8.0	n.a.		85.4
Chemical industry	100.0	93.3	6.7	2.7	2.6		94.3
Mechanical engineering	100.0	86.4	13.6	n.a.	n.a.		59.2
Motor vehicles	100.0	78.0	22.0	n.a.	n.a.		98.4
Electrical engineering	100.0	76.4	23.6	2.1	23.9		85.8
All sectors	100.0	84.1	15.9	7.5	5.4		84.9

Sources: SV Wissenschaftsstatistik 1995; DIW/ZEW calculations.

vehicle sectors, while German companies spend relatively more on R&D in the chemical and mechanical engineering industries. Foreign electrical engineering and motor vehicle companies can compete successfully in Germany if they conduct R&D in this country. In the chemical industry, local R&D is apparently not so important for ensuring the competitiveness of foreign companies in Germany.

About one-fifth of R&D resources in the motor vehicle industry in Germany is in foreign subsidiaries. The figure is not much lower for the electrical engineering sector. In both these areas foreign-owned companies thus make an essential contribution to the technological resources of the Federal Republic. At 15 per cent, the proportion of R&D personnel in

Table 5.10 *R&D personnel in full-time equivalent employment in selected major companies in Germany by predominant ownership, 1993*

Sector	Domestic companies	Selected companies of which German companies	Foreign companies	of which US	EC	note: All firms in Germany
Manufacturing	222,006	187,620	34,386	14,024	13,074	280,165
Chemical industry	49,801	46,548	3,253	n.a.	1,313	54,609
Mechanical engineering	18,262	15,928	2,334	341	412	35,264
Motor vehicles	48,666	39,150	9,516	8,143	n.a.	50,091
Electrical engineering	65,086	51,919	13,167	1,445	8,289	80,180
All sectors	228,980	195,368	34,612	14,024	13,121	293,775
		% share of total R&D personnel				Coverage
Manufacturing	100.0	84.5	15.5	6.3	5.9	79.2
Chemical industry	100.0	93.5	6.5	n.a.	2.6	91.2
Mechanical engineering	100.0	87.2	12.8	1.9	2.3	51.8
Motor vehicles	100.0	80.4	19.6	16.7	n.a.	97.2
Electrical engineering	100.0	79.8	20.2	2.2	12.7	81.2
All sectors	100.0	84.9	15.1	6.1	5.7	78.3

Sources: SV Wissenschaftsstatistik 1995; DIW/ZEW calculations.

foreign-owned companies is the same as that of employees in foreign affiliates to employees in the manufacturing sector as a whole (see table 5.8). This points to the same level of research intensity in foreign-owned companies and in all firms in the country. The SV-Wissenschaftsstatistik analysis reveals that in the electrical engineering, mechanical engineering, and motor vehicle industries there are no substantial differences in R&D intensity between German-owned companies and foreign subsidiaries (table 5.11). The R&D personnel intensity of foreign manufacturers is higher than in all other companies in Germany that engage in research. However, this may also be an expression of corporate economies of scale, since the SV-Wissenschaftsstatistik analysis included only larger companies.

Table 5.11 *R&D intensity of selected major companies in Germany by predominant ownership and selected industrial sectors, 1993*

| | Selected major companies | | | note: |
| | Domestic companies | of which | | All firms in |
		German companies	Foreign companies	Germany engaged in R&D
	R&D intensity of workforce (%)			
Manufacturing	8.9	9.3	7.2	7.0
Chemical industry	11.4	11.9	7.2	10.2
Mechanical engineering	5.7	5.8	5.4	4.8
Motor vehicles	7.9	8.0	7.6	7.5
Electrical engineering	10.8	10.8	10.9	9.9
	R&D intensity of turnover (%)			
Manufacturing	6.1	7.1	3.7	4.9
Chemical industry	5.9	7.5	1.5	4.9
Mechanical engineering	4.0	4.0	4.0	3.3
Motor vehicles	6.3	6.8	5.0	6.1
Electrical engineering	7.8	7.9	7.4	7.1

Sources: SV-Wissenschaftsstatistik, 1995; DIW/ZEW calculations.

A comparison of the fields of technology in which foreign and all companies conduct R&D in Germany reveals a relatively high degree of similarity of focus (figure 5.4). New materials, production engineering, environmental technology and software predominate in both foreign and domestic companies. Overall it appears that German and foreign companies are engaged primarily in the same fields of research. There are no substantial differences in the concentration of R&D activities on technology fields. This is an indication of the similarity of research-intensive foreign and domestic companies in Germany.

Foreign-owned manufacturers spend a slightly higher proportion of their total R&D expenditure externally than do German-owned companies. This is attributable especially to the high proportion of external R&D spending by foreign motor vehicle manufacturers, which at 22 per cent is markedly higher than the 12 per cent spent on external R&D by German firms in this sector. This shows that firms in multinational automobile groups are integrated in the global R&D organisation, and can make use of the R&D resources of related and parent companies abroad. This is

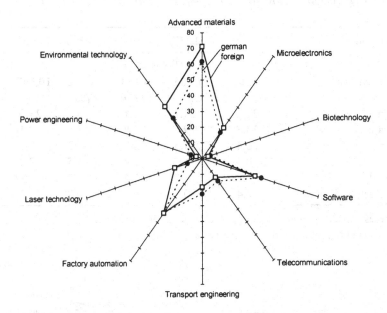

Figure 5.4 *R&D focus of German and foreign companies in Germany, 1993*
(share of companies engaged in R&D in technological fields in %)
Source: ZEW Mannheim Innovation Panel.

confirmed by the international payments for R&D services reported in the balance of payments (see table 5.6).

R&D of US multinationals in Germany

About a quarter of the R&D expenditure of US companies outside the United States is invested in Germany, which has thus been the most important single location for US research abroad for a considerable period (table 5.12).[10] This also applies when exchange rate effects are taken into account. R&D intensity, measured as the share of R&D expenditure in gross product, is higher in American-owned companies in Germany than in other countries (figure 5.5). In recent years, however, the R&D intensity of US companies has increased strongly in Japan. In 1993 R&D intensity in manufacturing affiliates in Japan exceeded the level in Germany for the first time. This was primarily a result of greater and growing R&D

Table 5.12 *Spending on R&D by US companies abroad, manufacturing 1966–94*

Host country	1966	1977	1982	1990	1994[a]
			US$ million		
All countries	528	1,785	3,123	8,468	10,147
		share in selected countries (%)			
Germany	22.3	24.1	27.1	28.7	25.9
Britain	23.5	19.7	22.8	18.7	19.1
France	6.4	14.5	6.3	8.2	11.3
Japan	0.6	1.5	2.3	4.5	7.8
Canada	29.5	10.7	12.3	11.7	9.2[b]
Total selected countries	82.4	70.5	70.7	71.7	73.3

Sources: US Department of Commerce; DIW/ZEW calculations.
Notes: (a) Preliminary estimates. (b) 1993.

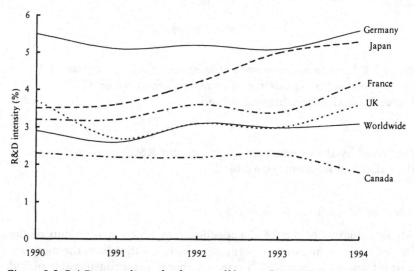

Figure 5.5 *R&D expenditure for foreign affiliates of US MNCs as percentage of gross product in selected countries*
Source: US Department of Commerce.

intensity in American chemical companies in Japan. Over a long period, automobile affiliates in Germany recorded the highest R&D intensities.

Table 5.13 *Share of R&D expenditure for affiliates of US MNCs in Germany in spending of affiliates worldwide (per cent)*

Sector	1977	1982	1990	1994[a]
Total industry	22.3	24.5	25.1	23.2
Manufacturing industry	24.1	27.1	28.7	25.9
Food and kindred products	19.7	12.6	17.6	9.5
Chemicals and allied products	12.4	11.3	11.6	9.5
Primary and fabricated metals	26.2	22.4	28.2	26.4
Non-electrical machinery, office machinery	18.3	21.2	27.7	26.1
Electric and electronic equipment	28.0	34.5	16.6	16.1
Transport equipment	n.a.	46.1	55.8	51.0
Other manufacturing	n.a.	12.4	20.7	18.7

Sources: US Department of Commerce; DIW/ZEW calculations.
Note: (a) Preliminary estimates.

In the early 1990s, American firms invested over half their total motor-vehicle R&D expenditure abroad in Germany. They invested roughly the same amount of money for R&D activities in electrical engineering in Germany and Japan (table 5.13).

R&D of Japanese companies in Germany

According to the Japanese External Trade Organisation JETRO, Germany ranked second to Britain in Europe as host to Japanese producers with research divisions. The proportion of Japanese affiliates engaged in production that have their own research facilities is highest in Germany (table 14). With eighteen research centres independent of production, Germany was the second most important location for Japanese companies in Europe after the UK. Indeed, Germany has the largest proportion of research centres to Japanese-owned producer affiliates in Europe. However, since 1990 the number of Japanese research centres has grown more rapidly in Britain than in Germany.

Financing of R&D

The high receipts from R&D shown in the German balance of payments for office and computing machinery and motor vehicles is attributable largely to the involvement of subsidiaries of US companies in Germany in

Table 5.14 *R&D of Japanese companies in Europe 1990–5*

	December 1990	December 1995
Share of Japanese affiliates engaged in R&D in all production affiliates (%)		
Total	35.4	42.2
of which:		
Britain	41.8	50.2
France	27.7	35.8
Germany	45.8	59.0
Netherlands	31.0	36.0
Belgium/Luxembourg	37.8	38.6
Spain	35.4	40.0
Number of independent research centres in proportion to the number of Japanese affiliates engaged in production (%)		
Total	7.0	9.8
of which:		
Britain	8.2	11.2
France	6.0	11.0
Germany	12.0	17.1
Netherlands	0.0	6.0
Belgium/Luxembourg	8.1	6.8
Spain	0.0	1.7

Sources: JETRO; DIW/ZEW calculations.

group R&D projects. In the electrical engineering industry, too, income levels reflect extensive R&D activities by foreign-owned affiliates. Lower receipts in the chemical industry in comparison to total inward direct investment confirm the low R&D intensity of foreign companies in this sector (see table 5.6). Income flows especially from countries where fellow affiliates of multinational enterprises exploit the R&D results of associated companies in Germany for production purposes (Spain, Austria). Low revenues from Japan are indicative of the hitherto relatively small Japanese R&D units in Germany.

The interrelationships between trade, direct investment and R&D in multinational enterprises

In Germany, as in other industrial countries, the internationalisation of R&D in multinational enterprises has reached a relatively high level. R&D

Table 5.15 *Share in employment and R&D spending of foreign affiliates in manufacturing in selected countries, 1993 (per cent)*

Country	Total employees	R&D expenditure by industry	R&D personnel	R&D financed from abroad
Germany	15.9	15.8	15.5	2.0
France	23.9	15.2	14.0	12.0
Britain	20.0	25.8	22.6	15.4
US	11.6	14.9	13.4	–
Japan	1.1	5.2	1.7	0.1
Canada	46.0	40.6	34.7	18.0

Source: Compilation by ZEW/DIW from national and OECD statistics.

expenditure by German companies abroad and by foreign companies in Germany is comparable in volume. It amounts to 15 per cent of domestic industrial spending on R&D. German corporate R&D abroad is concentrated in the chemical and electrical engineering industries, sectors that also have a high share of total R&D expenditure in Germany.

According to SV-Wissenschaftsstatistik the share of foreign-owned companies in Germany in total industrial R&D spending in Germany was just under 16 per cent in 1993. In the United States and France the proportion was 15 per cent, in Britain 26 per cent, and in Japan 5 per cent (table 5.15). Industrial R&D in Germany is thus already comparatively highly internationalised.

In Germany the R&D intensity of German-owned and foreign-owned firms in the manufacturing industry is approximately equal. In the US and Japan foreign firms have a little higher average R&D intensity, in France and Canada a little lower average R&D intensity than firms owned by nationals. This seems to be mostly due to the sectoral structure of foreign-owned firms.

Foreign companies in Germany have been conducting R&D in the Federal Republic on a relatively large scale for a considerable time. Their average R&D intensity in the large, research-intensive sectors, apart from the chemical industry – namely electrical engineering, motor vehicles, and mechanical engineering – are approximately equal to the R&D intensity of German firms in Germany. In their affiliates in Germany, foreign firms engage in R&D especially in electrical engineering (European and US companies), and motor vehicles (US firms).

The available data do not yet permit assessment of the extent to which foreign companies contribute to changing R&D resources in Germany. A comparison of R&D expenditure by American and Japanese companies in Germany with their involvement in production makes it clear that Germany occupies an outstanding position internationally as a centre for multinational R&D. This still holds even as other locations gain in attractiveness as production and research are progressively internationalised.

For globalising multinational enterprises market entry by means of trade and investment is essential. Especially in high technology sectors trade and direct investment appear to be complements rather than alternatives (Ostry 1996). For the period 1991–4 our work suggests that there is a positive correlation between the growth of the weight of foreign companies in the manufacturing sectors in Germany, as measured by their share in employment and sales in domestic firms, and the growth of the import penetration of these sectors. We also found a positive association between the growth of the weight of German affiliates abroad in German companies worldwide, measured by their share in employment and sales in German companies world-wide, and the growth of the export dependence of the manufacturing sectors in Germany.

The information on the activities of multinational companies in the industrialised countries shows a clear correlation between firms' foreign commitment to production and to research (table 5.16). The relatively high R&D expenditure by German firms located abroad compared with that by German firms on the domestic market is not least an expression of the strength of German exports. Yet in terms of the high level of German exports, direct investment by German industrial firms remains low in international comparative terms (table 5.16). As foreign markets grow it is to be expected that the production and research activities of German firms abroad will intensify. International comparison reveals a correlation between the relative importance of imports for the national economy (import penetration), the relative importance of foreign firms for the national industry and the proportion of R&D expenditure in the host country performed by foreign firms (figure 5.6).

On the basis of the available data, a close relationship between the scale and growth of production and R&D spending in foreign affiliates can be demonstrated. R&D conducted by foreign-owned firms is thus predominantly market and production related, although within larger market regions (countries, trade blocs) there are often no close spatial links between R&D and production facilities for individual innovation processes. Since the vital innovative stimuli come from regional markets, multinational enterprises are increasingly obliged to orient their international organisational structures towards these markets.

Table 5.16 *Indicators of the internationalisation of production and R&D in manufacturing industries of selected countries, 1993 (per cent)*

	Germany	US	Japan	France	UK	Canada
Activities abroad						
Exports as a share of gross output (export dependence)	29.9	12.3	11.6	30.2	29.7	44.8
Employees abroad as a proportion of domestic employment	23.5	2.4	8.1	32.5	–	–
Direct investment stocks abroad as a proportion of exports	26.2	51.7	32.6	30.9	59.0	34.1
R&D expenditure abroad as a proportion of domestic R&D expenditure	15.0	10.0	2.0	–	–	–
Share of patents registered by domestic firms with the location of invention given as abroad (US Patent Office, 1985–90)	14.9	7.8	1.0	14.3	2.1	33.0
Activities at home						
Imports as a share of domestic demand (import penetration)	25.4	15.9	5.7	28.8	33.7	46.2
Employees in foreign-owned firms as a share of domestic employment	15.9	11.6	1.1	23.9	20.0	46.0
Foreign direct investment stocks as a proportion of imports	19.5	32.2	10.3	20.9	31.7	48.4
R&D expenditure by foreign-owned firms as a share of domestic R&D expenditure	15.8	14.9	5.2	15.2	25.8	40.6
Share of patents registered by foreign-owned firms with the location of invention given as in the country in question (European Patent Office, 1990)	17.0	–	–	18.0	41.0	–

Sources: OECD: STAN-Database for Industrial Analysis; *International Direct Investment Statistics Yearbook*, National Accounts; UNCTAD; national statistics; patent indicators: Patel (1995); Barré (1994), DIW/ZEW calculations and estimates.

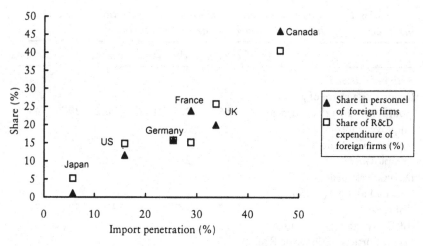

Figure 5.6 *Import penetration, share of employment and R&D expenditure of foreign affiliates in the manufacturing industry of selected countries, 1993*

Given that the main innovation impulses come from regional markets, multinational companies are increasingly obliged to adapt their international organisational structures to these markets. On the other hand, the need to raise the efficiency of R&D by reducing development times, removing duplication and exploiting economies of scale in R&D facilities, calls for a reconcentration of R&D within multinational corporations, although no longer merely at the parent company in the 'home country', but also at subsidiaries in the leading market regions. In a number of cases regional 'centres of competence' have arisen within multinational corporations, in which responsibility for R&D, production and sales is brought together. It is here that technological advances are made – not least due to the access to the global R&D potential of the corporation – and it is often here that they are first translated into actual production. The development of such centres of competence requires the spatial coincidence of market impulses, and productive and research-related competence. Thus the R&D potential of foreign companies in an industrialised country will be determined primarily by the market and production potential of these companies in that country, and less by the attractiveness of its research infrastructure.

German firms will continue to stabilise and extend their positions on foreign markets through direct investment. In the course of this process R&D activities will play an increasingly important role. By developing research centres abroad they will continue in their efforts to keep up with technological developments there, especially in new high-risk research fields where commercial exploitation is imminent (for example genetic technology in the pharmaceutical industry, and the development of new semiconductor components). In Germany an expansion of R&D activities in these and similar technological areas by multinational corporations can only be expected if, alongside the German market, a European market for new products develops and production centres are set up there. Once this is given, a sophisticated research and technology infrastructure conducive to cooperation between publicly financed research and firms located in the country constitutes a further important condition if Germany is to retain its importance to multinational corporations as a research location.

Notes

1   See the first case studies in Terpstra (1977), Ronstadt (1977) and Behrmann and Fischer (1980) and the statistical analysis in Creamer (1976). For a short survey see Belitz and Beise (1995).
2   In this case the third condition always applies with multinationals, since this is regarded as their *sine qua non*.
3   See, for example, Barrell and Pain (1997) and Chapter 2 in this volume.
4   See also Schumacher *et al.* (1995).
5   See Pausenberger (1982), Brockhoff and Boehmer (1993) and Wortmann (1990).
6   The production programmes of 217 American affiliates of German companies that engage in research were allwocated to technology fields. The shares in the technology fields of the companies in Germany were taken from the Mannheim Innovation Panel. See Harhoff, Licht *et al.* (1996).
7   SV-Wissenschaftsstatistik is an Essen-based, non-profit organisation that collects science-related statistics.
8   Foreign direct investment in Germany is recorded by the Bundesbank on the basis of reports from domestic companies with a balance sheet total in excess of DM 1 million, 20 per cent or more of whose capital or voting rights are owned by one or more foreigners. According to a special analysis of the Bundesbank, 92 per cent of inward direct investment in 1993 was in foreign-held subsidiary companies. In manufacturing the figure was 93 per cent and in the chemical industry 85 per cent. Companies in which foreigners hold a majority interest thus have slightly less weight than reported in the Bundesbank statistics on foreign direct investment, especially in the chemical industry.
9   The basis for determining the country of origin of direct investment was the first foreign owner. If direct investment totals are attributed to the last owner abroad, that is, to the parent company, the share of total direct investment in manufacturing from the United States increases to 33 per cent and from Japan to just under 3 per cent. The share of EC countries decreases to 36 per cent. The reason is that

118   Innovation, investment and technology in Europe

American and Japanese companies have interposed holding companies registered in European countries.

10 The US Department of Commerce reports R&D expenditure *for* affiliates, which in industrial countries generally corresponds to R&D performed *by* affiliates.

References

Barré, R. (1994), *Science & Technologie Indicateurs*, Paris, Observatoire des Sciences et des Techniques.
  (1995), 'Relationships between multinational firms' technology strategies and national innovation systems', in OECD, *Innovation, patents and technological strategies*, Paris, pp. 201-22.
Barrell, R. and Pain, N. (1997), 'Foreign direct investment, technological change and economic growth within Europe', *Economic Journal*, 107, pp. 1770-86.
Bartlett, C. and Ghoshal, S. (1990), 'Managing innovation in the transnational corporation', in Bartlett, C., Doz, Y. and Hedlund, G. (eds), *Managing the Global Firm*, London, pp. 215-55.
Behrman, J. and Fischer, W. (1980), *Overseas R&D Activities of Transnational Companies*, Cambridge, Mass, Oelgeschlager, Gunn & Hain.
Belitz, H. and Beise, M. (1995), 'Internationalisation of research and development in multinational corporations in the Federal Republic of Germany', DIW Discussion Paper No. 106, Berlin.
Brockhoff, K. and Boehmer, A.v. (1993), 'Global R&D activities of German industrial firms', *Journal of Scientific & Industrial Research*, 52, June, pp. 399-406.
Cantwell, J. (1995), 'The globalisation of technology: what remains of the product cycle model?', *Cambridge Journal of Economics*, 19/1, pp. 155-74.
Coe, D. and Helpman, E. (1995), 'International R&D spillovers', *European Economic Review*, 39, pp. 859-87.
Creamer, D. (1976), 'Overseas research and development by United States multinationals, 1966-1975', *The Conference Board*, Report No. 685, New York.
Dalton, D.H. and Serapio, M.G. (1995), *Globalizing Industrial Research and Development*, Washington, US Department of Commerce, Office of Technology Policy.
Dörrenbächer, Ch., Scheike, I., Schmitt, A. and Wortmann, M. (1995), *Internationaler Investitionsmonitor '95*, Forschungsgemeinschaft für Aussenwirtschaft, Struktur- und Technologiepolitik, Berlin.
Dunning, J. (1979), 'Explaining changing patterns of international production. In defence of the eclectic theory', *Oxford Bulletin of Economics and Statistics*, 41/4, pp. 269-95.
Harhoff, D., Licht, G. *et al.* (1996), 'Innovationsaktivitäten kleiner und mittlerer Unternehmen: Ergebnisse des Mannheimer Innovationspanels', *Schriftenreihe des ZEW*, 8, Baden-Baden.
Jungnickel, R., Krägenau, H., Lefeldt, M. and Holthus, M. (1977), *Einfluß*

multinationaler Unternehmen auf Außenwirtschaft und Branchenstruktur, Hamburg, Weltwirtschaftsarchiv.

Lichtenberg, F. and van Pottelsberghe de la Potterie, B. (1996), 'The channels of international R&D spillovers', paper prepared for the OECD Conference on New Indicators for the Knowledge-based Economy, Paris, 19–21 June.

Mansfield, E. and Romeo, A. (1984), 'Reverse transfer of technology from overseas subsidiaries to American firms', *IEEE Transactions on Engineering Management*, 31/3, pp. 122–7.

Ostry, S. (1996), 'Technology issues in the international trading system', *Market Access after the Uruguay Round*, Paris, OECD.

Patel, P. (1995), 'Localised production of technology for global markets', *Cambridge Journal of Economics*, 19/1, pp. 141–53.

Pausenberger, E. (1982), 'Technologiepolitik internationaler Unternehmen', *Zeitschrift für betriebswirtchaftliche Forschung*, 34/12, pp. 1025–54.

Ronstadt, R. C. (1977), *Research and Development Abroad by U.S. Multinationals*, New York, Preager.

Schumacher, D. *et al.* (1995), 'Technologische Wettbewerbsfähigkeit der Bundesrepublik Deutschland. Theoretische und empirische Aspekte einer international vergleichenden Analyse', DIW-Beiträge zur Strukturforschung no. 155, Berlin.

Terpstra, V. (1977), 'International product policy: the role of foreign R&D', *Columbia Journal of World Business*, 12/4, pp. 24–32.

Vernon, R. (1966), 'International investment and international trade in the product cycle', *Quarterly Journal of Economics*, 88, May, pp. 190–207.

Wortmann, M. (1990), 'Multinationals and the internationalisation of R&D: new developments in German companies', *Research Policy*, 19/2, pp. 175–83.

6 Foreign activities by Swedish multinational corporations: the role played by large European host countries

PONTUS BRAUNERHJELM and KAROLINA EKHOLM

1 Introduction

In comparison with most other countries, Sweden has an impressive number of large multinational firms, despite its limited size. These corporations account for the overwhelming part of domestic manufacturing production, employment and exports. They also have a long tradition of extensive foreign operations and several of them have undertaken production abroad since the 19th or early 20th century. Throughout the years the foreign activities of Swedish multinational corporations (MNCs) have grown markedly while inward investment by foreign firms has until recently been negligible.

In the wake of the unprecedented increase in foreign direct investment (FDI) flows in the 1980s, propelled by the dismantling of trade barriers and deregulation of capital markets, locational issues have become a prominent topic on the international research agenda. The most significant theoretical contributions emanate from important developments in trade theory, such as the extension of trade theory models to take into account the influence of economies of scale and trade costs on the location of economic activities (for example, Brainard, 1993; Markusen and Venables, 1994, 1996). The development of economic geography models intended to address issues related to agglomeration of economic activity, core and periphery effects, has also been very insightful. Work by Krugman (1991) and Venables (1993) has been particularly influential.

The IUI has conducted research on multinational corporations for a long time, taking advantage of a unique IUI data set based on a questionnaire sent to all Swedish MNCs approximately every fourth year since the 1960s (1965, 1970, 1974, 1978, 1986, 1990 and 1994).[1] The questionnaire contains detailed information on the parent company as well as on the operations of each individual subsidiary.[2] Research has focused on the home country effects of foreign activities by Swedish MNCs, particularly the extent to which FDI has substituted for or complemented production in domestic plants (Swedenborg, 1979; Eliasson et al., 1985; Svensson, 1996). Furthermore, more macro-oriented issues have also been examined, such as the implications of FDI for the allocation of production and the pattern of trade (Braunerhjelm, 1990, 1996; Andersson et al., 1996).

The purpose of the present study is to document the most recent trends in foreign activities by Swedish MNCs and to discuss the underlying forces, and consequences, of FDI. Emphasis will be on the distribution of production and R&D between foreign and domestic units of Swedish MNCs, the distribution of foreign production within industries, and the development of trade – within firms as well as to third markets. Particular attention will be paid to whether a large-country effect can be discerned in the Swedish MNCs' foreign operations. One important result from the economic geography literature is that if firms operate under increasing returns to scale and there are costs associated with shipping goods across national borders, a large home market will tend to attract production.[3] In this study, we examine whether the three large European countries – France, Germany and the United Kingdom – have attracted a disproportionately large share of Swedish firms' foreign activities.

The approach taken here is purely descriptive in the sense that there will be no rigorous modelling or testing of hypotheses. We focus on the period 1986–94, although the development of foreign activities since the 1960s will also be discussed. The evolution of the Swedish MNCs' activities in the European Union (EU) is of particular interest, since Sweden switched from being an outsider to becoming a full member in January 1995. The application for membership was submitted in mid-1991. These changes in the institutional framework that firms operate within may well have influenced the pattern of foreign trade and investment.

The chapter is organised to give, in Section 2, a brief overview of the important policy changes in Sweden during the last decade, and a description of the general pattern of outward and inward FDI for Sweden and other OECD countries. In Section 3, we show the overall geographical and sectoral allocation of affiliate production, trade patterns and R&D activities. Section 4 narrows down the analysis to the three large European countries referred to above. Finally, in Section 5, we conclude by relating the pattern of Swedish FDI to the policy changes that have taken place internationally and in Sweden.

2 Background

It seems obvious that in a globalised economy firms will locate production where the prerequisites for production are the most favourable. The
dismantling of trade barriers and deregulation of capital markets bring
two important consequences. First, competition for both national and
multinational firms will become intensified in the short run and, second,
firms will be induced to locate production into regions where profit
opportunities are the highest in the long run. The lower are transportation costs in relation to sales values, and the larger the differences in
production costs between regions, the more prone firms will be to
relocate to where production costs are the lowest. Therefore, in a global
economy with high mobility of goods and factors, countries with relatively
high production costs and an adverse institutional setting may find it hard
to attract investment. Furthermore, if agglomeration influences the
location of production, countries may find themselves 'trapped' in virtuous or vicious investment cycles that tend to be self-enforcing.

   In the following sub-section we shall give a brief account of recent policy
changes in Sweden. We will argue that some of the changes should tend
to improve Sweden's potential status as a host country for industrial investment, although Sweden has kept struggling with economic problems
that may work in the opposite direction.

Domestic policies

From a political point of view, the period 1990–94 saw several dramatic
changes. During this period Sweden experienced its deepest recession since
the Depression of the 1930s. The crisis of the 1990s was manifested in
decreasing GDP for three years, 1991–3, and the loss of 250,000 jobs in
the manufacturing sector. This downturn of the economy was paralleled
by previously unmatched productivity increases in the manufacturing sector. As a result of the large depreciation of the Swedish krona, the economy
switched into an export-led boom in 1994 that persisted well into 1995.
Domestic demand, however, continued to lag behind.

   Among the more decisive and far-reaching political events in the early
1990s was Sweden's application in 1991 to become a member of the
European Union. The EU, the successor to the European Community (EC),
was established in 1993 and Sweden was accepted as a full member in
1995. Between 1993 and 1995 the EES (European Economic Space) agreement replaced the old free trade agreement between the EFTA states and
the former EC. Although the EES-agreement gave Swedish firms roughly

the same access to the EU market as insider firms, some differences still prevailed, for instance with regard to border crossings and public procurement. In addition, the EFTA countries had no say in the political process of the EU. Hence, to some extent, outsiders still ran the risk of being discriminated against when compared to insider firms.

Some major changes in economic policy also took place in the 1980s and the early 1990s, particularly regarding Sweden's monetary policy. Sweden left the European currency snake in 1977 after a series of devaluations. The krona was then pegged unilaterally to a trade-weighted currency basket.[4] However, in the early 1980s there were further devaluations of the krona, including a devaluation of 16 per cent in 1982. This action was considered aggressive because it more than compensated for the cumulated difference in inflation compared with other countries, and thus caused a substantial depreciation of the real exchange rate. This, in combination with relatively high inflation, produced a view among economists and politicians that Sweden had a credibility problem with regard to its commitment to a fixed exchange rate. Therefore, for the rest of the 1980s, Sweden's monetary policy was largely devoted to building up confidence in the commitment of keeping the exchange rate fixed.

In 1991, as it became evident that Sweden would apply for membership of the EU, the Swedish krona was pegged to the ECU instead of the earlier currency basket. Under pressure from high levels of domestic inflation and a strong German mark, massive speculation against the krona took place and in November 1992 Sweden was forced to let the krona float. The immediate response was a depreciation of approximately 20 to 25 per cent against most other currencies. Since then, the Swedish krona has appreciated somewhat, but compared to most other currencies it is, at the time of writing, below the 1992 value by between 10 and 25 per cent.

A third important policy change in Sweden was the restructuring of the tax system at the beginning of the 1990s. The major ingredients of the tax reform were a reduction of statutory tax rates, comprising corporate as well as individual tax rates, combined with reduced deduction possibilities. As a result, Sweden's corporate tax rate now stands out as being fairly competitive in a European perspective.

However, irrespective of these policy improvements, other problems remain for the Swedish economy that may have an adverse effect on investments. High levels of unemployment and weak domestic demand persist. Despite tight fiscal policies during the last few years, budgetary problems and an increasing public debt – at present around 80 per cent of GDP – severely restrict the scope for expansionary economic policy. Still, it seems reasonable to expect that the overall long-run effects of the policy

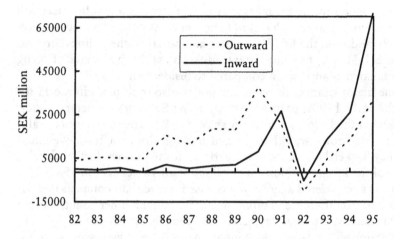

Figure 6.1 *Outward and inward flows of FDI in the Swedish manufacturing sector, 1980–95*
Source: Riksbanken (1982–1995).

changes in the 1990s, in particular EU membership, the floating of the krona with its resulting real depreciation, and the shift in tax policies, should make Sweden more attractive for investments by domestic as well as foreign firms. Thus, when looking at the activities by Swedish firms it seems reasonable to expect a moderation of the expansion abroad in favour of domestic production after 1990.

Trends in FDI

Turning to the development of FDI since 1980, figure 6.1 depicts the flows of inward and outward FDI according to the balance of payments statistics. Evidently, Swedish firms considerably stepped up their outward FDI in the middle of the 1980s and from then until 1990 FDI continued to grow. This trend came to a halt at the beginning of the 1990s when outward FDI fell sharply for two years. Inward FDI followed a similar pattern with a one-year lag. Thereafter both inward and outward FDI picked up again, but with a substantially changed relationship between inward and outward FDI. Since 1992, inward flows have exceeded outward flows.

The overall increase in FDI around the mid-1980s and a downturn in the early 1990s is clearly an international trend that embraces a large number of countries. However, the change in the relation between

Table 6.1 *The ratio of outward FDI stock to inward stock of FDI for a selected number of countries, 1981–92*

	1981	1985	1990	1992
Australia	0.17	0.27	0.43	0.37
Austria	0.17	0.31	0.43	0.64
Belgium/Luxembourg	0.83	0.53	0.79	0.81
Canada	0.44	0.62	0.69	0.72
Denmark	0.29	0.50	0.80	0.97
Finland	1.36	1.38	2.36	2.32
France	1.04	1.11	1.27	1.35
Germany	1.18	1.62	1.27	1.38
Italy	0.78	0.86	0.97	1.09
Japan	0.53	1.27	5.85	6.47
Netherlands	2.20	1.92	1.48	1.57
Norway	0.35	0.97	1.27	1.45
Spain	0.24	0.23	0.23	0.24
Sweden	1.68	2.60	4.24	3.56
Switzerland	2.53	2.12	2.13	2.27
UK	1.28	1.62	1.12	1.28
US	2.65	1.36	1.09	1.17

Source: United Nations (1994).

outward and inward FDI that occurred in Sweden at the beginning of the 1990s was probably influenced by two policy events: the large depreciation of the krona in 1992, and the application for membership of the EU in 1991. This change in pattern may also reflect in part the effects of the removal of capital market barriers to inflows that has taken place during the development of the European Single Market.

Table 6.1 illustrates the ratio of outward to inward stocks for a selected number of countries. A ratio of one implies that the stock of outward FDI is matched by an inward stock of equal size. As can be seen, Sweden has among the highest ratios during the entire period and is only exceeded by Japan in 1992. This indicates that Sweden is one of the most outward-oriented countries as far as FDI is concerned. This picture is reinforced by the fact that, in contrast to Japan, Sweden's position as a net direct investor abroad cannot be explained by any current account surpluses during this time period.

To summarise, Sweden has undergone some major policy changes, particularly during the 1990s, that could perhaps be expected to make

Table 6.2 *Shares of MNCs' employees and output 1965–94 (per cent)*

	Employees		Output	
	Sweden	Abroad	Sweden	Abroad
1965	66.1	33.9	74.1	25.9
1970	n.a.	n.a.	72.9	27.1
1974	59.8	40.2	71.1	28.9
1978	57.6	42.4	64.6	35.4
1986	50.8	49.2	57.7	42.3
1990	39.4	60.6	48.6	51.4
	(34.1)	(65.9)	(43.2)	(56.8)
1994	38.9	61.1	47.8	52.2

Source: IUI database.
Note: Figures in parentheses are percentages including Asea Brown Boveri in the sample.

Sweden a more attractive host country for FDI in the 1990s as compared to the 1980s. An increase in inward FDI flows from 1990 onwards can also be observed. At the same time, international trends point to generally increasing overall flows of FDI.

3 Foreign production by Swedish MNCs

This section gives an overview of the regional and sectoral pattern of the Swedish MNCs' foreign production, R&D, and trade, both within and outside the firm.[5]

The geographical and sectoral distribution of production

The number of employees and output levels can be used to capture the geographical distribution of production within Swedish MNCs. The latter is measured as total affiliate sales corrected for intra-firm deliveries from the parent company. Henceforth, when we refer to foreign production, we mean only output of affiliates where production is the dominant activity; sales affiliates are disregarded. The allocation of Swedish MNCs' production between foreign and domestic units since 1965 is depicted in table 6.2. There has been a continuing decline in the proportion of the Swedish MNCs' employees and output located in Sweden. This decline appears to have been particularly large between 1986 and 1990. One possible explanation is that plans to deepen European integration may have

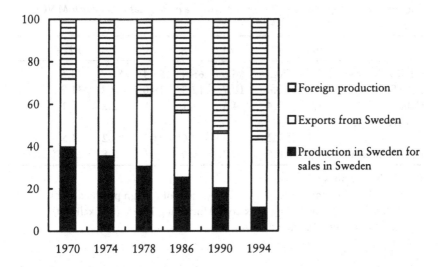

Figure 6.2 *Distribution of Swedish MNCs' production in Sweden and abroad, selected years 1970–94 (per cent)*
Source: IUI database.
Note: Figures are net of intra-firm transactions.

had an effect on the locational decisions of Swedish MNCs. As illustrated in the table, the negative trend in the Swedish share of employment and output has continued in the 1990s.

We can divide MNCs' total production into foreign production, domestic production for exports, and domestic production aimed for sale in the home country market. As a result we get an overall picture of the MNCs' dependence on foreign markets. The sum of affiliate production abroad and exports from Sweden has increased from about 60 per cent of the total in 1970 to approximately 85 per cent in 1994. Even though the share of domestic production geared for exports increased between 1970 and 1994 (from 45 to 75 per cent), exports from Swedish units as a share of the MNCs' total production diminished in the period between 1974 and 1990. This pattern is mirrored by a decline in the share of total home country production (exports plus production for domestic sales) by Swedish MNCs from over 70 per cent in 1970 to 48 per cent in 1994, although between 1990 and 1994 there was an increase in the share of exports from the Swedish units, which was most likely a consequence of large depreciation of the krona in 1992. However, since the share of home country

Table 6.3 *The regional distribution of affiliate employees in Swedish MNCs, percentage of total, 1965–94[a]*

	1965	1970	1974	1978	1986	1990	1994
OECD Europe	72.1	70.3	66.6	66.4	55.4	58.7	53.5
NAFTA[b]	13.4	10.6	10.7	12.3	28.0	29.2	31.3
Other OECD[c]	1.9	3.4	4.5	3.1	4.5	2.2	2.1
Eastern Europe	–	–	–	–	–	–	3.3
Asia[d]	7.7	7.2	7.4	2.6	3.0	3.2	4.5
Latin America[e]	4.9	8.5	10.7	15.6	9.1	6.8	5.3

Source: IUI database.
Notes: (a)These regions contain over 99 per cent of foreign production by Swedish MNCs. (b) Including Mexico. (c) Including Japan. (d) Excluding Japan. (e) Excluding Mexico.

production for domestic sales continued to decrease, the share of total home country production remained relatively constant between these two years. Thus, an unambiguous pattern of continued internationalisation of Swedish MNCs emerges, paired with a corresponding decrease in the share of domestic sales.

As illustrated in table 6.3, foreign production, as approximated by the number of affiliate employees, has been concentrated in OECD Europe.[6] The share has remained well over 50 per cent in the period 1965–94. Since 1970, however, it has decreased in a trendlike fashion, with the exception of 1990 when there was a considerable increase in the operations of Swedish MNCs in OECD Europe. One likely reason for this peak is the uncertainty in that period surrounding Sweden's future relationship to the EU and the risk for firms of being exposed to discriminatory measures if Sweden were to have chosen to stay outside the Union.

An opposite pattern is observed for the NAFTA region, where Swedish MNCs have expanded their activities since the early 1970s. From hosting about 13 per cent of employees in Swedish affiliates in 1965, this share rose to 31 per cent by 1994. The other regions display a more irregular pattern, except for Latin America where the share of employees in Swedish affiliates has decreased since the late 1970s. Moreover, there has been a marked increase in the activities by Swedish MNCs in the formerly closed Eastern European countries in the 1990s.

Turning to the distribution of Swedish MNCs' affiliate employees by industry (table 6.4), it is evident that engineering accounts for the overwhelming part.[7] Its dominance seems to have decreased somewhat,

Table 6.4 *Distribution of affiliate employees by industry, 1965–94*

Industries	1965	1970	1974	1978	1986	1990	1994
Basic	1.3	2.4	3.2	4.8	2.8	13.5	9.7
Chemicals	17.4	14.4	10.6	7.9	11.1	7.0	10.4
Engineering	74.8	71.8	74.8	75.6	71.3	68.2	68.4
Other	6.5	11.4	11.4	11.7	14.8	11.3	11.5
All industries	100.0	100.0	100.0	100.0	100.0	100.0	100.0

Source: IUI database

falling from 75 per cent of affiliate employees in 1965 to 68 per cent in 1994. A noticeable change in the industry pattern is the increased share of affiliate employees in the basic industries, although these industries still have most of their activities in Sweden. Almost the entire increase in affiliate employees in basic industries took place between 1986 and 1990 (it rose from 2.8 to 13.5 per cent). This was a period when the paper and pulp industry was involved in some very large acquisitions of foreign companies.

Swedish MNCs and the pattern of trade

As can be seen from table 6.5, in 1994 OECD Europe was the main recipient of exports from the domestic units of Swedish MNCs. In 1994, about 65 per cent of total exports were destined for Europe, predominantly the EU countries. The other large recipients of Swedish exports were the NAFTA countries (Canada, Mexico and the United States), to which almost 15 per cent was exported,[8] and Asia, which received about 10 per cent of total exports. It is also evident that MNCs in the engineering industry have the most geographically dispersed exports, while the MNCs in the basic products industry have the least dispersed exports. The basic industry's exports were strongly concentrated in OECD Europe, with more than 90 per cent of parent company exports destined for this region. The other industries rank somewhere in between in terms of the geographical dispersion of parent company exports.

It is useful to divide exports into intra-firm exports and other exports, and figure 6.3 does this. The share of parent company exports to sales affiliates shows a particularly pronounced increase in 1978–86, as well as in 1990–94, two periods characterised by a major fall in the value of the Swedish krona. It is evident from figure 6.3 that the share of parent company exports to manufacturing affiliates has grown over time as well.

Table 6.5 *Exports from parent companies of Swedish MNCs, by industry and region, 1994 (per cent of total)*

Region	Engineer-ing	Chemicals	Basic	Others	All Swedish MNCs	Total Swedish exports
OECD Europe	57.9	70.6	90.3	75.1	65.5	70.0
NAFTA	19.2	12.7	3.1	14.3	15.6	9.6
Other OECD	3.1	3.2	0.4	0.6	2.6	1.6
Eastern Europe	3.5	2.1	2.1	3.9	3.1	3.7
Asia	12.2	10.1	3.4	2.0	10.2	12.0
Latin America	2.0	0.4	0.0	0.0	1.3	1.7
Other	2.1	0.9	0.7	4.1	1.7	1.5
Total	100.0	100.0	100.0	100.0	100.0	100.0

Source: IUI database and Statistics Sweden.

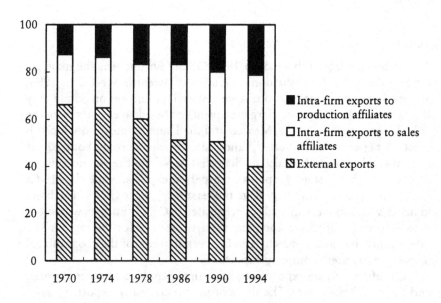

Figure 6.3 *Composition of exports from parent companies of Swedish MNCs, selected years 1970 and 1994, per cent of parent exports*
Source: IUI database.

Table 6.6 *Parent company exports to production affiliates by industry,*
1970–94 (per cent of total parent company exports)

Industry	1970	1974	1978	1986	1990	1994
Basic	12.9	10.9	14.4	7.3	5.3	8.4
Chemicals	15.7	18.4	16.0	9.5	14.8	27.3
Engineering	14.6	18.4	20.8	20.3	29.8	23.9
Metal products	10.7	10.3	13.9	31.8	46.1	40.2
Machinery	23.5	20.6	25.5	26.2	22.3	28.4
Electronics	18.8	24.0	15.2	18.1	32.0	21.5
Transport	7.8	13.9	23.6	18.4	26.8	21.9
All industries	12.7	14.0	16.9	16.5	20.1	20.8

Source: IUI database.

Out of total parent company exports, 34 per cent was shipped to affiliates in 1970, while in 1994 the corresponding figure was 60 per cent.

When we analyse intra-firm exports to production affiliates by industry (table 6.6), we find that all industries, except basics, have experienced an increase between 1970 and 1994. However, the figures reveal considerable fluctuations between different years. There are also distinct differences between industries: the basic, chemical and machinery industries report an increase in the share of exports to foreign affiliates between 1990 and 1994, while the remaining four industries report a decrease. Not only do changes over time differ between industries, but the overall level of the shares of the intra-firm exports differ as well. These shares range between less than 10 per cent (the basic industries) and over 40 per cent (metal products).

The trade patterns of the foreign affiliates of Swedish MNCs are plotted in figure 6.4, which shows that the share of intra-firm imports from the parent company fell from around 17 per cent of affiliate turnover in 1974, to about 12 per cent in 1990. Between 1990 and 1994 this trend reversed and intra-firm imports by foreign affiliates increased. Figure 6.4 also reveals that the export intensity of foreign affiliates, as measured by exports as a percentage of total affiliate sales, has increased throughout the entire period. The overall export intensity has almost doubled between 1974 and 1994 (from 19 to 33 per cent). There has also been a marked increase in the share of exports from foreign affiliates back to Sweden between 1990 and 1994 (from 5 to 9 per cent). Even though intra-firm trade is less likely to be sensitive to exchange rate changes than trade between unaffiliated parties, this development is somewhat surprising

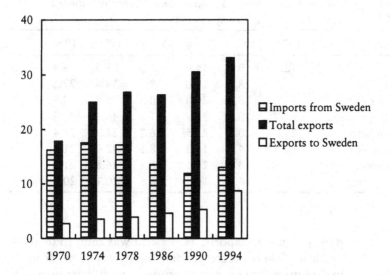

Figure 6.4 *Exports and intra-firm trade by manufacturing foreign affiliates in relation to the affiliates total sales, 1970–94 (per cent)*
Source: IUI database.

considering the large depreciation of the Swedish krona and the subsequent boost in Swedish manufacturing exports. A possible interpretation is that the integration among the different units of the MNCs is so significant that increased exports from the Swedish units also boost imports from the foreign units.

R&D in Swedish MNCs

The location of R&D is often considered to be of special importance for both home and host countries. This topic is discussed at length by Heike Belitz and Marian Beise in this volume (Chapter 5). A widespread view is that R&D generates spillovers of importance for other firms and, therefore, may encourage other, R&D-intensive, firms to locate in the same place. Table 6.7 shows how R&D expenditures were divided among different industries in the Swedish manufacturing sector in 1994. R&D expenditures are concentrated in the chemical, electronic and transport industries. These industries accounted for almost 90 per cent of the Swedish MNCs' total R&D in 1994, whilst their employment share was only about 58 per cent of the total.

Table 6.7 *Total R&D and employment by industry, 1994 (per cent of total for all MNCs)*

Industries	R&D	Employment
Basic	3.3	14.2
Chemical	23.1	10.1
Metal products	2.5	7.6
Machinery	4.4	12.1
Electronics	46.3	33.9
Transport	19.2	13.9
Other	1.2	8.1
All industries	100.0	100.0

Source: IUI database.

Table 6.8 *R&D expenditures as a percentage share of total turnover, 1965–94*

Industries	1965	1970	1974	1978	1986	1990	1994
Basic	1.4	1.2	1.1	0.7	0.7	0.9	0.9
Chemical	3.9	4.7	3.7	4.6	6.7	6.8	9.4
Metal products	1.8	1.4	1.7	3.1	2.5	2.4	2.0
Machinery	2.5	2.5	1.9	2.4	2.7	2.6	2.3
Electronics	5.2	6.5	4.1	3.8	4.5	4.6	8.1
Transport equipment	1.1	1.3	2.7	2.4	5.9	8.4	4.2
Other industries	0.9	1.5	2.8	1.2	0.9	0.5	0.7
All industries	2.0	2.1	2.1	2.2	3.9	3.9	4.7

Source: IUI database.

Table 6.8 shows R&D expenditures as a share of total turnover for Swedish MNCs over the period 1965–94. For the group as a whole this has increased over time. As may be expected, the industries in which a growing proportion of available resources have been allocated to R&D include chemicals and engineering. Indeed, the overall increase in R&D intensity stems exclusively from these industries, whereas the share of R&D spending in basic industries and in other industries (for example food, textiles and clothing) does not appear to have altered much over this time period. A striking change in this pattern is the relatively strong increase in the share of R&D expenditure in the transport equipment sector, a change that is particularly marked between 1978 and 1990. This is most likely to have been a consequence of the increased importance of

Table 6.9 *Swedish MNCs' R&D expenditure abroad as a percentage share of total R&D expenditure, 1965–94*

Industries	1965	1970	1974	1978	1986	1990	1994
Basic	1.6	0.1	9.8	3.5	2.1	25.0	24.2
Chemical	8.3	9.7	13.3	12.7	13.2	17.0	28.7
Metal products	2.1	1.3	0.0	9.4	15.8	21.4	32.3
Machinery	6.6	13.8	34.5	37.4	45.3	55.7	64.3
Electronics	19.5	16.2	15.2	9.9	21.1	25.5	25.2
Transport equipment	0.0	0.3	8.9	3.8	3.6	5.6	8.1
Other industries	23.8	11.1	12.8	17.4	27.0	38.6	37.1
All industries	9.7	9.3	15.1	14.0	13.6	18.6	24.7

Source: IUI database.

R&D as a competitive tool in the motor industry elsewhere in Europe, which has led to a competitive response by Swedish firms.

Considerable concern has been expressed in the policy debate in Sweden about the location of R&D departments; and in particular about the implications of their location abroad. As can be seen from table 6.9, there is a clear tendency towards an increased proportion of the Swedish MNCs' R&D being located outside of Sweden in all industries. Yet, it is also evident from this table that there have been considerable fluctuations within some of the industries during the period 1965 to 1994. The role played by the engineering sector is once again noteworthy. For instance, firms in the machinery industry undertook almost two-thirds of their R&D abroad in 1994[9]. However, the most striking change in the distribution of R&D between domestic and foreign units is reported for the basic industries. Between 1986 and 1990, a ten-fold increase in the share of foreign R&D occurred in this sector. The share then remained constant between 1990 and 1994. This dramatic increase in the share of foreign R&D is probably explained by the major acquisitions of foreign firms, especially in the pulp and paper sector, that have occurred over this period. In addition the level of R&D in these industries was relatively modest at the start of our sample period.

4. Is there a large-country bias in the location of foreign activities?

In the preceding sections, it has been apparent that the dominant host region for Swedish MNCs is Western Europe. It would be useful to know whether a large-country effect can be detected in the pattern of location

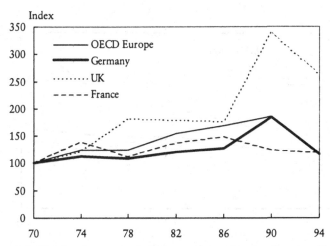

Figure 6.5 *The development of affiliate output related to host country GDP,*
1970=100
Source: IUI database.

of foreign activities by Swedish MNCs in this region. If there is, then we
can provide some evidence to support the implications of modern trade
and location theories. Given the gradual reduction of barriers within the
region over the last thirty years, if large-country bias has existed it should
be declining over time, and locations should become more dispersed.
Hence, it is important to examine how the initial relative shares of production, R&D and trade have developed since the 1970s in the three large
countries, France, Germany, and UK, as compared to total Western
Europe.

The pattern in terms of output for the three large countries is given
in figure 6.5. Affiliate output here refers to net foreign affiliate sales,
implying that intra-firm deliveries of goods from the parent company are
excluded. These figures have all been divided by the GDP of the respective host country or region in order to normalise figures for output,
expenditure and exports. We have also presented the data as indices with
the starting year set to 100.

As shown in figure 6.5, foreign production in Germany, when adjusted
for host country market size, has lagged behind the average for the OECD
Europe area for the whole period up until 1990. Between 1986 and 1990
there was a strong increase in Swedish affiliate production in Germany,
which to some extent probably reflects the Swedish firms' strategies to
position themselves before the completion of the internal European

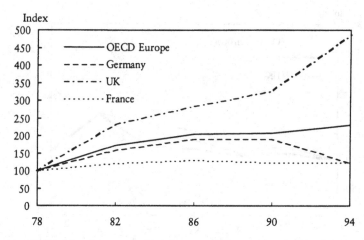

Figure 6.6 *The development of R&D expenditures abroad related to host country GDP, 1978=100*
Source: IUI database.

market. From 1990, foreign production in Germany declined together with the OECD average and in 1994 it was back to its 1986 level. This perhaps reflects the effects of both EU membership and a more competitive home country exchange rate.

Foreign production in France lagged behind the OECD Europe average for most of the period 1970 to 1994 (except for the period 1970–4). In 1994, the market size adjusted index was the same as for both Germany and the OECD Europe average, which means that, between 1970 and 1994, both France and Germany conform completely to the development for the Western European average. For all three regions, there is a slight increase in the market size adjusted level of foreign production by Swedish MNCs between these two years.

Development in the UK, however, contrasts sharply with developments in Germany and France. During the last two decades, affiliate output in the UK has clearly increased more than for the OECD Europe region as a whole. After an initial jump following UK entry into the EU in 1973, the difference accelerated between 1986 and 1994, although, just as for the whole OECD Europe region, there was a decrease between 1990 and 1994 in the index for foreign production in the UK. From these data, it thus seems as if there has been an increasing bias towards locating production in the UK for the Swedish MNCs. However, we are not able to detect any change in the potential bias towards either of the other two large

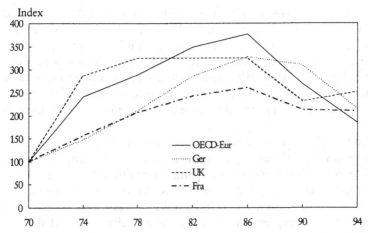

Figure 6.7 *The development of exports by parent companies of Swedish*
MNCs related to host country GDP, 1970=100
Source: IUI database.

European countries. Hence there may be some support for the
suggestion that changes in the UK's institutions have helped it attract further inward FDI.

Concerning the location of foreign R&D activities, there are also distinctive differences across regions. These differences work in the same direction as those just shown for affiliate production. According to figure
6.6, the growth of R&D expenditures in France and Germany relative to
market size lag behind that in OECD Europe, while the opposite holds
for the UK.[10] Indeed, there is a very pronounced increase in the index of
R&D located by Swedish MNCs in the UK, an increase that is particularly strong between 1990 and 1994. For Germany, on the other hand,
there is a fall in the index of R&D expenditure at the beginning of the
1990s, while, for France, the development has been stable over the whole
time period. We can conclude that, overall, there seems to be a strong correlation between the development of the pattern of location of production and the pattern of location of R&D. The growth in R&D does not
appear to be concentrated in centres where R&D activities are particularly strong. If this had been the case, we would have expected more of
the increase in R&D activities to be located in Germany than in the UK.

Figure 6.7 shows the development of parent company exports divided
by host country GDP to the three large European countries and OECD
Europe as a whole. Host market adjusted exports to the whole OECD
Europe region increased between 1970 and 1986, but thereafter they have

declined. Again, this is somewhat surprising, considering the substantial depreciation of the Swedish krona in the 1990s. For France and Germany, host market adjusted exports also increased up until 1986, but not as much as for OECD Europe. Since then, the export index has fallen for both countries. Looking at the whole time period 1970–94, the relative increase in host market adjusted exports has been the same for France and Germany, whereas this increase has been slightly less for the whole OECD Europe region.

For the UK, the relative increase in host market adjusted exports was higher than for both Germany and France (and OECD Europe) over the whole time period 1970–94. At the beginning of the period, there was a large increase in the export index for the UK. As for the other countries, there was a decrease from 1986, but unlike in Germany, France, and OECD Europe, the export index for the UK actually increased slightly between 1990 and 1994.

Generally, we do not find that the large European countries have attracted a disproportionately high share of the increase in Swedish MNCs' foreign activities in Europe from 1970 and onwards. France and Germany almost consistently lag behind OECD Europe in terms of affiliate production, R&D and exports by Swedish firms. The UK, however, displays a distinctly different pattern. We do find some evidence of a disproportionately high share of foreign activities in the UK. Thus, there seems to be a UK effect rather than a large-country effect in the Swedish MNCs' activities. This may reflect changes in the UK institutional environment over the period we have studied, making that country a relatively more attractive location within the European market.

5   Concluding remarks

The results from IUI's most recent (1994) questionnaire to Swedish MNCs suggests that the trend towards greater internationalisation continues. Despite a number of recent policy changes, such as entering as a full member into the EU and a tax reform that seems to have benefited firms, and despite the large depreciation of the Swedish krona, the share of foreign production has actually increased in the 1990s. However, other developments have changed the regional pattern of investment.

In the 1980s, the deepening of the process of European integration appears to have fostered an increase in the share of foreign production located in member countries of the EU. However, in the 1990s, this trend was broken and the share of foreign production returned to the level of the early 1980s. Once membership of the Union had been agreed it appears that it was no longer so important for Swedish firms to locate in other parts of Europe in order to gain guaranteed market access.

The opening up of the former communist countries has had a noticeable, but modest, effect on the location of foreign operations by Swedish MNCs. Furthermore, South-East Asia seems to be attracting a larger share of Swedish affiliate production, as are the NAFTA countries. Thus, the overall picture that emerges from this study is that the relative importance of foreign operations has continued to increase in the 1990s for Swedish MNCs, but that other regions than Europe have emerged as attractive sites for locating production and R&D.

When we consider the industry distribution of foreign production, the engineering industry dominates over other manufacturing industries. Yet basic industries, which have traditionally had the major part of their production in Sweden, have undertaken a rapid expansion in foreign production since 1986. A similar pattern for the basic industries emerges with regard to the distribution of R&D activities abroad, where the share of foreign R&D has increased very sharply since 1986.

Another aspect of the increased internationalisation of the firm is the intensified integration of Swedish and foreign production units. This intensified integration is reflected in the increase in intra-firm trade. Between 1990 and 1994 the trend of decreasing imports by affiliates from parent companies was reversed, and imports increased by almost 14 per cent. Similarly, exports from the foreign affiliates back to the parent company as a share of total affiliate sales almost doubled in that period. This may reflect changing patterns of specialisation that have developed as a consequence of Swedish membership of the EU.

In the final section we examined the role played by large European countries as home countries of Swedish MNCs. No systematic large-country bias could be detected in a comparison between France, Germany and the UK on the one hand, and the whole of Western Europe on the other. However, when looking at developments since 1970, the UK seems over-represented as a recipient of affiliate production, R&D and parent country exports. It is possible to conclude that changes in the UK environment may have influenced the pattern of location by Swedish firms in Europe.

APPENDIX

The database

The database comprises all manufacturing Swedish MNCs with more than fifty employees, having established foreign affiliates. The questionnaire consists of two parts where one is answered by the parent company and the other by each foreign affiliate involved in manufacturing production. Information on sales companies is more limited and is provided by the parent company. All values are expressed in terms of the Swedish krona, and the firms themselves have converted the values of their foreign activities by implementing the exchange rate at the respective year of the questionnaire. Consequently large swings in exchange rates will affect the values of several of the variables. At the level of aggregation presented here, this is unlikely to seriously convey or distort information.

The total number of firms covered in the 1994 survey is approximately 170 parent companies and 800 foreign affiliates. The results presented here for 1994 are based on interim response rate of about 75 per cent and are thus preliminary. However, most of the large Swedish corporations are included.[11] Therefore we do not expect any substantial changes in the results obtained as the response rate increases to its usual level of almost 100 per cent.

The classification of industries and regions is as follows:

- Asia: India, Pakistan, Burma, Sri Lanka (Ceylon), Thailand, Philippines, Malaysia, Singapore, Japan, Lebanon, China, Indonesia, Hong Kong, Democratic People's Republic of Korea, Republic of Korea, Taiwan.
- EU: Belgium, Denmark, France, Germany (exc. former East Germany), Greece, Ireland, Italy, Luxembourg, Netherlands, Portugal, Spain, UK.
- EFTA: Austria, Finland, Iceland, Norway, Switzerland, Sweden (and Denmark, Ireland, and United Kingdom before 1973).
- Eastern Europe: Former Soviet Union, the Baltic States, East Germany, Hungary, Czech Republic, Poland.
- NAFTA: Canada, Mexico, United States.
- Latin America: Argentina, Brazil, Chile.
- OECD Europe: EU, EFTA (exc. former East Germany), Turkey, Cyprus, Malta.
- Other OECD: Australia, Japan, New Zealand.

The classification of industries is as follows:

- Basic: Paper and pulp industries, iron and steel industries.
- Chemicals: Chemical plastic and rubber industries.
- Engineering: Fabricated metal products industry, machinery industry, electronics and electrical machinery industry, transport equipment industry, ship and boat-building industry.
- Other: Food, beverages and tobacco industries, textile, wearing apparel and leather industries, paper products and printing industries, wood and wood products industry, non-metallic mineral products industry (except products of petroleum and coal), industries for measuring and controlling equipment, photographic and optical goods.

Notes

1 Valuable comments on earlier drafts of this paper have been provided by Roger Svensson and other IUI researchers. Financial support from Marianne & Marcus Wallenbergs Foundation is gratefully acknowledged.
2 See Braunerhjelm, Ekholm, Grundberg and Karpaty (1996) for detailed information on the questionnaire.
3 This so-called home market effect was originally shown by Krugman (1980) and it is present in many of the recent economic geography models.
4 The US dollar entered this basket with double weight.
5 In this section, figures for Asea Brown Boveri are excluded for the years 1990 and 1994, if not mentioned otherwise. Note also that some of the figures will be influenced by exchange rate fluctuations. For a brief description of the database and the questionnaire, see appendix.
6 For definitions of the regions used in the tables, see appendix.
7 For definitions of industry classifications, see appendix.
8 The lion's share of the exports to NAFTA is of course destined for the US and Canada.
9 According to the data (not presented here), the EU has received an increasing share of R&D in the machinery industry.
10 Data on the distribution of R&D by countries are unfortunately not available before 1978.
11 The large Swedish firms not included are Assi-Domän and AGA. ABB is not included in the figures for 1990 and 1994, while Asea are contained in the figures preceding 1990.

References

Andersson,T., Fredriksson, T. and Svensson, R. (1996), *Multinational Restructuring Internationalisation and Small Economies. The Swedish Case*, London, Routledge.

Brainard, S. (1993), 'A simple theory of multinational corporations and trade with a trade-off between proximity and concentration', NBER Working Paper No. 4269.

Braunerhjelm, P. (1990), 'Svenska industriföretag inför EG 1992', IUI and ÖEB, Stockholm.

(1996), 'Regional integration and the location of multinational production', Dissertation, IUI, Stockholm.

Braunerhjelm, P., Ekholm, K., Grundberg, L. and Karpaty, P. (1996), 'Swedish multinational corporations: recent trends in foreign activities', Industrial Institute for Economic and Social Research Working Paper No. 462.

Eliasson, G., Bergholm, F., Horwitz, E.V. and Jonung, L. (1985), 'De svenska storföretagen', IUI, Stockholm.

Krugman, P. (1980), 'Scale economies, product differentiation, and the pattern of trade', *American Economic Review*, 70, pp. 950–9.

(1991), 'Increasing returns and economic geography', *Journal of Political Economy*, 99, pp. 483–500.

Markusen, J. (1996), 'Incorporating the multinational enterprise into the theory of international trade', *Journal of Economic Perspectives*, 9, pp. 169–89.

Markusen, J. and Venables, A. (1994), 'Multinational firms and the new trade theory', NBER Working Paper No. 5036.

(1996), 'The theory of endowment, intra-industry, and multinational trade', NBER Working Paper No. 5529.

OECD (1994), *International Direct Investments Statistics Yearbook*, Paris, OECD.

Statistics Sweden, various issues, Örebro.

Riksbanken (1982–1995), *Betalningsbalansen*, Riksbanken.

Svensson, R. (1996), 'Foreign activities of Swedish multinational corporations', Dissertation, IUI, Stockholm.

Swedenborg, B. (1979), 'The multinational operations of Swedish firms. An analysis of determinants and effects', Dissertation, IUI, Stockholm.

United Nations (1994 and 1995), *World Investment Report*, New York and Geneva, UNO.

Venables, A. (1993), 'Equilibrium locations of vertically linked industries', CEPR Discussion Paper No. 82.

7   European integration and German FDI: implications for domestic investment and Central European economies

JAMUNA PRASAD AGARWAL

Since the mid-1980s foreign direct investment (FDI) outflows from Germany have increased considerably. Germany ranks after the US, UK and Japan as the fourth most important global investor. The most rapid expansion of German FDI in the 1980s occurred in the EU; now it is happening in Central Europe (Czech Republic, Hungary, Poland, Slovakia and Slovenia). The question arises whether economic integration is a major stimulant of German FDI. The Single Market Programme was introduced in the EU in the 1980s and it increased the degree of integration of the markets of member countries. This was particularly important for the service industries that had hitherto been heavily protected from foreign competition. Economic integration of the Central European countries with the EU is now likely. They have already applied for EU membership. It is not clear when this will take place but, during the interim phase, some of the advantages of economic integration (free trade, capital movement, economic aid) are available through 'Europe Agreements' between the EU and Central European countries (Langhammer 1992), and through the Central Europe Free Trade Agreement (CEFTA).

It is also important to ask if the strength of capital outflows has impaired domestic investment in the German economy. This is especially relevant in the context of the continuing debate about the deteriorating attraction of Germany as a business location. Wages and taxes in Germany are rather high by international standards. Recorded inflows of FDI into Germany have also been very disappointing. The key objective of the recent decision of the German government to reform the tax system and reduce its incidence on enterprises is to regain the economy's attractiveness to foreign as well as domestic equity capital.

The rapid growth of German FDI in Central Europe also raises an

Table 7.1 *German share in global FDI outflows and stock 1984–95 ($ million and percentages)*

	FDI outflows		FDI stock		
	1984–9	1990–5	1980	1990	1995
Global FDI ($mn)	121,630	237,933	513,740	1,684,136	2,730,146
Germany	7.9	9.2	8.4	9.0	8.6
Developed countries	93.7	88.2	98.8	95.9	92.1
European Union	51.5	47.2	41.5	46.2	44.3
France	7.3	10.6	4.6	6.5	7.4
Netherlands	5.8	5.5	8.2	6.5	5.8
UK	19.1	10.1	15.7	13.7	11.7
US	13.9	21.7	42.9	25.8	25.8
Japan	17.1	11.8	3.7	12.2	11.2
Developing countries	6.3	11.7	1.2	4.1	7.9
Latin America	0.5	1.2	0.6	0.8	0.9
Asia	4.9	10.2	0.6	2.6	6.4
China	0.5	1.1	0.0	0.2	0.6
Hong Kong	1.5	5.4	0.0	0.8	3.1
Rep. of Korea	0.1	0.8	0.0	0.1	0.4
Singapore	0.2	0.8	0.1	0.3	0.5
Taiwan	1.6	1.2	0.0	0.8	0.9

Source: UNCTAD (1996a).

important question about its implications for the host countries. FDI brings not only capital, technology, managerial and marketing know-how to host countries but also promotes their integration into the international marketplace, which is essential for the efficient allocation of resources. This increased integration is evident from the rising level of trade between Germany and Central Europe. Central European countries do not appear to have doubts about advantages of FDI either. They have opened their markets for it, and adopted liberal promotional policies. If there has been disappointment, it is mostly because FDI inflows have been less than expected. Thus the question about the implications of German FDI in Central Europe boils down to its future prospects. A great part of FDI has been undertaken in the framework of privatisation of state-owned enterprises (Lansbury *et al.,* 1996), and hence there are fears that the growth of FDI in Central Europe may slow as privatisation programmes run out of steam.

Table 7.2 *Regional pattern of German FDI outflows 1983–94 (annual averages, DM million and percentage shares)*

	1983–6	1987–90	1991–4
Total	14,958.00	26,458.00	30,884.00
European Union	32.56	52.18	61.15
EU(8)[(a)]	26.94	45.87	55.04
Greece	0.43	0.27	0.49
Portugal	0.31	0.71	1.22
Spain	4.89	5.36	4.40
Austria	2.21	2.71	3.19
Finland	0.11	0.14	0.18
Sweden	0.29	0.34	2.01
Central Europe[(b)]	0.01	0.28	6.06
Eastern Europe	0.11	0.27	1.54
US	42.99	28.55	11.07
Developing countries[(c)]	10.56	4.50	7.86
Latin America	4.28	2.21	3.67
South and East Asia	2.05	1.46	3.64

Source: OECD, *International Direct Investment Statistics Yearbook* (various issues).
Notes: (a) EU-9 excluding Germany. (b) Czech Republic, Hungary, Poland, Slovakia and Slovenia. (c) Non-OECD Area + Mexico – Central and Eastern Europe.

German FDI: global and regional trends

Table 7.1 highlights the importance of Germany in global FDI outflows and stocks. Germany occupies fourth place behind the US, UK and Japan in terms of global stocks of FDI. Moreover, this position has not changed over the years. As far as FDI outflows are concerned Germany has recorded very rapid growth, second only to France in the EU. Outside Europe, US FDI outflows have risen faster, and those of developing countries still faster. The latter have, of course, started from a very low base. Nevertheless, Asian NICs have already accumulated considerable stocks of outward FDI.

More than three-fifths of recent German FDI outflows have been to other EU countries (table 7.2). This share has doubled since the mid-1980s. Another important feature of German FDI is that it is focused on more advanced members of the EU. The two Mediterranean countries, Greece and Portugal, have received only minor shares. Spain has attracted more

German FDI, but its share has not increased since the mid-1980s. In the case of three new members, Austria, Finland and Sweden, German FDI began rising before their formal accession in 1995. The Central European countries, particularly the Czech Republic, Hungary and Poland, are expected to become members of the EU, and German enterprises have begun to position themselves in these markets. Of course, FDI flows are conditioned by a variety of factors, but European integration appears to be a common stimulant of German FDI in the current and potential member countries. Compared with them, German FDI has declined in the US, the country with the world's largest domestic market, which also has good growth prospects. It had been the biggest host country for German multinational enterprises (MNEs), attracting as much as 43 per cent of the German FDI outflows in the mid-1980s. In the mid-1990s only 11 per cent of such flows are directed to the US, probably a sign of market saturation. The US still accounts for 21 per cent of the total stock of outward German FDI in spite of downward adjustments in the value of investments due to the falling long-term trend of US dollar exchange rate *vis-à-vis* the German currency.

Regional integration as a stimulant of German FDI

European integration has tended to intensify local competition. German enterprises have responded to it by extending the boundaries of the domestic market to the unified market. The search for scale economies and better market access has resulted in increased German direct investment in the member countries (Nunnenkamp *et al.* 1994). The increase in intra-Europe FDI may have been promoted by locational competition among the member governments, mostly in form of tax reductions, privatisation programmes and deregulations.

The restructuring of German and other European MNEs in the 1980s led to an unprecedented number of mergers and acquisitions (M&As), and the formation of new joint ventures in the EU. This activity peaked as early as 1989–90, much in advance of the completion of the single market (European Commission and UNCTAD 1996). Mergers and acquisitions were especially conspicuous in construction, banking and insurance.[1] In the service sector, barriers to trade were higher than in manufactured goods, which had been liberalised before 1985. Hence more competition was expected in the service sector. The pattern in relation to the likely eastward extension of the EU is similar. The liberalisation of goods trade between the EU and Central European countries has progressed further than that of trade in services. Complete integration of these countries would have a greater liberalising, and thus competition enhancing, effect in the services sector.

Economic integration generally tends to bolster intra-union as well as extra-union investment, although it has often been difficult to catch its effect in econometric analyses.[2] Classical cases of integration are found between the former imperial powers and their ex-colonies. Preferential trading and investment relations among them led to high FDI inflows into the ex-colonies. The preferential agreements between the EU and the Mediterranean countries resulted in many cases in more FDI from EU enterprises (Joekes, 1982; Pomfret, 1986). ASEAN seems to have promoted the intra-regional FDI of the member countries, although the numbers are as yet relatively small and subject to high volatility (UNCTAD, 1997a). Trade has accelerated recently among the Latin American MERCOSUR members, recording a growth of 250 per cent during 1990 and 1993 compared with 29 per cent growth in trade with the rest of the world. Flows of FDI are also expected to rise in the future as trade and FDI are widely seen as complementary in this context (UNCTAD, 1997b).

However, economic integration alone is not a sufficient condition for increased FDI inflows from the member countries. Greece has been, for example, a member of the EU since 1981, but FDI flows from other member countries have remained subdued. In the case of NAFTA, Canadian and Mexican shares in the total outward stock of the US declined from 19 per cent (1990) to 13 per cent in 1995 (OECD, 1996; Lowe and Bargas, 1996), although they might have been expected to rise because of their free trade agreement. The decline was particularly high (from 16 per cent to 11 per cent) in the Canadian case. The removal of trade barriers may have stimulated US firms to exploit scale economies at their home production bases rather than investing or remaining involved in Canada. NAFTA did not promote Canadian FDI in the US either. In 1994, the US share in Canadian FDI stock was 5 per cent lower than in 1991 (OECD, 1996).

Does FDI reduce domestic investment?

This question is addressed in the context of the continuing *relocation* debate in Germany and elsewhere. Many developed countries, including Germany, are faced with long-term unemployment. At the same time, their FDI outflows have been rising. This coincidence has fuelled the concern that FDI outflows could have reduced potential domestic investment in the home countries. This concern is exacerbated in Germany by low

Table 7.3 *FDI flows in and out of Germany, 1983–96, DM million*

	FDI inflows	FDI outflows	Net FDI (– outflows)
1983–6[a]	2,488	14,958	–12,470
1987–90[a]	5,635	26,458	–20,823
1991	6,785	39,276	–32,492
1992	4,158	30,499	–26,341
1993	2,944	25,344	–22,400
1994	1,118	27,032	–25,914
1995	12,914	49,998	–37,084
1996	–4,865	41,824	–46,689

Source: As table 7.2; Deutsche Bundesbank (1997).
Notes: (a) Annual average.

inflows of FDI. The rising net FDI outflow (table 7.3) is often considered to be a result of deteriorating attractiveness of the German economy for both domestic as well as foreign investors due to unfavourable labour market conditions, stringent environmental regulations, and taxes on corporate income higher than in many other competing host countries in Europe.[3] This applies particularly to the UK, which is often regarded by foreign investors as the most attractive location in the EU.[4]

As far as wage costs are concerned, it cannot be denied that Germany occupies top ranking among the relevant countries[5] (figure 7.1). The influence of wage costs on FDI decisions is likely to vary among industries depending on their factor combinations (labour or capital intensive) and investment motives (domestic or export market oriented). But other things being equal, high wage costs are likely to discourage foreign and domestic transnational corporations (TNCs) from investing in Germany (Beyfuss, 1996). Moreover, labour laws regulating hiring and firing practices in Germany are considered to be rigid. According to survey results, among relevant countries they were found more rigid only in Italy (WEF, 1996). In the same survey Germany received lower rankings than most of the developed countries with regard to environmental laws insofar as their compatibility with corporate competitiveness is concerned. Costs of labour and environmental protection are likely to weigh heavier in investment decisions after the completion of the Single Market Programme as investors have a greater scope to locate their plants in other EU countries and supply the German market from there without any barriers at the border. It is also suggested that because of high wage costs, the risk

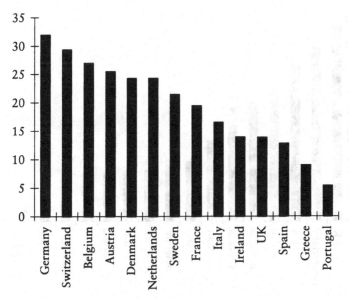

Figure 7.1 *Wage costs per hour 1995*
Source: US Department of Labor (1996).

perception by US investors of German assets has increased, and they are said to be asking for substantial discounts on offer prices of M&As (FAZ, 1996).

Among other reasons for low FDI inflows in Germany, the relatively strong technological competitiveness of German enterprises *vis-à-vis* foreign investors and difficulties of investing through M&As in Germany seem to be more decisive. This tends to reduce the overall scope for inward FDI in Germany.

Technological superiority can be side-tracked by acquiring the related enterprises. But foreign investors often find it hard to enter the German market through M&As, which are a popular mode of FDI among developed countries. They enable investors to buy ownership of specific asset and market shares, have local partners in place of competitors, and get access to supplier networks and distribution systems. Acquisition of German companies is rather difficult, particularly compared with UK and US companies. There are several reasons for this. First, stock market capitalisation (27 per cent) in Germany is very low (figure 7.2). At the end of 1996, Germany had nearly 3 million enterprises, of which only 0.13 per

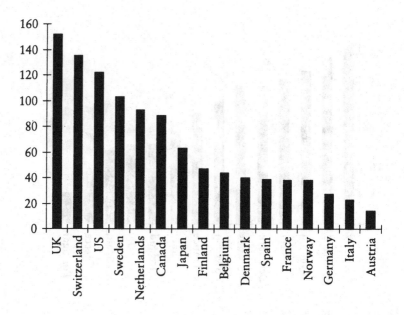

Figure 7.2 *Stock market capitalisation[a] (1996)*
Source: Deutsche Bundesbank (1997).
Notes: (a) Ratio of total value of listed shares at end of November 1996 to
nominal GDP of 1995.

cent were registered as joint-stock companies (Deutsche Bundesbank,
1997, p. 28). This restricts the scope for M&As. Second, cross holding of
shares is widespread among German enterprises. Third, the state and the
banking sectors[6] hold relatively high shares of company stocks (table 7.4).
This means that investors who wish to acquire German enterprises often
have to negotiate with management rather than buying through the stock
exchange. Moreover, management boards include employee representatives, who are generally apprehensive about lay-offs when M&As take
place. These problems add to transaction costs for investors, and it is not
surprising that hostile takeovers are almost non-existent in Germany.

Now, to come back to outward FDI, it is an open question whether and
how much FDI outflows are a drag on domestic capital formation. If just
the ratio of FDI outflows to gross fixed capital formation is considered, it
increased until 1990 in the wake of the Single Market Programme. Thereafter it declined until 1994. It rose again in 1995, but it was still below

Table 7.4 *Ownership structure[a] of joint stock companies in Germany, France, UK, US and Japan, 1995, per cent*

	Germany	France	UK	US	Japan
Enterprises	42.1	58.0	4.1	15.0	31.2
Banks	10.3	4.0	2.3	0.2	13.3
Public institutions	4.3	3.4	0.2	0.0	0.5
Insurance companies and pension funds	12.4	1.9	39.7	31.2	10.8
Investment trusts and other financial institutions	7.6	2.0	10.4	13.0	11.7
Private persons	14.6	19.4	29.6	36.4	22.2
Others	8.7	11.2	13.7	4.2	10.3

Source: Deutsche Bundesbank (1997).
Note: (a) Ratio of share capital owned.

Table 7.5 *Ratio of FDI outflows in gross fixed capital formation in Germany, 1981–95, DM billion, per cent*

	Gross fixed capital formation	FDI outflows	Share of FDI outflows
1981–5[a](average)	192.9	10.3	5.3
1986–90[a](average)	261.3	24.0	9.2
1991	655.3	39.3	6.0
1992	709.4	30.5	4.3
1993	689.2	25.3	3.7
1994	729.7	27.0	3.7
1995	751.1	50.0	6.7

Sources: Klodt and Maurer (1996); Deutsche Bundesbank (1996b); Statistisches Bundesamt (1995, 1996).
Note: (a) West Germany.

the 1986–90 level (table 7.5). By the early 1990s, German firms had already completed the restructuring of their European production bases that had been provoked by the Single Market Programme. New investment opportunities also emerged at home following German unification. Moreover, some of the important host countries were faced with reces-

Table 7.6 *FDI outflows and income of Germany and US, 1989–95*

	1989	1990	1991	1992	1993	1994	1995
Germany (DM million)							
FDI outflows	28,539	38,691	39,276	30,499	25,344	27,032	49,998
Equity capital	21,031	31,162	31,127	26,211	23,109	23,525	41,457
Reinvested							
earnings	5,000	5,000	6,000	1,500	−1,500	0	2,000
Other investments	2,508	2,529	2,150	2,787	3,735	3,507	6,541
Income	8,870	9,293	9,378	7,210	5,950	8,429	10,830
Royalties, etc.	n.a.	n.a.	n.a.	1,696	1,545	1,747	2,074
US ($ million)							
FDI outflows	37,604	30,982	32,696	42,647	77,247	53,078	93,406
Equity capital	6,395	8,739	17,682	14,647	24,565	12,749	36,292
Reinvested							
earnings	12,697	21,436	18,327	16,294	30,014	32,075	52,367
Intercompany							
debt	18,512	807	−3,313	11,705	22,668	8,254	4,747
Income	53,929	58,004	52,087	50,565	59,381	65,994	85,538
Royalties, licence fees							
and charges for							
other services	14,347	16,197	17,404	19,124	19,149	21,231	23,955

Source: Deutsche Bundesbank (1994; 1996b; 1996d); USDOC (1996).
Note: n.a. = not available.

sion in the early 1990s. This could have contributed to the decline of FDI outflows from Germany from 1992–4.

The above ratio is, however, flawed as an appropriate indicator of the relation between domestic and foreign capital formation by national firms. First, FDI outflows include reinvestments of profits earned in host countries. This amounted to 34 per cent of the German outward stock in 1994 (latest year available, Deutsche Bundesbank, 1996a). FDI flow data for the recent years reveal, however, a substantially lower contribution (7.5 per cent) of reinvestment to outward German FDI (table 7.6). Inclusion of reinvestment in FDI makes it questionable to compare total FDI outflows with domestic investment. Second, foreign affiliates repatriate profits and other income (patent and licensing fees and so on) to the head offices. The former averaged (1989–95) about 25 per cent of total recorded German FDI, and the latter was about 5 per cent (1992–5, earlier data not available). These two add to funds available for capital formation in the domestic economy rather than reducing them. Excluding reinvestments, repatriated earnings and other income from FDI outflows, 70 per cent (1992–5) of recorded FDI outflows remain to be considered as a diversion of investment from the German domestic economy, provided outward FDI was not financed from foreign borrowing routed through the domestic capital market.[7]

In comparison, the US has a longer history of outward FDI, and provides a larger scope for examining the effect of outward FDI on domestic investment. During the seven years from 1989 to 1995, US outward FDI was $368 billion, and total earnings on the stock of assets were $425 billion (table 7.6), yielding a 'surplus' of $57 billion. Over this period $183 billion of total earnings were reinvested in the host countries. If they are excluded from total FDI outflows, the repatriated earnings ($242 million) exceeded the outflows of equity capital and inter-company debt ($184 billion) by 32 per cent during this period. In addition, US firms had received $131 billion for royalties, licence fees and so on from their foreign affiliates. Indeed, during this seven-year period, earnings exceeded FDI outflows in every year except 1993. If royalties, licence fees and so on are taken into account, the US had a 'surplus' even in this year. Thus, it seems that foreign involvement of US firms makes a substantial contribution to funds available for domestic capital formation in the US rather than reducing them. It is suggested that, in the early stages of the investment development cycle, FDI outflows may reduce domestic capital formation (Dunning and Narula, 1996). During this stage, the FDI outflows from a country may far exceed its FDI earnings, but in a sufficiently longer period of time, earnings may outstrip FDI outflows. Then the net balance of these two variables begins to have a positive rather than a negative impact on home country investment.

An indirect effect on domestic investment through trade

Outward FDI may affect domestic investment negatively through the effects of export substitution and re-imports from the foreign affiliates, and positively through the effects of additional exports of goods and services to their host countries. The net balance of these two effects in a country is essentially an empirical question, and it is likely to differ from case to case at the micro level. At the macro level, positive effects are expected to outweigh negative ones. In the absence of hard facts, the following discussion of the trade-related effect of FDI on domestic investment is primarily analytical, drawing on existing literature.

Export substitution is one of the two main channels through which FDI may reduce investment in the home country. This is likely to occur in 'product cycle' and 'efficiency-seeking' investments. In the former case, it is however important to remember that the original producer is forced by competition to locate new plants in host markets (Vernon, 1966, 1979; Hirsch, 1967; Hufbauer, 1966). The choice in this case is not between continuation of exports and FDI, but between FDI and loss of host markets.

Efficiency-seeking FDI refers to relocation of existing or future production capacity to host countries offering lower land, labour, raw material or environmental costs than in the home country. US direct investment in maquiladoras in Mexico or German investment in the clothing sector of Mediterranean or Central European countries are prominent examples of efficiency-seeking FDI. If FDI results in relocation of existing production capacity, export substitution may or may not reduce capital stock depending on the written down value of plant and machinery. Thus, the investment effect is different from the employment effect of export substitution by FDI (Agarwal, 1996a). In the latter, relocation means retrenchment of existing jobs. However, in the former, the capital stock may have already been written down or be obsolete, and relocation makes no difference to the domestic capital stock. By contrast, if the investor relocates future investments, that is, creates production capacity abroad in place of home country capacity, then domestic fixed capital formation is negatively affected by outward FDI. This is observed in labour intensive industries such as clothing, textiles and leather. However, developed countries like Germany have been losing comparative advantage in such industries. The newly industrialising countries from Asia have particularly strengthened their competitive position for these products even on the home markets of developed countries. Hence if the enterprises from the latter do not invest abroad to improve their cost efficiency, they stand to lose markets for the related products. This would in turn affect domestic investment in those branches negatively. Thus, in this case too, the choice may often be not between domestic and foreign investment, but between no investment and foreign investment.

The other trade channel likely to encroach upon domestic output and hence investment is that of re-imports of goods and services produced by the foreign affiliates abroad. In this case, investors go far beyond export substitution. They not only substitute exports by local production in host countries, but also re-import the goods produced there into the home country. Re-imports may reduce actual or potential domestic production and investment. The negative effect of re-imports on domestic investment has drawn considerable attention in the recent relocation debate. Compared with Germany, it has been of a greater concern in Japan because of re-imports by Japanese TNCs from their affiliates in East Asian countries. In electronics and electrical machinery, for instance, around 25 per cent of Japanese imports from Asian countries are products of the subsidiaries of Japanese enterprises (UNCTAD, 1996b).

On the positive side of trade effects of outward FDI on domestic invest-ment stand exports of capital goods, spare parts, raw materials, and so on, to the foreign affiliates. This applies particularly to greenfield efficiency-seeking FDI. But import ratios of foreign affiliates in market and resource-seeking FDI in developing countries are also generally very high. Japanese 'transplants' set up in the US as well as in Europe to cir-cumvent import restrictions in automobile and consumer electronic indus-tries are known to raise exports of components and spare parts from Ja-pan (OECD, 1994). In addition, FDI stimulates exports of other products to the host country that are neither produced by the foreign affiliate nor exported by the parent firm prior to the establishment of that foreign af-filiate. This can be traced back to the publicity effect of the new affiliate in the home market, and the new affiliate is also usually able to offer closer servicing and marketing relationship to customers in the host country. The new exports initiated by FDI are likely to have a positive impact on domestic investment of the home country.

The net balance of negative (export substitution and re-imports) and positive (associated exports) trade effects of FDI on domestic investment may vary from case to case. A firm, for example, producing only one good and exporting to only one country may have to scale down its domestic investment if it starts production of the same good in the same foreign location, because its exports will be substituted by host country produc-tion. It will not be able to compensate the export substitution by exports of FDI associated goods since it does not produce them. But if the invest-ing firm is a conglomerate producing and trading a large number of pro-ducer as well as consumer goods and services, substitution of exports of one product by production in the host country may be more or less com-pensated for by associated exports with a corresponding effect on domestic investment of the related enterprise. The more diversified a firm, the greater is the likelihood that the net trade effect of its FDI on its domestic invest-ment will be positive.

As in the case of a firm, FDI of a narrowly defined industry may result in reduced domestic investment via export substitution and re-imports. But if an industry is defined broadly or if the manufacturing sector as a whole is considered, exports induced by FDI may exceed the sum of ex-port substitution and re-imports creating more demand for domestic

Table 7.7 *Intra-firm trade in the US and Japan, 1983, 1989 and 1992*

	United States			Japan[a]		
	1983	1989	1992	1983	1989	1992
Exports by parent firms to their foreign affiliates ($ billion)	47	89	106	31	63	86
Imports by parent firms from their foreign affiliates ($ billion)	39	74	94	5	19	16
Balance of intra-firm trade in home country of parent firms ($ billion)	8	15	12	26	44	70
Share of affiliates in total exports of parents (per cent)	31	40	42	28	40	32
Share of affiliates in total imports of parents (per cent)	36	42	46	21	30	29

Source: UNCTAD (1995, pp. 194–5).
Notes: (a) excluding commerce.

investment. In Germany, outward FDI is dominated by diversified con-
glomerates. Shares of their foreign affiliates in their total exports is likely
to be high. However, data on intra-firm trade for Germany are not readily available. The figures for the US and Japan reveal that the affiliates
have increased their shares in total exports of their parent firms (table 7.7),
while outward FDI of these two countries also increased during the same
period. This means that increased FDI outflows were correlated with more
associated exports. Moreover, the balance of intra-firm trade is in favour of
home economies. In both the countries, re-imports increased as well, but they
were exceeded by exports to foreign affiliates. Recently, Hufbauer and Schott
(1993) estimated that US exports of capital goods, components and other associated goods and services to Mexico following US FDI due to NAFTA would
more than compensate for re-imports from Mexico to the US. A similar result is reported by Hanson (1995) for US FDI in Mexican maquiladoras. Thus
export creation substitutions and re-imports caused by its FDI should *ceteris
paribus* lead to more domestic investment in home countries.

German FDI in Central Europe

Germany is by far the biggest direct investor in Central European coun-

Table 7.8 *Countries of origin of FDI in Central European countries, latest year available,*[a] *per cent*

	Czech Rep.	Hungary	Poland	Slovakia[b]
EU	54.6[c]	53.8	63.4	30.6[d]
Belgium, Luxembourg	7.1	3.9	1.5	n.a.
France	12.6	5.2	5.2	4.6
Germany	31.2	22.3	22.9	13.7
Italy	3.7	4.7	19.3	1.6
Netherlands	n.a.	11.1	8.3	5.0
UK	n.a.	4.5	2.6	5.7
Other Europe	10.5[e]	25.1	13.9	17.7[e]
Austria	6.1	19.9	5.0	16.8
Switzerland	4.4	3.8	2.1	0.9
US	27.9	14.3	16.4	9.0
Japan	n.a.	1.9	0.2	n.a.

Sources: For Czech Republic: UN (1994); Hungary: OECD, *International Direct Investment Statistics Yearbook (*various issues); Poland: Central Statistical Office; Slovakia: *PlanEcon Report* (1996).
Notes: (a) Czech Republic and Poland: end of 1993, Hungary: end of 1994, Slovakia: end of 1995. (b) Czech Republic had 30.3 per cent share, of which 63 per cent is recorded as portfolio investment. (c) Belgium, France, Germany and Italy. (d) France, Germany, Italy, Netherlands and UK. (e) Austria and Switzerland.

tries. In the Czech Republic, German enterprises account for about one-third of the FDI stock (table 7.8). In Hungary and Poland, this share has been smaller, but it is higher than that of any other country.[8] In Slovakia, the contribution of Germany ranks behind Austria. Most of the reasons for strong involvement by Germany in FDI in Central Europe also apply to Austria. In passing it is worth noting that Slovakian FDI data include portfolio investment from the Czech Republic, probably a pre-partition relic. If they are excluded, Austrian and German shares would be considerably higher in the FDI stock of Slovakia. Compared with other OECD countries, investors from these two countries have recently directed considerably more of their equity capital to Central and East European countries (CEECs).

One of the reasons for the relatively strong involvement of German investors in Central Europe is geographical proximity. Germany shares

Table 7.9 *Trade relations of Central Europe with Germany and Austria, 1928, 1989 and 1994, per cent*

	Czechoslovakia				Hungary			Poland		
	1928	1989	1994[a]	1994[b]	1928	1989	1994	1928	1989	1994
Germany										
Exports	27	8	43	44	12	12	28	35	14	36
Imports	39	9	40	36	20	18	24	27	13	28
Austria										
Exports	15	3	9	12	34	5	10	12	3	2
Imports	7	2	9	11	16	7	11	7	5	3

Source: Piazolo (1996).
Notes: (a) The Czech Republic excluding trade with Slovakia. (b) Slovakia excluding trade with the Czech Republic.

common borders with Poland and the Czech Republic, and this generally exercises a strong positive influence on FDI flows between the countries (Agarwal, 1994). Austria shares this advantage in respect of the Czech Republic, Hungary, Slovakia and Slovenia. Austria is the second biggest investor in Hungary after Germany, and as in Slovakia Austria ranks above Germany. Geographical distance constitutes an important element of transaction costs for investors. Investors from bordering countries have a comparative advantage over others. Cultural barriers, which also tend to raise transaction costs for investors, are relatively low between Germany and other Central European countries. Thus, Germany is apparently a natural investment partner for these countries after the removal of the artificial barriers to capital movement created by the former political system of CEECs.

Investment and trade between countries are in the long run interdependent unless constrained by legal barriers. Germany has long standing trade relations with Central Europe. Before the Second World War, Czechoslovakia, Hungary and Poland were important trading partners of Germany. After the war the eastern part of Germany was a member of the former trade bloc of communist countries (Council of Mutual Economic Assistance, CMEA), and had a large part of its trade with them. West German shares in Central European trade declined (table 7.9), but it remained the most important Western economic partner of the CMEA. Since the demise of the CMEA in 1989, Germany has again evolved into the dominant trading partner of the CEE economies. Moreover, it is now the most important aid donor and creditor of Central European countries (Hoey, 1996). Besides trade, aid and other financial links also tend to promote FDI (Agarwal, 1990).

German FDI in Central Europe is very likely also to have been facilitated by the envisaged economic integration of the countries of this region in the EU. The 'Europe Agreements' of these countries allow them to become full members depending on their achievements in terms of economic and political convergence. Meanwhile, they have preferential market access to the member economies, and benefit from investment promotion and economic and technical aid as well as scientific, industrial and monetary cooperation. Trade preferences and economic integration, as already discussed, tend to strengthen FDI flows among the partners. Barrell *et al.* (1996) and the chapter by Hubert and Pain in this volume provide evidence that economic integration can have a sizeable positive impact on inward FDI from German corporations.

Heightened growth prospects of Central European countries can be safely assumed to have further stimulated FDI inflows in this region. Market size and its growth prospects are often found as significant determinants of FDI inflows. This also applies to Central European countries (Wang and Swain, 1995). The five members of CEFTA have a total population of over 66 million. They have already been able to achieve respectable rates of economic growth (Deutsche Bundesbank, 1996c). Prospects for the future are good as judged from the ongoing progress in macroeconomic reforms. However, FDI inflows in Central Europe have been more volatile than should have been expected on the basis of potential growth scenarios because of the high share of privatisation-based FDI inflows. Privatisation-based equity investments are usually lumpy, and can produce heavy swings in FDI inflows in smaller economies. Privatisation accounted for 60 per cent of all FDI inflows to CEECs during 1991–3 (UNCTAD, 1995, p. 18). A year later, they amounted to only 18 per cent of them (UNCTAD, 1996a, p. 65). The link between FDI and economic growth can be found only for non-privatisation FDI inflows.

Privatisation and growth are likely to have encouraged FDI from all sources in Central Europe. However, it is possible that German investors have been able to take a greater advantage of them owing to their lower transaction costs. As mentioned earlier, German investors have a comparative advantage based on geographical and cultural proximity, and intensive trade relations involving established distribution and servicing networks in this region. All these factors reduce transaction costs for German investors in Central European economies. Austria enjoys similar competitive advantages in this region. As already stated, it has common borders with more countries of the region than Germany, and it is not surprising that 43 per cent of Austria's FDI outflows in 1994 were directed to CEECs compared with 13 per cent for Germany (OECD, 1996). The total volume of German FDI in Central Europe is, however, greater than that of Austria because of the former's greater investing capacity resulting from the size of its economy.

Most of German FDI in CEECs appears to have been financed by mobilisation of additional equity capital, and not by diversion from other host countries (Agarwal, 1997) or from domestic fixed capital formation in Germany (table 7.5). Additional support for this hypothesis comes from the fact that the great majority of German FDI in Central Europe is market rather than cost oriented. Market-seeking FDI tends to create and not divert investment from other targets (Agarwal, 1996b). A recent survey (Beyfuss, 1996) of German enterprises[9] marked penetration and preservation of markets as the dominating motivation of investments in CEECs. Wage and other cost related motivations were assigned lower rankings. The same result was obtained a year earlier in another survey of British and German companies (Meyer, 1995). Nine-tenths of all German FDI in CEECs is concentrated in Hungary, the Czech Republic and Poland.[10] All three countries offer good prospects of expanding markets. Many Bavarian firms in southern Germany have invested across the border in the Czech Republic (DIHT, 1996). Most of them are of small or medium size investing for the first time abroad. They would probably have not invested in another country if the barriers at the Czech border had not been dismantled. This means new, additional equity capital has been mobilised for direct investment. However, some of this investment may be motivated by a desire to exploit cost advantages in the Czech Republic.[11] Indeed, senior figures in some of the counties in southern Germany are worried about an exodus of productive capital to areas across the border. But the weight of such cases in total German FDI in Central Europe is expected to be low. Moreover, the cost advantages of Central European countries based on low wages is likely to disappear as their income levels converge towards West European levels in the course of joining the EU as full members, and as exchange rates of their currencies move upwards to realistic levels.

FDI inflows in Central Europe including those from Germany can be expected to increase further in future. Central Europe appears to play the role of hinterland for German and other EU investors, as South- and South-East Asia do for Japanese investors, and Latin America for US investors. Asian and Latin American shares in Japanese and US FDI stocks amount to nearly 16 per cent (table 7.10). In comparison, CEE accounts

Table 7.10 *Share of neighbouring regions in outward stock of FDI of Germany, EU, Japan and US, 1990 and 1995, per cent*

	1990	1994
South- and South-East Asian share in Japanese FDI	15.3	16.4
Latin American share in US FDI	14.2	15.5
CEE share in EU FDI	n.a.	1.3
CEE share in German FDI	0.2	2.3

Source: OECD (1996).

only for 2.3 per cent of German, and 1.3 per cent of EU FDI stock as yet. From this perspective, there is enough room for German and other European direct investment in this region.

The apprehension that abatement of privatisation of state-owned enterprises, which attracted a major portion of the FDI inflows into Central Europe, would drastically cut FDI inflows does not appear realistic. As pointed out earlier, privatisation-based FDI inflows in 1995 declined by a quarter compared with the preceding year. However, FDI inflows in the five Central European countries jumped by a factor of 2.6 (IMF, 1996). Latin American experience shows that FDI continues to flow in the post-privatisation period (UNCTAD, 1995, pp. 77–8). Post-privatisation FDI may sometimes exceed the initial sums owing to investments required for rationalisation and modernisation of acquired enterprises. This applies especially in telecommunication and energy sectors. The Australian Bond corporation, for example, after having acquired the CTC telecommunication company of Chile in 1987, invested $400 million per annum in the following seven years (UNCTAD, 1997b). Moreover, privatisation-related FDI often leads to reinvestments, and improves the climate for more FDI, reassuring investors about the continuation of liberal policies in future. Furthermore, privatisation-based foreign investment may lead to follow-up investment by input and service suppliers of parent companies and to FDI by rival firms. This is rather conspicuous in the car industry of Central European countries. The acquisition by Volkswagen of Skoda in the former Czechoslovakia was followed by direct investment by dozens of their component suppliers from Germany.[12]

Optimism about sustainability of FDI inflows in Central Europe is also based on good prospects of GDP growth. Increasing market size should attract more FDI. The Economist Intelligence Unit (1996) has estimated that yearly FDI inflows in the five Central European countries would increase from $5 billion in 1990–5 to $11 billion in 1996–2000. For the Czech Republic, Poland and Slovakia, they are expected nearly to triple, and in Slovenia they may increase by a factor of six according to the above estimates. Only for Hungary, which attracts the highest levels of FDI at present, is a slower growth of FDI inflows forecast.

Conclusions

German FDI is definitely guided by European economic integration. Market deepening through the Single Market Programme of the mid-1980s, especially in services, led to accelerated FDI outflows from Germany to the member countries. The prospect that the Central European countries might join the EU and the granting of some integration-related advantages through Europe Agreements have boosted German direct investments in the Czech Republic, Hungary, Poland, Slovakia and Slovenia.

Economic integration is, however, not a sufficient condition for attracting FDI. As a member of the EU, Greece did not receive much German FDI. Nor do Bulgaria or Romania attract substantial amounts even though they are signatories of Europe Agreements. The strong growth of German FDI in Central Europe is additionally supported by geographical and cultural proximities, long standing trade relations, and an improving local investment climate in the host countries.

FDI outflows have presumably benefited the home as well as host economies. The restructuring of German manufacturing inspired by the Single Market Programme as well as Europe Agreements is associated with the achieving of economies of scale. Moreover, FDI outflows do not appear to have impaired domestic fixed capital formation in Germany. They may indeed have had a positive effect on it through induced demand for capital goods and intermediate products net of export substitution and re-imports. In addition, FDI is followed by receipts of earnings and other income such as licence fees, royalties and so on. In the US, these receipts already exceed FDI outflows. German outward FDI can be expected to follow suit as it moves to correspondingly higher stages of the investment development cycle.

In Central Europe, FDI inflows have added considerably to fixed capital formation. In the Czech Republic, Hungary and Poland, FDI-related investment shares are higher than in the group of developed or developing countries as a whole. German FDI has made a substantial contribution to this development. FDI is an efficient means of facilitating the international division of labour. From one-fourth (Hungary) to two-fifths (the Czech Republic and Slovakia) of their world trade is already with or through Germany.

FDI inflows to Central Europe can be expected to keep growing in the near future. The scope for privatisation of public enterprises, which contributed a great deal to inward FDI in the past, has not yet been exhausted. Utilities, railways, banks and so-called strategic industries remain largely under state control (EBRD, 1996). Beyond that, the dynamics related to already privatised enterprises are going to accelerate the FDI of input suppliers from home countries including Germany, and of rival firms. In addition we should note that the present income level in the best performing Central European country – Hungary – is only half that of the poorest EU economy – Greece. Thus, there is large scope for income growth in Central Europe, and it will pull more equity capital from abroad, especially from neighbouring Germany. Good prospects for FDI inflows depend, of course, on macroeconomic performance, political stability and the institutional development of Central European economies. The latter should, *inter alia,* guarantee healthy competition. This is in the interests of domestic and foreign investors alike.

Notes

1 Disaggregated data for Germany are readily available only to a limited extent for total FDI and not for M&As. The share of the banking sector in the total outward stock increased from 13.6 per cent (1985) to 15.2 per cent (1994). In addition, the insurance sector accounted for 5.7 per cent of total FDI in 1994. But the 1985 share of insurance has not been disclosed. The manufacturing share decreased from 54.2 per cent (1985) to 44.4 per cent (1994) (Deutsche Bundesbank, 1996a).

2 For a survey of related studies see Agarwal (1980) and UNCTC (1992) and, for a recent study on German FDI, Barrell *et al.* (1996). Lorz (1993, p. 63) estimated that EU membership and geographical proximity of host countries to Germany raises their chances of receiving German FDI by 1.4 and 1.5 times respectively.

3 Corporate tax has been reduced in Germany since 1980, but it is still higher than in some competing countries like France, the Netherlands and the UK (Klodt and Maurer 1996, pp. 28–9). Presently, the government has proposed to reduce it further, which should improve locational attractiveness of Germany.

4 Between 1992 and 1994 France hosted more FDI than the UK, but in 1995 the latter regained its position as the biggest receiver of FDI in the EU (IMF, 1996).

5 Before adjusting for productivity differences.

6 In addition, bank credits (domestic and foreign) cover nearly half the financial needs of German enterprises (Deutsche Bundesbank, 1997).

7 The existence of this latter channel of finance should indicate that caution is needed in interpreting FDI data in the context of domestic capital formation.
8 These rankings are not stable over time. Even one big investment may change the relative position of the investing country. In 1995, the US became the biggest investor in Poland (FAZ, 1997).
9 Both MNEs and SMEs, which have invested and which have not yet invested in CEECs, were included in the survey. Moreover, investors from all the three sectors – primary, secondary and services – were included in the sample.
10 Total German FDI in CEECs from 1989 to 1995 was DM12,750 million. Of this Hungary accounted for 40 per cent, the Czech Republic and Poland for 34 per cent and 16 per cent, respectively (Beyfuss, 1996).
11 The Czech Republic appears more attractive than other Central European countries for German investors looking for relocation sites for their labour intensive products and processes (Beyfuss, 1996; Meyer, 1995).
12 The same applies to General Motors' investment in the Hungarian automobile industry and to Ford's and FIAT's FDI in Poland (UNCTAD, 1995, p. 103).

References

Agarwal, J.P. (1980), 'Determinants of foreign direct investment: a survey', *Weltwirtschaftliches Archiv*, 116/4, pp. 739–73.
(1990), 'Determinants of foreign direct investment in Pacific-Rim countries', *Asian Economic Review*, 32/1, pp. 83–100.
(1994), 'The effects of the single market programme on foreign direct investment into developing countries', *Transnational Corporations*, 3/2, pp. 29–44.
(1996a), 'Does foreign direct investment contribute to unemployment in home countries? – An empirical survey', Kiel, Institute of World Economics, Discussion Paper No. 765.
(1996b), 'Impact of "Europe Agreements" on FDI in developing countries', *International Journal of Social Economics*, 23/10–11, pp. 150–63.
(1997), *German MNEs: Consequences of Eastward Drive for Developing Countries*, revised version of the paper written for the International workshop on FDI, technology transfer and export orientation in developing countries organised by the United Nations, Institute for New Technologies, Maastricht, 15–16 November 1996.
Barrell, R., Pain, N. and Hubert. F. (1996), 'Regionalism, innovation and the location of German direct investment', NIESR Discussion Paper No. 91.
Beyfuss, J. (1996), 'Erfahrung deutscher Auslandsinvestoren in Reformländern Mittel- und Osteuropas', Beiträge zur Wirtschafts- und Sozialpolitik 232, Institut der deutschen Wirtschaft, Cologne: Deutscher Institutsverlag.
Deutsche Bundesbank (1994), *Technologische Dienstleistungen in der Zahlungsbilanz*, Statistische Sonderveröffentlichung 12, Frankfurt.

(1996a), *Kapitalverflechtung mit dem Ausland*, Statistische Sonderveröffentlichung 10, Frankfurt.

(1996b), *Zahlungsbilanzstatistik*, Statistisches Beiheft zum Monatsbericht 3, December.

(1996c), *Neuere Tendenzen in den wirtschaftlichen Beziehungen zwischen Deutschland und den mittel- und osteuropäischen Reformländern*, Monatsbericht, July, pp. 31–47.

(1996d), *Technologische Dienstleistungen in der Zahlungsbilanz*, Statistische Sonderveröffentlichung 12, Frankfurt.

(1997), *Die Aktie als Finanzierungs- und Anlageinstrument*, Monatsbericht, January, pp. 27–41.

Deutscher Industrie- und Handelstag (DIHT) (1996), *Produktionsverlagerung als Element der Auslandsinvestitionen, Ergebnisse einer Unternehmungsbefragung im Herbst 1996*, Bonn.

Dunning, J.H. and Narula, R. (1996), 'The investment development path revisited, some emerging issues', in Dunning, J.H. and Narula, R. (eds), *Foreign Direct Investment and Governments, Catalysts for Economic Restructuring*, London/ New York, pp. 1–41.

The Economist Intelligence Unit (EIU) (1996), Economic forecast, *Economies in Transition, Eastern Europe and the Former Soviet Union: Regional Overview*, 1st Quarter, pp. 25–35.

European Bank for Reconstruction and Development (EBRD) (1996), *Transition Report 1996, Infrastructure and Savings*, London, EBRD.

European Commission and UNCTAD Division on Transnational Corporations and Investment (EU–UNCTAD) (1996), *Investing in Asia's Dynamism: European Union Direct Investment in Asia*, Luxembourg, European Commission.

Frankfurter Allgemeine Zeitung (FAZ) (1996), 'Deutschland für ausländische Firmenkäufer attraktiv', 6 July, p. 11.

(1997), 'Direktinvestitionen in Polen verdoppelt', 8 February, p. 16.

Hanson, G.H. (1995), 'The effects of off-shore assembly on industry-location: evidence from US border cities', NBER Working Paper No. 5400.

Hirsch, S. (1967), *Location of Industry and International Competitiveness*, Oxford, Clarendon Press.

Hoey, J. (1996), 'Germany's new drive eastwards', *Economies in Transition, Eastern Europe and the Former Soviet Union: Regional Overview*, 1st Quarter, pp. 5–16.

Hufbauer, G.C. (1966), *Synthetic Materials and the Theory of International Trade*, London.

Hufbauer, G.C. and Schott, J.J. (1993), *NAFTA – An Assessment*, Washington, D.C, Institute for International Economics.

International Monetary Fund (IMF) (1996), *Balance of Payments Statistics Yearbook*, Washington, D.C.

Joekes, S. (1982), 'The multifibre arrangement and outward processing: the case of Morocco and Tunisia', in Stevens, C. and Themat, J.V. (eds), *EEC and the Third World: A Survey*, pp. 102–12, London/Sydney, Hodder & Stoughton.

Klodt, H. and Maurer, R. (1996), 'Internationale direktinvestitionen: determinanten

166   Innovation, investment and technology in Europe

und konsequenzen für den standort Deutschland', Kiel, Institute of World Economics Discussion Paper No. 284.

Langhammer, R.J. (1992), 'Die assoziierungsabkommen mit der CSFR, Polen und Ungarn: wegweisend oder abweisend?', Kiel, Institute of World Economics, Discussion Paper No. 182.

Lansbury, M., Pain, N. and Smidkova, K. (1996), 'Foreign direct investment in Central Europe since 1990: an econometric study', *National Institute Economic Review*, 156, pp. 104–14.

Lorz, J.O. (1993), 'Direktinvestitionen des verarbeitenden gewerbes in industrieländern', *Die Weltwirtschaft* 2, pp. 149–66.

Lowe, J.H. and Bargas, S.E. (1996), 'Direct investment positions and historical-cost basis', *Survey of Current Business* 76/7, pp. 45–60.

Meyer, K.E. (1995), 'Business operations of British and German companies with the economies in transition: first results of a questionnaire survey', Discussion Paper series 19, London Business School, CIS–Middle Europe Centre.

Nunnenkamp, P., Gundlach, E. and Agarwal, J.P. (1994), 'Globalisation of production and markets', Kieler Studien 262, Tübingen.

OECD (1994), *Trade and Investment: Transplants*, Paris.

(1996), *International Direct Investment Statistics Yearbook*, OECD, Paris.

Piazolo, D. (1996), 'Trade integration between Eastern and Western Europe', Kiel, Institute of World Economics, Working Paper No. 745.

PlanEcon Report (1996), 36/9–10, p. 36.

Pomfret, R. (1986), *Mediterranean Policy of the European Community*, London.

Statistisches Bundesamt (1995, 1996), *Statistisches Jahrbuch für die Bundesrepublik Deutschland*, Wiesbaden.

UN (1994), *East–West Investment News, Economic Commission for Europe*, Geneva, UN.

United Nations Centre on Transnational Corporations (UNCTC) (1992), *The Determinants of Foreign Direct Investment: A Survey of the Evidence*, New York, UN.

UNCTAD (1995), *World Investment Report 1995: Transnational Corporations and Competitiveness*, New York and Geneva.

(1996a), *World Investment Report 1996: Investment, Trade and International Policy Arrangements*, New York and Geneva, UN.

(1996b), *Trade and Development Report, 1996*, Geneva, UN.

(1997a), *Sharing Asia's Dynamism: Asian Direct Investment in European Union*, Geneva, UN.

(1997b), *FDI Determinants and TNCs' Strategies: The Case of Brazil*, Interim version, Geneva, UN.

US Department of Commerce (USDOC) (1996), 'US direct investment abroad: detail for historical-cost position and related capital and income flows, 1995', *Survey of Current Business* 76/9, pp. 98–128, Washington, D.C.

US Department of Labor (1996), *International Comparison of Hourly Compensation Costs for Production Workers 1975–1995, Supplementary Tables for BLS Report 909*, Washington, D.C.

Vernon, R. (1966), 'International investment and international trade in product cycle', *Quarterly Journal of Economics*, 70/2, pp. 190–207.

(1979), 'The product cycle hypothesis in a new international environment', *Oxford Bulletin of Economics and Statistics*, 41/4, pp. 255–67.

Wang, Z.-Q. and Swain, N.J. (1995), 'The determinants of foreign direct investment in transforming economies: empirical evidence from Hungary and China', *Weltwirtschaftliches Archiv*, 131/2, pp. 359–82.

World Economic Forum (WEF) (1996), *The Global Competitiveness Report 1996*, Geneva.

8 Innovation and the regional and industrial pattern of German foreign direct investment

FLORENCE HUBERT and NIGEL PAIN

1 Introduction

The growth of FDI over the past decade has led to renewed interest in the impact of multinational enterprises on growth and employment in developed economies. Microeconomic evidence on licensing and direct investment suggests that inflows of new technology and working practices from the affiliates of multinational firms create a significant potential for spillovers to local firms in the host country. This makes it important to understand the factors that lead firms to invest overseas, rather than at home, and the characteristics that attract investment to particular locations.

This chapter addresses these issues using a panel data set to analyse the determinants of foreign direct investment by German manufacturing corporations from 1977 to 1994. World-wide, German firms have the fourth largest stock of overseas assets of all investing countries. Within Europe they are the second most important investors after the United States. At the end of 1994 just under 1.2 million workers were employed in the foreign affiliates of German firms located in Europe. However, comparatively little research exists on the determinants of their foreign investment decisions. One striking feature of German FDI, as with that of many other large foreign investors, is the extent to which it became increasingly concentrated in the developed world over the 1980s. The vast majority of new investments in that decade took place in other European countries, particularly within the EU. An important question of interest is whether these observed changes in the pattern of direct investment are related to regional-specific factors or simply to differences in national characteristics.

168

Our panel consists of six EU countries (or country blocs) plus an EFTA bloc comprising Austria, Sweden and Switzerland, who were all outside the EU over the sample period, North America, Latin America and East Asia, reflecting the primary locations of German foreign investment. Around 90 per cent of German manufacturing FDI is sited in these locations. Within the EU we distinguish France, Italy, the British Isles, Belgium, the Netherlands and the Iberian peninsula. We examine investments undertaken in four broad sectors, chemicals, mechanical engineering, electrical engineering and road vehicles. Together investments in these four sectors account for around 70 per cent of outward manufacturing direct investment from Germany.

In practice there are a wide range of factors that may determine the pattern of specialisation and location over time. Multinational enterprises arise through a combination of industrial organisation motives that result in a number of activities being placed under common ownership and control, and comparative advantage reasons that cause these activities to be placed in separate countries (Krugman, 1995). Our results provide evidence that the development of firm-specific assets, measured by the cumulated stock of R&D expenditures of German corporations, has had a significant influence on the level of outward investment from Germany. To this extent high levels of outward investment could be construed as a sign of competitive health rather than a sign that Germany is an unattractive business location (Jungnickel, 1995). More importantly it suggests that German foreign direct investment may be an important vehicle for the transmission of firm-specific innovations throughout Europe and the wider world economy.

We also highlight the extent to which heterogeneity can arise within dynamic panel data models of FDI from regional and industrial factors. Failure to allow for such heterogeneity could result in biased parameter estimates. Our findings suggest that there are significant differences in the factors driving investment decisions within and outside the EU economies. These largely appear to arise from the factors affecting investment in the transport sector in these two regions.

The remainder of the chapter is as follows. Section 2 provides an outline of the model on which we base our empirical work. Section 3 discusses the trends in German direct investment over our sample period. Section 4 contains the main empirical results both for the basic model and for one which allows for differences across regions and industries. Some concluding comments are made in Section 5.

2 A model of foreign direct investment

The decision to invest abroad reflects choices over the optimal scale and location of production, the means and availability of finance for such investments, and the perceived need to develop facilities that promote and support overseas sales whilst safeguarding firm-specific assets. Our analysis attempts to allow for these various influences.

Market size and relative costs

Conventional supply-side models of the location of production consider the first and second aspects above. Typically they determine direct investment using indicators of market size and relative production costs (see for instance Barrell and Pain, 1996). Given that there is a cost advantage to producing outside the home country of the investor, growth in market size would be expected to raise the level of foreign investment. Jost (1997) illustrates the significant relationship between the aggregate level of FDI by German residents and measures of foreign income.

In the empirical work we proxy market size by industrial production in the host location. To capture the role of relative costs we use 'normalised' trend unit labour cost data for manufacturing produced by the IMF, converted into a common currency.[1] This provides a measure of the real exchange rate. Unit costs are used so as to allow for differentials in productivity levels as well as wages and payroll taxes. In principle a more extensive measure of costs could also be used so as to allow for the impact of any differences in the user cost of capital across countries. We do not pursue this issue in the present paper. The preliminary findings of Pain and Young (1996) and Hubert and Pain (1997) suggest that attempts to allow for international differences in the cost of capital make little difference to the results reported here.

Firm-specific assets

The decision to establish foreign operations may also reflect factors internal to the firm, in particular the existence of firm-specific knowledge based assets (Markusen, 1995). Such assets might include process innovations, marketing skills or managerial expertise. All serve to give economies of scale at the level of the firm rather than at plant level by acting as a joint input across plants. Multinational firms thus have lower variable costs but higher fixed costs than national firms in different locations.

The basic supply-side model does not formally consider the choice over the means of foreign production. In practice, whilst there may be locational advantages to having multiple production facilities, the firm could still choose to permit a foreign manufacturer to produce the required output by licensing the firm-specific technology required to do so, rather than undertake foreign direct investment. This may appear to be particularly attractive if licensees have greater experience of operating in the overseas product market. The trade-off between the two can be shown to be dependent upon the costs of licensing relative to the factor costs of foreign production (Barrell et al., 1996).

Full licensing arrangements can give rise to a variety of transactions costs. Typically these arise from the difficulties of writing state-contingent contracts (Horstmann and Markusen, 1987) to ensure the maintenance of product quality and to guard against the appropriation by potential competitors of the rents accruing from firm-specific knowledge. In practice the costs of licence agreements cannot be directly observed; however it is probable that the costs of monitoring such agreements will be associated with the extent to which firm-specific assets and knowledge are being transferred (Markusen, 1995).

In this chapter we proxy the 'stock' of firm-specific assets by a seven-year cumulative, sector-specific, moving average of German R&D expenditure (in real terms).[2] R&D intensity has been found to be closely related to the level of FDI in a number of earlier empirical studies, notably Clegg (1990) and Pain (1997). Many German corporations, especially in industries such as automobiles and mechanical engineering, have been at the forefront of important innovations in business practice (Patel and Pavitt, 1989), with the level of business enterprise expenditure on research and development having risen sharply over our sample period from 1¼ per cent of GDP in the early 1970s to over 2 per cent of GDP by the late 1980s.

Financial factors

A number of studies suggest that the investment decisions of companies, both at home and abroad, are affected by domestic financial conditions, although there appears to be little agreement as to how these are best measured. Carlin (1996) provides an extensive overview of the impact of corporate profitability on the pattern of domestic investment within Germany. Heiduk and Hodges (1992) also suggest that investment activity is dependent upon the development of profits. Their case studies of the foreign investment strategies of Daimler-Benz and the BASF Group suggest that the (procyclical) volatility of foreign investment is greater than that of domestic investment, suggesting that planned foreign investments are reduced before domestic ones at times of financial distress. Here we concentrate on a measure of corporate interest gearing, measured as debt interest payments relative to cashflow for the corporate sector as a whole. Fluctuations in interest gearing have already been shown to have a significant effect on the level of foreign investment by UK firms (Pain, 1997).[3]

Even if production costs are equalised across locations, international differences in corporate taxes may still affect the location decision if they affect the post-tax return available in different locations. To investigate this hypothesis we include a measure of bilateral tax competitiveness based on that used in Pain and Young (1996), with:

$$TAX_{jt} = (1 - t_i{}^j) \, / \, (1 - t_i{}^j) \qquad\qquad (8.1)$$

where:

$t_i{}^j$ = tax rate on profits earned in host country by a German firm

$t_i{}^j$ = tax rate on profits earned in Germany by a German firm

Profits generated by cross-border investments may be subject to taxation in three main ways before they are distributed to shareholders. Profits are subject to corporation tax as they accrue in the host country. Repatriated profits may also be subject to additional tax from the government of the host country if withholding taxes are levied. Finally, the foreign source income of domestic parent companies may be subject to further tax from the government of the home country. In practice this is not applicable for Germany, as most foreign source income is exempt from domestic taxation (Weichenrieder, 1996).

Sufficient data are available to enable us to calculate this measure for all panel members with the exception of Latin America. For East Asia we use data on Japan, and for the Iberian countries we use Spain. We expect the variable to have a positive coefficient, so that a reduction in the host country tax rate stimulates inward investment. Our data on tax rates extend from 1975 to 1992; we thus take no account of the impact of subsequent tax reforms in Germany, with domestic tax rates being lowered in 1994, although we do capture the earlier tax reforms in 1990.

Labour relations and technology sourcing

We have also included two variables designed to capture other characteristics of the labour markets in potential host economies. Investment may depend upon the flexibility and quality of the workforce as much as its basic cost. It is widely claimed that the greater flexibility of the UK labour market has been a primary factor behind the growth in inward investment (Eltis and Higham, 1995). Flexibility is affected by a large number of institutional features in labour, product and housing markets, and it is unlikely that it can be captured fully in any empirical study of this sort. Here we follow Moore (1993) and Jun and Singh (1996) and utilise data on the number of days lost through strikes in each of the host economies (denoted STR_j). We expect that more strike-prone locations will receive less inward investment, although it remains possible that labour disruption could simply encourage capital–labour substitution.

Technology sourcing may also be an important determinant of FDI, with firms investing in locations in which they can acquire or utilise technical knowledge from indigenous producers (Neven and Siotis, 1993). To some extent, differences in labour quality and average productivity levels are already reflected in our model through the use of unit labour costs. However the technology sourcing hypothesis is broader than this, reflecting the potential for investing firms to either benefit from an existing research base or be able to establish their own operations using skilled personnel. Studies have thus either used information on numbers of scientific and engineering personnel or on domestic research outputs. Here we use information on patents registered by host country firms in the United States.[4] As with the German R&D series we use a seven-year cumulative series which varies by sector (denoted $PAT7_{ij}$).

Exchange rate volatility

The FDI literature suggests a variety of ways in which currency variability might affect direct investment. Simple portfolio models would imply that a rise in the risk associated with a particular asset might reduce the level of investment in that asset, although this is dependent on the extent to which the risks associated with different assets are correlated. Whilst it is possible to insure against currency risk, this is not without cost. Volatility in the exchange rate may directly contribute to uncertainty over the timing of planned transactions. If companies are risk-averse then uncertainty over future exchange rate movements may act as a barrier to foreign purchases. For instance, Barrell and Pain (1996) illustrate that expectations of future movements in the dollar have a significant effect on the level of current investments by US parent companies.

Alternatively, if the cost of exchange rate variability largely arises because production is being undertaken in one location whilst sales are primarily elsewhere, then variability may actively promote direct investment and production diversification. Volatility in labour costs, and hence the real exchange rate, is more difficult to hedge than volatility in market exchange rates. The results of Cushman (1988) and Stokman and Vlaar (1996) suggest that exchange rate variability has acted to raise inward investment in the United States and the Netherlands.

It may also be the case that the impact of currency variability on investment from a particular location is dependent upon the importance of that location within the wider regional market. This is particularly true of Germany, since the German market will be the primary destination for many tradable goods produced elsewhere, especially within Europe.[5] An implication of this is that German firms may prefer to produce in countries whose nominal exchange rates are closely linked to the DM.[6]

In this chapter we follow Stokman and Vlaar (1996) and investigate measures of both nominal and real exchange rate volatility in an attempt to discriminate between the uncertainty and production shifting hypotheses. There is no unique way of measuring exchange rate volatility. Here we use a three year moving sample standard deviation of the rate of change of the bilateral exchange rate of the host economy with Germany. Letting $e_{j,t}$ denote the nominal, bilateral DM exchange rate of the host country (or region) j at time t, nominal volatility is given by:

$$NVOL_{j,t} = \left[(1/m) \sum_{k=1}^{m} [\Delta \ln(e_{j,t+1-k})]^2 \right]^{0.5}$$ (8.2)

This measure will be zero for any county whose exchange rate is fully pegged against the DM, and a constant for any country whose bilateral exchange rate changes at a constant rate. The equivalent measure for the real exchange rate, denoted $RVOL_{j,t}$ was calculated using unit labour costs in the host country relative to Germany (RLC_j), so that:

$$RVOL_{j,t} = \left[(1/m) \sum_{k=1}^{m} [\Delta \ln(RLC_{j,t+1-k})]^2 \right]^{0.5}$$ (8.3)

As our unit labour cost series are all in a common currency, volatility in the real exchange rate is determined both by movements in relative inflation as well as by the nominal exchange rate.

The basic model

The basic form of the model we initially employ is thus given by:

$$FDI_{ij,t} = a_{ij} + \beta_1 Y_{j,t} + \beta_2 RLC_{j,t} + \beta_3 RD7_{j,t} + \beta_4 INT_{t-1}$$

$$+ \beta_5 TAX_{j,t-2} + \beta_6 STR_{j,t-1} + \beta_7 PAT7_{ij,t-1} + \beta_8 NVOL_{j,t}$$

$$+ \beta_9 RVOL_{j,t} + \beta_{10} FDI_{ij,t-1} + v_{ij,t} \qquad (8.4)$$

where $FDI_{ij,t}$ denotes the stock of foreign direct investment in sector i in country (or region) j at time t, Y_j is a measure of market size, RLC_j is relative German-host labour costs, $RD7_j$ is the measure of R&D expenditure in Germany and INT is a measure of interest gearing. The number of strikes and the research base of the host country are denoted as STR_j and $PAT7_j$ respectively. The sector and location specific fixed effects a_{ij} allow for unobserved influences that remain constant over the whole of the sample period. All other influences will be contained in the disturbance term n_{it}. The fixed effects may capture factors such as contiguous borders and language that are not reflected in the other variables.

The model includes a lagged dependent variable. The existence of adjustment costs arising from factors such as delivery lags and delays in finding suitable investments overseas, means that the desired and actual stocks of investment are unlikely to be equal period by period. We therefore estimate a dynamic, partial adjustment, panel model whereby the aggregate change in the investment stock (that is, the flow of new direct investments) is a function of the discrepancy between the current desired stock of direct investment and the actual stock at the end of the previous period:

$$\Delta \ln(FDI_{ij,t}) = \omega[\ln(FDI^*_{ij,t}) - \ln(FDI_{ij,t-1})] \qquad (8.5)$$

or, equivalently:

$$\ln(FDI_{ij,t}) = \omega \ln(FDI^*_{ij,t}) + (1 - \omega)\ln(FDI_{ij,t-1}) \qquad (8.6)$$

This is a potentially important distinction between our model and that of Moore (1993), who simply relates the current *change* in the investment stock to the factors that determine the desired stock, even though the standard neoclassical model relates the investment stock to relative costs. Omission of the lagged stock ignores potentially valuable information and could potentially generate misspecification.

Estimation is undertaken over a sample period running from 1977 to 1994. With ten separate country (or regional) groupings and four separate manufacturing sectors there is a total sample size of 720 annual observations. Although our panel has a relatively rich time dimension, with eighteen observations per panel member, the inclusion of a lagged dependent variable may induce small sample bias into panel estimates produced using OLS (Nickell, 1981), so that an instrumental variable estimator has to be employed. There are a number of potential instruments that can be used for the lagged dependent variable. In this paper we employ two additional instruments, a simple linear time trend and the rank order of the lagged dependent variable (Durbin, 1954). This latter instrument is clearly strongly correlated with the variable being instrumented, but has been 'cleaned' of the lagged disturbance term.[7]

We initially estimate a model with fixed effects for each panel member, but with common slope parameters imposed across all host locations and sectors. We subsequently examine whether there is any evidence of differential effects between regions or sectors. Most of the main explanatory variables are entered in logarithmic form, permitting direct estimates of their elasticities. We use constructed data on the stock of direct investment at constant prices. This was obtained by deflating the nominal (dollar) value of the FDI stock by the national GDP deflator of each host location.

3 The regional and industrial pattern of German FDI

Table 8.1 illustrates how the location of total manufacturing direct investments by German companies has evolved over time, with a marked rise in the share of investment in North America and, since the mid-1980s, in the EU, and a gradual fall in the proportion in Latin America. In 1994 some 45 per cent of investments were in the EU locations we show, compared with 35 per cent in 1982. Within the EU, France has consistently attracted the largest single proportion of investment, although the share of investment in the British Isles (UK and Ireland) and, to a lesser extent, Iberia (Spain and Portugal) has risen noticeably over the sample period. Investment within the EFTA members, Austria, Sweden and Switzerland, has also risen sharply since the late 1980s. Overall, the aggregate stock of German manufacturing FDI has risen by over 10 per cent per annum since 1976, broadly in line with the growth rate observed over the most recent sub-period from 1988 to 1994.[8]

In 1994 some 88 per cent of German manufacturing direct investments were located in the ten host locations we consider. This was a little lower than in 1988, reflecting the rapid growth in investments in Central and Eastern Europe since that time. The accompanying Chapter 7 in this volume by Jamuna Agarwal provides a more detailed discussion of the evolution in the pattern of German FDI.

Table 8.1 *Geographical distribution of German manufacturing FDI stocks (DM, millions)*

	1976	1982	1988	1994
Belgium	2,012	2,684	4,093	8,344
Netherlands	1,012	1,450	2,149	4,685
UK/Ireland	548	1,630	3,662	10,157
France	2,469	3,692	6,488	12,650
Italy	784	1,268	3,560	4,913
Spain/Portugal	1,770	2,919	6,992	10,213
EFTA[a]	2,366	3,515	6,191	12,177
North America[b]	4,445	16,725	26,696	37,839
Latin America[c]	5,003	9,197	11,744	17,564
South-East Asia[d]	415	1,189	2,728	4,742
Total of above	20,824	44,269	74,303	123,284
Total manufacturing	23,711	49,702	80,946	139,777

Source: Deutsche Bundesbank *Kapitalverflechtung mit dem Ausland*, various issues.
Notes: (a) Austria, Sweden and Switzerland. (b) USA and Canada. (c) Argentina, Brazil and Mexico. (d) Japan, Singapore and India.

In table 8.2 we show the sector breakdown of manufacturing FDI in a number of regions. The vast majority of manufacturing investments in the former Soviet-bloc economies has been in the road vehicles sector, with around 8¼ per cent of the stock of investments in that sector located in these countries by 1994.

The chemicals sector has consistently had the highest level of foreign investment out of the four we consider. German firms have followed a consistent path towards globalisation in this sector (Allen, 1989), with the distribution of investments in each of the regional locations remaining broadly in line with the size of the overall market. In contrast the distribution of investments in the road vehicles and electrical engineering sectors is more skewed, with investments becoming increasingly concentrated within the EU. The motor vehicles sector is also notable for the high level of investment in Latin America, reflecting investments by VW to gain access to the potentially large regional market (Streeck, 1989).

Table 8.2 *Geographical and industrial distribution of German FDI stocks (DM, millions)*

Industry	Host country	1976	1982	1988	1994
Chemicals	European Union	3,357	5,694	10,308	15,489
	EFTA	538	600	767	1,677
	North America	3,117	7,882	13,530	19,231
	Latin America	859	2,095	3,069	3,894
	South East Asia	151	575	1,585	2,389
	Central and Eastern Europe	–	–	–	649
	Others	906	1,543	2,039	3,483
Mechanical engineering	European Union	676	1,196	2,249	4,030
	EFTA	366	446	749	1,597
	North America	283	1,489	2,358	4,603
	Latin America	578	1,260	1,031	1,904
	South East Asia	42	116	260	379
	Central and Eastern Europe	–	–	–	241
	Others	253	245	346	702
Electrical engineering	European Union	1,404	1,929	4,222	7,430
	EFTA	661	884	1,780	2,734
	North America	293	2,824	4,071	4,945
	Latin America	772	1,337	1,648	2,762
	South East Asia	205	257	326	841
	Central and Eastern Europe	–	–	–	589
	Others	582	1,191	1,160	2,347
Road Vehicles	European Union	841	1,609	3,580	9,951
	EFTA	59	310	798	1,887
	North America	138	1,419	2,062	3,104
	Latin America	1,920	2,773	4,511	6,687
	South East Asia	55	128	213	362
	Central and Eastern Europe	–	–	–	2,112
	Others	346	1,241	1,837	1,488

Source and notes: as table 8.1.

4 Empirical results

The basic model

The initial estimation results are summarised in table 8.3. The first column (hereafter (3.1)) reports the parameter estimates for the basic panel model. Overall, these are in accordance with our priors, suggesting that foreign investment by German firms is driven by strategic factors and firm-specific competitive advantages as well as by a desire to relocate to lower cost sites. There appears to be an important role for the accumulated sectoral level of R&D expenditure by German companies, with the absolute levels term possibly picking up some of the upward trend in FDI that might otherwise be attributed to the market size variable (Y), given the extent to which our sample period has been characterised by steady growth in the real level of resources devoted to R&D. The implied long-run elasticity is 1.25 per cent.

There are also well determined effects from labour costs and market size, with respective elasticities of 0.39 and 0.65 per cent. The restriction required to impose relative unit labour costs was readily accepted by the data, although a separate term in German labour costs was in fact insignificant. There is some evidence that labour relations in the host country are of importance, with an implied long-run elasticity on the strike variable of 0.09 per cent. However there is little evidence of technology sourcing, with the host country patents indicator being insignificant.

The corporate gearing measure appears to have a significant impact on the foreign investment decisions of German companies, with a rise in interest gearing leading to a reduction in investment. This term is primarily an indicator of the extent to which changes in domestic financial conditions affect the timing and the size of the flow of investment. As the gearing ratio cannot be expected to permanently trend over time,[9] it cannot be the primary factor behind the continuing upward trend in the stock of investment. The significance of financial factors confirms the findings from the case studies cited by Heiduk and Hodges (1992).

The bilateral tax variable is also correctly signed, but not particularly well determined. Taken together these results suggest that the impact of differences in national taxes on social security, reflected in the relative unit labour cost series, may be of greater importance than differences in other corporate taxes.[10]

The size of the coefficient on the lagged dependent variable suggests that there is some modest inertia in the pattern of outward investment. It is of interest to note that the coefficient is significantly different from unity, implying that the use of a model specified in first difference form, that is,

Table 8.3 *The determinants of German FDI: Dependent variable: ln(FDI)$_{ijt}$*
Sample period: 1977–94
Number of observations: 720

	(3.1)		(3.2)	
ln(FDI$_{ij}$)$_{t-1}$	0.3973	(7.4)	0.4059	(7.8)
ln(Y$_j$)$_t$	0.3935	(2.1)	0.3741	(2.0)
ln(GLC / HLC$_j$)$_t$	0.2366	(3.0)	0.2461	(3.1)
ln(RD7$_i$)$_t$	0.7508	(7.2)	0.7359	(7.2)
ln(INT)$_{t-1}$	−0.1069	(2.0)	−0.0947	(1.9)
ln(STR$_j$)$_{t-1}$	−0.0538	(2.1)	−0.0519	(2.1)
ln(PAT7$_{ij}$)$_{t-1}$	−0.0147	(0.3)		
TAX$_{j,t-2}$	0.1950	(1.6)	0.1980	(1.8)
NVOL$_{jt}$	−0.3700	(4.2)	−0.3796	(4.5)
RVOL$_{jt}$	0.5626	(2.1)	0.3796	(4.5)
$\overline{R}^2$	0.9680		0.9682	
Standard error	0.2581		0.2570	
Mean-group			Chi(6) = 42.34	
Elasticities[a]				
Output	0.65	(0.31)	0.63	(0.30)
R&D	1.25	(0.13)	1.24	(0.13)
Labour costs	0.39	(0.13)	0.41	(0.13)
Strikes	−0.09	(0.04)	−0.09	(0.04)
Gearing ratio	−0.18	(0.08)	−0.16	(0.08)
Corporate tax[b]	0.32	(0.20)	0.33	(0.18)

Variable definitions:

FDI$_{ij}$	Stock of FDI in sector i in host country j
GLC/HLC$_j$	Unit labour costs in Germany relative to host economy
INT	Ratio of interest payments to cashflow in corporate sector
NVOL$_j$	Bilateral nominal exchange rate volatility
PAT7$_{i,j}$	Stock of host country patents in sector i
RD7$_i$	Stock of domestic R&D in sector i
RVOL$_j$	Bilateral real exchange rate volatility
STR$_j$	Number of strikes in host country
TAX$_j$	Bilateral tax competitiveness of host country
Y$_j$	Industrial production in host country

Notes: (a) Standard errors in parentheses; (b) Semi-elasticity.

for the flow of new investments, without any effect from the stock level, would be rejected by the data.

The variable for nominal exchange rate volatility is well determined, and provides some evidence that, *ceteris paribus*, German companies may have been more inclined to invest in countries which have been able to maintain a greater degree of nominal exchange rate stability with the DM. The real exchange rate volatility measure is also significant and implies that a rise in the volatility of the real exchange rate of the host country will raise inward investment from Germany. This is consistent with a production shifting hypothesis. A similar result for foreign investment by Dutch companies was obtained by Stokman and Vlarr (1996). However, in contrast to their findings, the nominal exchange rate measure remains significant in our model. One possible explanation for this is that Germany remains an important final market for domestic producers that have chosen to relocate elsewhere within Europe.

A restriction of equal and opposite coefficients on the two volatility measures is data acceptable [Chi(1) = 0.51]. This is merely a simplifying restriction rather than one motivated by theoretical considerations. However it implies that volatility in the nominal exchange rate will not constrain inward investment by German companies if matched by similar volatility in the bilateral real exchange rate. This primarily applies to the North American locations over our sample period, where there is a high correlation between the two volatility measures. Thus whilst fluctuations in the dollar–DM rate have raised uncertainty over the timing of investments by German companies, they have also given German companies a greater incentive to invest in North America.

Discarding the insignificant patents variable and imposing the restriction on the two volatility terms gives (3.2) in table 8.3. The long-run elasticities are little changed from the previous equation. The bilateral tax variable is better determined, although the long-run tax semi-elasticity is still not significant at conventional levels.

Testing for heterogeneity

Whilst (3.2) appears to be a parsimonious, economically coherent equation, there remains some possibility that the reported coefficients may be subject to bias given that the panel regression pools investment across a number of different locations with different trade regimes and industries with different investment strategies. Pesaran and Smith (1995) illustrate that heterogeneity in dynamic panels can give rise to bias if 'slope homogeneity' is imposed. If sufficient observations are available, consistent

Table 8.4 *Testing for differential regional and industrial effects*

	Sector / industry	Test statistic
MODEL 1: *Regional & industrial disaggregation*		
Pooling regions	Chemicals (CH)	Chi(16) = 6.51
within industries	Mechanical engineering (ME)	Chi(16) = 6.87
	Electrical engineering (EE)	Chi(16) = 16.59
	Road vehicles (TR)	Chi(16) = 71.77*
	All industries	Chi(64) = 101.74*
	CH, ME & EE	Chi(48) = 29.97
	TR: EU	Chi(8) = 70.31*
	Non-EU developed	
	TR: EU	Chi(8) = 26.30*
	Non-EU developing	
	TR: Non-EU developed	Chi(8) = 13.74
	Non-EU developing	
Pooling industries within regions	All industries	Chi(72) = 88.49
Pooling industries and regions	CH, ME & EE	Chi(64) = 35.17
MODEL 2: *Regional disaggregation*		
Pooling regions	All regions	Chi(16) = 45.45*
	EU	Chi(8) = 30.05*
	Non-EU developed	
	EU	Chi(8) = 23.35*
	Non-EU developing	
	Non-EU developed	Chi(8) = 11.31
	Non-EU developing	

estimates of the long-run parameters can be obtained using a mean-group estimator.[11] An attempt at jointly imposing the non-linear restrictions required to yield the long-run parameters from the mean-group estimates in (3.2) was decisively rejected by the data [Chi(6) = 42.34], suggesting that there is some evidence of unmodelled heterogeneity.[12] A similar result was previously obtained by Barrell *et al.* (1996) using a data set disaggregated by location, but not by industry.

Over our sample period the host locations can be classified as EU member states, developed economies outside the EU region who are members of regional free trade areas (the United States, Austria, Sweden and Switzerland), and developing regions (Latin America and East Asia). To investigate whether the combination of these divergent locations with the four separate sectors leads to heterogeneity we re-estimated (3.2) allowing for separate slope parameters in each of the distinct country and sector groups. In effect this decouples the individual regions and industries, although this is unavoidable if we are to test for common slope parameters. With three regions, four sectors and eight explanatory variables, a model with ninety-six slope parameters was initially estimated.

In table 8.4 we report the results of imposing the restrictions required to give common slope coefficients between the particular regional and industrial groups in the re-estimated version of (3.2). The first set of tests investigate whether it is possible to pool regions within industries. For each industry we test whether it is possible to impose common parameters on the factors that affect investment in each of the three regions. The results indicate that regional differences do not appear to be significant, either individually or jointly, in the chemicals, mechanical engineering and electronics sectors, but are significant in the road transport sector. The hypothesis that there are no regional differences in any of the four sectors is also rejected [Chi(64) = 101.74], largely because of the influence of the road transport sector.

In contrast it is not possible to reject the hypothesis that there are no significant differences between the four sectors within each of the three individual regions [Chi(72) = 88.49]. These findings are consistent with those in our earlier work (Barrell *et al.*, 1996). It is clear that the finding of significant differences between regions largely arises through the behaviour of the road transport sector. The pairwise comparisons between regions for the transport sector suggests that the primary differences arise from the factors influencing investment in the EU and non-EU locations. The restrictions required to give common slope parameters in the non-EU panel members cannot be rejected [Chi(8) = 13.74].

The lower panel of table 8.4 repeats our previous analysis in a model allowing for regional disaggregation alone, with twenty-four separate slope parameters. Again we find that the restrictions required to return to a single set of slope parameters common to all three regions are rejected at conventional significance levels. The subsequent pairwise comparisons suggest that the primary reason for this finding arises from differences between the EU and the other panel members; we cannot reject the restrictions required to give common slope parameters in the non-EU panel members. These results are consistent with the notion that membership of a customs union has differential effects on inward investment from membership of a free trade area.

Table 8.5 *Model 1. Regional and industrial disaggregation:*
Dependent variable: ln(FDI)$_{ijt}$
Sample period: 1977–1994
Number of observations: 720

Variable	Industry / region	(5.1)
$\ln(FDI_{ij})_{t-1}$	CH, ME, EE	0.4738 (6.7)
	TR/EU	0.2677 (3.4)
	TR/NON-EU	0.3641 (3.5)
$\ln(Y_j)_t$	CH, ME, EE	0.6277 (2.7)
	TR/EU	1.5408 (2.4)
	TR/NON-EU	0.1231 (0.2)
$\ln(GLC / HLC_j)_t$	CH, ME, EE	0.2042 (2.3)
	TR/EU	0.8108 (2.7)
	TR/NON-EU	0.2837 (1.4)
$\ln(RD7_j)_t$	CH, ME, EE	0.5121 (3.4)
	TR/EU	0.4139 (1.6)
	TR/NON-EU	0.7426 (2.5)
$\ln(INT)_{t-1}$	CH, ME, EE	−0.0286 (0.5)
	TR/EU	−0.4009 (2.9)
	TR/NON-EU	0.0515 (0.3)
$\ln(STR_j)_{t-1}$	CH, ME, EE	−0.0369 (1.3)
	TR/EU	−0.4123 (5.4)
	TR/NON-EU	0.0738 (1.2)
$TAX_{j,\,t-2}$	CH, ME, EE	0.0183 (0.2)
	TR/EU	1.0600 (3.7)
	TR NON-EU	−0.0999 (0.2)
$NVOL_{jt} - RVOL_{jt}$	CH, ME, EE	−0.2319 (2.5)
	TR/EU	−0.6543 (0.5)
$\overline{R}^2$	TR/NON-EU	−0.5416 (2.6)
		0.9702
Standard error		0.2491

Note: All variables as defined in table 8.3.

Models with differential industrial and regional effects

It is clear from the results in table 8.4 that two types of model are supported by the data. The first would have common effects in the chemicals and engineering sectors with separate effects for transport sector investments inside and outside the EU. The second would have common effects across all industries, but allow separate effects for investment inside and outside the EU. The results from allowing for differential effects within

Table 8.6 *Long-run elasticities, table 8.5 equation*

Variable	Industry / region	
Output	CH, ME, EE	1.19 (0.43)
	TR/EU	2.10 (0.94)
	TR/NON-EU	0.19 (1.00)
Host labour costs	CH, ME, EE	−0.39 (0.17)
	TR/EU	−1.11 (0.43)
	TR/NON-EU	−0.45 (0.32)
R&D	CH, ME, EE	0.97 (0.24)
	TR/EU	0.57 (0.32)
	TR/NON-EU	1.17 (0.43)
Strikes	CH, ME, EE	−0.07 (0.05)
	TR/EU	−0.56 (0.11)
	TR/ NON-EU	0.12 (0.10)
Interest gearing	CH, ME, EE	−0.05 (0.11)
	TR/EU	−0.55 (0.18)
	TR/NON-EU	0.08 (0.24)
Taxes[a]	CH, ME, EE	0.03 (0.23)
	TR/EU	1.45 (0.35)
	TR/NON-EU	−0.16 (0.68)

Notes: Standard errors in parentheses. (a) Semi-elasticity

the transport sector alone are shown in table 8.5, with the implied long-run elasticities summarised in table 8.6. It is clear that there are significant differences in the factors that appear to determine investment within the transport inside and outside the EU. Within the EU there are significant roles for interest gearing, strikes and bilateral corporate taxes. All three variables are insignificant for investment outside the EU, and for investment by firms in the other three sectors.

Market size matters for transport sector investment within the EU, but not outside it, where domestic technological developments provide the primary impetus for investment. Investment within the EU by the transport sector also appears to be considerably more sensitive to labour costs than investment elsewhere, with a long-run elasticity of over one. In contrast the elasticities for investment in the other three sectors appear broadly in line with the earlier evidence from the aggregate panel models, although the R&D and output elasticities are now both around unity. There are also some interesting differences in the responses to exchange rate volatility, with volatility having little effect on investment within the EU by the transport sector, but a large significant effect on investment outside the EU. We would expect the volatility measure to be significant for other industries, notably chemicals, where risk diversification is an important motivation for foreign investment (Allen, 1989). Fluctuations in the (dollar) price of oil have, for instance, acted to encourage petrochemicals investment in the United States, so that costs and revenue are denominated in the same currency.

One possible explanation for the differences observed for the road transport sector is that the organisation of the production process differs significantly from that in other sectors. Relocation of activities within the firm can take place more easily in response to changes in national tax systems and labour markets. Cars can be produced for different segments of the market with only minor modifications to production processes. Many producers typically have a portfolio of plants within large regional markets, with production being switched in response to cost changes or product market developments. The recent expansion of investments within the EU may also reflect the growing impact of competition by other producers in the high quality market segments occupied by some of the leading German car manufacturers.[13]

The case studies of Daimler-Benz and BASF in Heiduk and Hodges (1992) also highlight a number of interesting differences between the globalisation strategies of firms in different manufacturing sectors. The foreign investments of BASF have largely been driven by the need to expand market size for a given range of products, with investments concentrated in North America. In contrast Daimler-Benz has sought to establish strategic alliances, particularly within Europe, and diversify into a number of other engineering industries. Mason and Wagner (1994) highlight differences in the education and training of the workforces in two chemicals and engineering industries in Germany and the UK, with the engineering sectors having a greater demand for intermediate craft skills, where differences between the UK and German workforces are particularly marked. In contrast the chemicals industry relies more heavily on highly qualified personnel, where cross-country differences are less apparent. This provides a further reason why the location strategies of firms in the two sectors may differ.

The results from allowing for differential effects between regions, but not industries, are summarised in tables 8.7 and 8.8. It is clear that the transport sector has a significant effect on the findings within this model, and can explain many of the results from our earlier work which only allowed for regional disaggregation. Strikes, interest gearing and (to a lesser extent) taxes only matter within the EU, whilst the volatility measures are

Table 8.7 *Model 2. Regional disaggregation*

Variable	Region		
$\ln(FDI_{ij})_{t-1}$	EU	0.3843	(6.2)
	Non-EU	0.4164	(7.3)
$\ln(Y_j)_t$	EU	0.5226	(1.9)
	Non-EU	0.7644	(4.4)
$\ln(GLC / HLC_j)_t$	EU	0.3020	(2.3)
	Non-EU	0.1988	(2.8)
$\ln(RD7_j)_t$	EU	0.7316	(4.5)
	Non-EU	0.4942	(4.7)
$\ln(INT)_{t-1}$	EU	−0.1999	(2.4)
	Non-EU	0.0066	(0.2)
$\ln(STR_j)_{t-1}$	EU	−0.1648	(2.5)
	Non-EU	0.0143	(0.7)
$TAX_{j, t-2}$	EU	0.1670	(1.2)
	Non-EU	−0.1544	(0.9)
$NVOL_{jt} - RVOL_{jt}$	EU	−0.0082	(0.1)
	Non-EU	−0.2492	(3.9)
$\bar{R}^2$		0.9692	
Standard error		0.2533	

Notes: All variables as defined in table 8.3.

only significant for investment outside the EU. In line with our earlier work, German direct investment is found to be much more sensitive to differentials in unit labour costs with EU panel members than with non-EU ones. There is thus little evidence that investments outside the EU have been primarily motivated by a need to relocate to sites with lower labour costs.

An important issue is why there should be any differences in the observed investment patterns within the EU. It has long been recognised that changes in regional trade arrangements and technical and social standards can have an important effect on both the level and location of overseas investments. There are many different forms of regional integration agreements in operation. Some regions, such as the European Union, have chosen to augment their common customs union with a liberalised internal market whilst retaining a common external barrier to foreign producers. In such cases firms may have an incentive to establish and maintain operations within such relatively 'closed' regions in order to ensure unimpeded access either to the region-wide market or to large national markets within the region. This may be a particularly important consid-

Table 8.8 *Long-run elasticities, table 8.7 equation*

Variable	Region	(8.1)	(8.2)
Output	EU	0.85 (0.45)	1.06 (0.48)
	Non-EU	1.31 (0.28)	1.33 (0.28)
Host labour costs	EU	−0.49 (0.20)	−0.91 (0.26)
	Non-EU	−0.34 (0.12)	−0.51 (0.14)
R&D	EU	1.19 (0.21)	1.29 (0.22)
	Non-EU	0.85 (0.17)	0.94 (0.17)
Strikes	EU	−0.27 (0.11)	−0.30 (0.11)
	Non-EU	0.02 (0.04)	0.002 (0.04)
Interest gearing	EU	−0.32 (0.12)	−0.69 (0.15)
	Non-EU	0.01 (0.07)	−0.16 (0.08)

Note: Standard errors in parentheses.

eration for German investors in some sectors such as vehicles, with foreign investments undertaking production for sales in the German domestic market. In other sectors, such as chemicals, foreign production may be largely designed to support and enhance sales in foreign markets.

Accounting for inward investment growth in Europe

The estimated equations can be used to calculate the effects of actual changes in the factors determining inward investment from Germany over the sample period. Taking the output term as an example, the reported regressions can be expressed as:

$$\ln(FDI)_{ijt} = \beta_{10}\ln(FDI)_{ijt\text{-}1} + \beta_1\ln(Y_j)_t \tag{8.7}$$

Any quantitative evaluation of the estimated impact of the impact of changes in the market size of particular host countries has to take account of the presence of the lagged dependent variable. At any given period the overall implied direct effect of host output on the stock of direct investment in that location can be calculated from the regression coefficients using:

$$\text{OUTPUT EFFECT} = \beta_1 \sum_{k=1}^{n} \beta_{10}^{(k-1)} \ln(Y_j)_{t+1\text{-}k} \tag{8.8}$$

where n denotes the number of periods over which the impact of output is assessed. Separate effects can be calculated for each of the four sectors; these are then weighted together using the share of each individual sector in total investment in a particular location. Our illustrative calculations

Table 8.9 *Accounting for inward investment growth in Europe: percentage change in stock of FDI during each period due to movements in each factor*

Host location	Period	Host output	Relative labour costs	Host strikes	German R&D
Belgium	1984–9	14.7	4.7	0.4	22.9
	1989–94	1.6	3.0	3.8	18.1
Netherlands	1984–9	13.4	5.0	–7.9	18.1
	1989–94	9.0	4.1	4.9	15.9
UK/Ireland	1984–9	20.5	7.4	3.2	18.5
	1989–94	4.7	8.0	8.2	14.8
France	1984–9	10.1	4.6	3.0	21.0
	1989–94	1.7	3.9	1.5	16.4
Italy	1984–9	18.4	3.1	2.6	19.9
	1989–94	2.9	8.4	3.0	17.7
Spain/Portugal	1984–9	19.4	2.1	2.4	23.7
	1989–94	1.4	1.0	–0.2	21.5
EFTA	1984–9	17.7	2.6	–2.4	22.3
	1989–94	7.4	6.7	8.8	18.2

shown in table 8.9 set $n = 5$, and use coefficients from the equation in table 8.5. We compute the extent to which changes in output, R&D, relative labour costs and strikes changed the stock of inward FDI between 1984 and 1989 and between 1989 and 1994. Because of the use of a distributed lag, our estimates for changes between, say, 1984 and 1989 reflect the extent to which a weighted average of the level of output from 1985 to 1989 differed from a weighted average of the level of output from 1980 to 1984.

Results for four European locations, the British Isles, France, Italy and the Iberian countries, are summarised in table 8.9. These reveal some interesting differences between countries. For example, whilst it is clear that the growth in R&D undertaken by German firms has had a large effect on the level of inward investment received in all locations, the effects have been consistently smaller for the UK and Ireland than for the other locations. In part this reflects the relatively low share of the two sectors whose R&D expenditure has grown most rapidly, electrical engineering and road vehicles, in German investments in these countries. However it may also reflect perceived differences in the quality and skills of the domestic workforce in different locations. Output growth is found to have contributed more to the growth of FDI in the UK than elsewhere, with the exception of the EFTA bloc in the latter sub-sample.

The labour relations effect also appears to have been particularly beneficial for the UK, reflecting the relatively sharp falls in the level of strikes since the middle of the 1980s. This is estimated to have raised the stock of inward investment by over 8 per cent between 1989 and 1994. However, once again it is worth noting that a similar outcome was achieved by the EFTA members, even though labour market institutions in these countries are very different from those in the UK. Investment in the other locations has also risen as a result of a decline in strike activity, with the exception of Spain and Portugal where strikes have discouraged investment since 1989.

Perhaps the most interesting results are obtained for host country labour costs relative to those in Germany. All seven locations in Europe are estimated to have gained investment in both sub-periods as a result of movements in this measure of the real exchange rate. However there are some interesting distinctions to be drawn between the various locations. Trend unit labour costs in countries such as the Netherlands, France and Austria, whose currencies have maintained a close link with the DM, are estimated to have risen less rapidly between 1984 and 1994 than those in Germany. In contrast, unit costs in countries such as the UK, Spain, Italy and Sweden actually rose more rapidly than German costs over this period. However this was more than offset by the depreciation of their nominal bilateral exchange rates against the DM, particularly in the early 1990s, resulting in a depreciation of the real exchange rate. Thus whilst movements in relative labour costs have helped to raise the level of overseas investment by German companies since the mid-1980s, this has as much, if not more, to do with movements in market exchange rates than with the high basic wage costs in Germany.

5 Conclusions

This chapter has investigated the factors determining the scale and location of German manufacturing foreign direct investment, with allowance being made for differential effects between regions and sectors. The approach used augments a conventional supply-side model of production location with measures to reflect both domestic financial conditions and internal firm-specific developments within industries. We also seek to control for a number of host country characteristics which are often believed to be important determinants of the level of inward investment. Our panel data results extend previous findings, largely from cross-sectional studies and case studies of individual multinational enterprises, and suggest that investment overseas by German firms may be closely related to both technological developments in the domestic economy and the financial health of the corporate sector.

In addition we find evidence which suggests that membership of a common customs union with Germany can have an important impact on the factors which influence the likely scale of inward direct investment from German corporations. There is evidence of regional and industrial heterogeneity, which largely appears to arise from the investments undertaken by firms in the road vehicles sector. The extent to which greater domestic innovation is associated with additional foreign investment suggests that there are limits to the economies of scale available within a single plant, leading firms to establish multiple production facilities to help maximise the rents accruing to their firm-specific assets. The importance of trade arrangements at the regional level may be particularly apparent in sectors such as road vehicles, characterised by a greater degree of intra-firm trade. In contrast the production process in other sectors such as chemicals is more typically concentrated in a single site.

The growth in the net level of outward FDI from Germany over the 1980s has led to widely expressed concerns about a possible deterioration in the competitiveness of the German economy (Jungnickel, 1995; Jost, 1997). To address this issue fully a detailed study of inward FDI in Germany would be required to complement any analysis of outward FDI. However our results do suggest that some of the concerns over the locational attributes of the German economy are misplaced; whilst differences in unit labour costs do help to determine the level and location of outward FDI, the extent to which they did so in the 1980s and early 1990s does not appear to have been particularly different from the findings from earlier studies of the 1960s and 1970s (Goldsbrough, 1979). In part this is undoubtedly because the high level of wage costs in Germany is no more than the counterpart to a higher level of basic skills and labour productivity. The evidence that outward FDI has been partially motivated by the development of firm-specific products and processes also suggests that high levels of outward investment could be construed as a sign of competitive health rather than weakness.

Overall, our results suggest that the foreign investments undertaken by German companies may be an important channel for the diffusion of new technology and management techniques in the European economies. This raises important questions about the form and type of operations located within separate national economies. The importance of potential spillovers from knowledge-based assets suggests that more research be directed towards the types of investment taking place in particular locations and the

192   Innovation, investment and technology in Europe

role of labour quality in the investment decision. The existence of significant differences in the factors influencing investment decisions at the sectoral level suggests that it would be of considerable interest to seek to augment the findings from broader econometric analyses of this type with those from more detailed plant-level studies.

Notes

1 For Latin America we use constructed data on manufacturing unit labour costs in Argentina, Brazil and Mexico. For East Asia we use equivalent series for Singapore and India plus the normalised trend unit cost series for Japan.
2 Comparisons with our earlier study (Barrell *et al.* 1996) indicate that the degree of cumulation makes little difference to the results obtained.
3 If capital markets were perfect then, given the Modigliani-Miller theorems, the cost of capital should be independent of the capital structure of the firm. However if there are dead-weight costs associated with bankruptcy, then companies' real decisions may not be independent of their financial situations.
4 This is a widely used preferred source of patent data as it includes patents originating in a large number of countries which are internationally comparable.
5 Pain (1996) presents econometric evidence that outward direct investment from Germany has a significant positive effect on the level of imports of goods into Germany.
6 In our earlier work (Barrell *et al.*, 1996) we found some evidence in favour of this hypothesis by including a dummy variable set to unity for those countries who are members of the Exchange Rate Mechanism of the EMS, plus Austria which has pursued a policy of closely shadowing the DM since 1982. This variable, based on nominal exchange rate commitments, had a positive coefficient, implying that, other things being equal, German firms may prefer to produce in countries whose nominal exchange rates are closely linked to the DM.
7 The rank order may be a weak instrument if there is substantial measurement error present in the instrumented variable and, hence, in the associated rank order. There are a number of alternative estimators available, but most would force us to estimate an equation for the investment flow rather than the investment stock as first differences of the data would have to be employed. This could result in the incorrect omission of significant long-run information.
8 Jost (1997) provides a detailed overview of the different sources of statistics on Germany's direct investment position.
9 Standard tests indicate that the series does not have a unit root.
10 The impact of social security taxes depends on the incidence of the tax and in particular the extent to which changes in non-wage costs are offset by changes in wage costs in the wage bargain between employers and employees.
11 The mean-group estimator is calculated as an average of the parameters obtained from separate regressions for each panel member. Such an estimator is consistent

under both the null of parameter homogeneity as well as the alternative of heterogeneity, whereas the fixed-effects estimator is only consistent under the null.

12 Some care is required in interpreting this test as only eighteen observations are available for each of the individual regressions. Whilst this offers sufficient degrees of freedom to estimate the required parameters, some small sample bias may remain because of the presence of the lagged dependent variable.

13 Streeck (1989) discusses the possible evolution of the German automobile industry in the face of the changing strategies and locations of Japanese producers.

References

Allen, C.S. (1989), 'Political consequences of change: the chemical industry', in Katzenstein P.J. (ed.), *Industry and Politics in West Germany: Toward The Third Republic*, Ithaca and London, Cornell University Press.

Barrell, R. and Pain, N. (1996), 'An econometric analysis of US foreign direct investment', *Review of Economics and Statistics*, 78, pp. 200–7.

Barrell, R., Pain, N. and Hubert, F. (1996), 'Regionalism, innovation and the location of German direct investment', NIESR Discussion Paper No. 91.

Carlin, W. (1996), 'West German growth and institutions, 1945–90', in Crafts, N. and Toniolo, G. (eds), *Economic Growth In Europe Since 1945*, Cambridge, Cambridge University Press.

Clegg, L.J. (1990), 'The determinants of multi-national enterprise: a comparative study of the US, Japan, UK, Sweden and West Germany', in Casson M. (ed.) *Multinational Corporations*, Aldershot, Edward Elgar.

Cushman, D.O. (1988), 'Exchange rate uncertainty and foreign direct investment in the United States', *Weltwirtschaftliches Archiv*, 124, pp. 322–36.

Durbin, J. (1954), 'Errors in variables', *Review of the International Statistical Institute*, 22, pp. 23–32.

Eltis, W. and Higham, D. (1995), 'Closing the UK competitiveness gap', *National Institute Economic Review*, 154, pp. 71–84.

Goldsbrough, D. (1979), 'The role of foreign direct investment in the external adjustment process', *IMF Staff Papers* 26, pp. 725–54.

Heiduk, G. and Hodges, U.W. (1992), 'German multinationals in Europe: patterns and perspectives', in Klein M.W. and Welfens, P. J. J. (eds), *Multinationals in the New Europe and Global Trade*, Berlin, Springer-Verlag.

Horstmann, I. and Markusen, J.R. (1987), 'Licensing versus direct investment: a model of internalization by the multinational enterprise', *Canadian Journal of Economics*, 20, pp. 464–81.

Hubert, F. and Pain, N. (1997), 'Economic integration in Europe and the pattern of German foreign direct investment', NIESR mimeo, forthcoming in *Economic Integration*, London, Macmillan Press.

Jost, T. (1997), 'Direct investment and Germany as a business location', Economic Research Group of the Deutsche Bundesbank, Discussion Paper 2/97.

Jun, K.W. and Singh, H. (1996), 'The determinants of foreign direct investment: new empirical evidence', *Transnational Corporations*, 5, pp. 67–106.

Jungnickel, R. (1995), 'Foreign direct investment, trade and employment: the experience of Germany', in OECD, *Foreign Direct Investment, Trade and Employment*, Paris, OECD.

Krugman, P.R. (1995), 'International trade theory and policy', in Grosman, G. and Rogoff, K. (eds), *Handbook of International Economics Volume III*, Amsterdam, Elsevier.

Markusen, J.R. (1995), 'The boundaries of multinational enterprises and the theory of international trade', *Journal of Economic Perspectives*, 9, pp. 169–89.

Mason, G. and Wagner, K. (1994), 'Innovation and the skill mix: chemicals and engineering in Britain and Germany', *National Institute Economic Review*, 148, pp. 61–72.

Moore, M.O. (1993), 'Determinants of German manufacturing direct investment 1980–1988', *Weltwirtschaftliches Archiv*, 129, pp. 120–38.

Neven, D. and Siotis, G. (1993), 'Foreign direct investment in the European Community: some policy issues', *Oxford Review of Economic Policy*, 9/2, pp. 72–93.

Nickell, S. (1981), 'Biases in dynamic models with fixed effects', *Econometrica*, 49, pp. 1399–416.

Pain, N. (1993), 'An econometric analysis of foreign direct investment in the United Kingdom', *Scottish Journal of Political Economy*, 40, pp. 1–23.

(1996), 'Foreign direct investment, trade and economic growth within Europe', paper presented at ESRC Macroeconomic Modelling Bureau Annual Seminar, University of Warwick, July.

(1997), 'Continental drift: European integration and the location of UK foreign direct investment', *The Manchester School*, Supplement 65, pp. 94–117.

Pain, N. and Young, G. (1996), 'Tax competition and the pattern of European foreign direct investment', paper presented at 52nd Congress of International Institute of Public Finance, Tel Aviv, August, and IFS conference on Public Policy and the Location of Economic Activity, November.

Patel, P. and Pavitt, K. (1989), 'A comparison of technological activities in West Germany and the United Kingdom', *National Westminster Bank Quarterly Review*, May, pp. 27–42.

Pesaran, M. H. and Smith, R. (1995), 'Estimation of long-run relationships from dynamic heterogeneous panels', *Journal of Econometrics*, 68, pp. 79–114.

Stokman, A.C.J. and Vlaar, P.J.G. (1996), 'Volatility, international trade and capital flows', De Nederlandsche Bank Reprint Series No. 453.

Streeck, W. (1989), 'Successful adjustment to turbulent markets: the automobile industry', in Katzenstein P.J. (ed.), *Industry and Politics in West Germany: Toward The Third Republic*, Ithaca and London, Cornell University Press.

UNCTAD (1996), *World Investment Report 1996*, Geneva, UN.

Weichenrieder, A. (1996), 'Fighting international tax avoidance: the case of Germany', *Fiscal Studies*, 17, pp. 37–58.

Printed in the United States
By Bookmasters